MODERN JEWISH CLASSICS

THE WORLD IS A WEDDING

The Vallentine, Mitchell

MODERN JEWISH CLASSICS

A Selection of titles in the series

Sholom Aleichem
The Old Country
Tevye's Daughters

Bernice Rubens
Set On Edge

Mordecai Richler
The Apprenticeship of
Duddy Kravitz

Dannie Abse
Ash On A Young Man's
Sleeve

Brian Glanville
Diamond

Bernard Kops
The World Is A Wedding

Isaac Babel
Benya Krik, The Gangster
And Other Stories

Chaim Raphael
Memoirs Of A Special
Case

Dan Jacobson
The Price Of Diamonds

Frederic Raphael
The Limits Of Love

THE WORLD IS
A WEDDING

BERNARD KOPS

VALLENTINE, MITCHELL
LONDON

This edition first published in 1973 by
VALLENTINE, MITCHELL & CO. LTD.
67 Great Russell Street,
London WC1B 3BT

ISBN 0 85303 179 7

Printed in Great Britain by
Lewis Reprints Ltd.
member of Brown Knight & Truscott Group
London and Tonbridge

FOR ERICA

CONTENTS

The world is a wedding
THE TALMUD

1

Child in the Family

Take one Jew and immediately you have an opposition party. In
our family it was no exception. Our home was like a Yiddisher
parliament, with seven opposition parties. Plus my mother and
father, who were trying to govern and be in the opposition at the
same time. Each of us constantly talked, fifty to the dozen, trying
to be heard, pulling each other's garments, arms, and even faces,
to make the others listen. And we shouted most of the time, mainly
to ourselves. There was always someone laughing or crying at any
given moment.

We each lived in our own world, except for my mother who lived
in all our worlds. But each of our worlds was held together by our
home in Stepney Green. Twenty-three, Stepney Green Buildings
—right at the top of seven flights, a red-brick tenement erected
eighty or so years ago.

There were seven children sharing two beds in that buggy attic,
two single beds, beds without sheets, whose springs scratched our
bodies, springs that were victims of relentless pillow-fights and our
jumping up and down. From the windows I could see as far as
Tower Bridge, its arms opening and closing several times a day,
as if welcoming in new immigrants.

My father had come from Amsterdam, from poverty, and he
settled near the docks, like most of the Jews before him, who stayed
near the river, I suppose, to keep as close as possible to the Old
Country. On his first morning in London he got on a tram in the
Mile End Road and said to everyone, 'Good morning, all'—the
only words of English he knew. They ignored him, thought he was
mad.

A couple of weeks later he met my mother in Forest Gate, of all
places. She too came from a Dutch Jewish family, though slightly
better off than his. They married at the synagogue in Stepney

Green, both of them about five feet three inches tall—though later they shrank to five feet. My mother's width, however, made up for her height.

The first war brought a certain physical prosperity, and my father, a leather worker, made jerkins for soldiers. That sort of prosperity seems to go with war; for when the war finished so did work. I was born in the middle of the General Strike. My father, prolific in giving my mother children, seemed to be the only one not on strike. All those days were a tremendous struggle to get money, a struggle largely falling on the shoulders of my mother, who lived for each moment, scheming and dreaming—who, in the words of mothers of her sort, and though not actually believing in God, would often say: 'God is good, something will turn up.' But the only thing that seemed to turn up was more children and more poverty.

My first concrete memory was waiting for a new child to arrive. My sister Phoebe, my brother Dave and myself were sitting on the stairs eating ice-cream cornets. This was a rare treat, so something obviously was up, and we knew my father had given us the money to get out of the house. I had heard my mother moaning during the day, from the bedroom; but because I had been told the usual stupid stories about the stork, the gooseberry bush and the doctor's little black bag, I asked my sister why she needed to go on so. The doctor came shuffling up the stairs, and as he passed us Phoebe said, 'The baby's in that case.'

'I know—I can see the arms and the legs sticking out.'

She told me not to be so silly, so I rejected the case theory, and the stork came back into favour. When we went inside the house we all thought it a great giggle, because Marie, my eldest sister, told us we would all be eating upstairs in our room.

My mother moaned throughout the night, and I kept awake until the dawn. When I went into her room, I expected to see feathers all over the place. There was my mother, and Rose.

'God bless you,' my mother said to me.

'Yes, He does owe me something,' I would like to think I replied.

There were seven of us. I was the seventh, but Rose was the eighth child. The first had died at the age of three, and lay buried in a little Christian cemetery in Leicester, in a special corner that had been consecrated Jewish, just for her. I often thought of her lying there, all alone, and I remember my mother crying about her quite often. 'To lose a parent is the worst thing in the world; but to lose a child is even worse.'

Despite her obsessive involvement with us, my mother tried to emulate the birds. She loved her children, lived for us and through us, tried to provide for us, to prepare us for flight, to provide us with the strength to reject her. But blood is very much thicker than water in a Jewish family. One day my melancholy Aunt Esther came, my father's eldest sister. I could hear them having a row. Aunt Esther was childless, but she had some money saved, and she chided us on our poverty. 'I've got the quids,' she said.

'And I've got the kids,' my mother replied, equally as nasty. But neither of them had other weapons to use. Aunt Esther died in a mad house. When they went through her furniture, they found millions of pieces of paper that had been torn up methodically. Nobody knew why.

There were no books in my house. Lots of laughter and language, but no books. Except the dreaded rent book, and the insurance book—for my parents, no matter how hard-up they were, were already insuring themselves against the day when they would die, so that they wouldn't be a burden upon us, and there would be enough money to pay for the ground, the coffin and the stone. But books weren't missed, because they never occurred to me. Hunger did—and not only the hunger for food, which was bad enough, but the hunger for things that I couldn't fathom.

My father was unemployed and on the means test, and was somehow expected, God knows how, to bring us up on twenty-eight shillings a week. A woman who lived nearby sometimes brought us in potatoes. She worked Up West, my mother told me—'Up West' was that fabulous world beyond, our Eldorado. It was only years later that I guessed what sort of work the woman did—for who in the Buildings could afford to give their neighbours potatoes in those days?

Yet it was a happy childhood, almost idyllic, and I was practically the happiest child of the whole family. I used to enjoy running around to my aunt's to try to borrow a shilling. My father would bring the money from the Labour Exchange on Friday; it was gone by Sunday, and by Monday my mother was already on the borrow. So when my father came with money on the Friday, most of it had to be paid back. A pair of shoes, or the one good suit in the family, or the wedding ring, was the pawnable article. And I used to love to go to the pawn-shop with my mother, though she hated it. Everyone was pawning; yet everyone was ashamed of it. I suppose that's why the pawning entrance was always tucked away. Soon as we entered the pawn-shop, the man knew exactly how much to give us, and would hand us the money even before the shoes were on the counter. With the few shillings would come a certain relief to my mother's face, and she'd always sing me the same song on the way home:

> Mary, Mary, at the pawn-shop door,
> A bundle in her hand and a parcel on the floor
> She asked for seven-and-six but they only gave her four,
> So she pulled the blinkin' handle off the pawn-shop door.

We would sometimes get food parcels from the Jewish Board of Guardians: demerara sugar, butter beans, and margarine. Now I come to think of it, a strange combination. And meat, bread, and coal tickets from another Jewish organization. But there were so many Jewish families in the same position that this help was very spasmodic. In winter we used to burn old shoes in the fireplace, and I would often search the streets, where the sight of a solitary, dirty shoe would be like a gift of manna. Shoes, in the streets of the East End, were few and far between.

And I would go with my father to the soup kitchens. We'd walk all the way to Aldgate with a saucepan, and return with pea soup and black bread, after waiting hours in the queue, the long queue of tired, hungry people. I remember a friend suddenly didn't want to speak to me any more, so I collared him one day and asked him why. He said that he had actually seen my father eating the soup at the soup kitchen. I denied it indignantly, said, 'We never eat it there—we always bring it home!' Apparently, and for the life of me I can't see the reason, to have your soup there wasn't considered nice. This strange snobbery existed in all manner of things, even though we were all in it together. For instance, my mother hated to be seen taking me to the Jewish Board of Guardians, where I would receive clothing, clothing I needed desperately, clothing that everybody else also got, smelling of moth balls, clothing of the most wonderful cloth, but often five sizes too large for me, handed down by wealthy Jews the other side of nowhere.

It was a self-imposed ghetto, but a happy world. And there was a spirit of community as in a village. People were involved in each other's lives, and not for the wrong reasons. Now, looking back, I see it was a desperate time—but then it meant security, and happiness. It was my world, and Aldgate East was the outside frontier of that world, a world that consisted mainly of Jewish people. I had no chip on my shoulder about being Jewish, because I knew of nothing else that existed. The teeming streets sheltered the family, and poverty wasn't imposed by economics or society. It was just something to battle against.

Stepney Green was wide open, with a narrow park running the length of it, with trees that had stood there for perhaps a hundred years. My mother said she remembered the cows grazing there, although I believe they grazed only in her imagination.

My parents were not religious. My mother lit the candles on Friday because she said it was nice, and on this night we would have a proper meal. My father said poor people couldn't afford to be religious; yet we followed the Jewish festivals, and ceremony broke into the stark reality of day-to-day living. On Passover all the children of the Buildings used to play with cracker nuts in the playground, building little castles of nuts, and knocking them down with more nuts. And we would go from one aunt to another on these occasions, perhaps to show off a new pair of socks, and they would give us an orange, an apple, or sweets. It was worth running the gauntlet for such gifts: I say gauntlet, because visiting my aunts entailed being pinched on the cheeks until we were almost black-and-blue, them saying atavistically, 'You're so lovely I could eat you' or 'I could pinch you to bits'. Kosher cannibalism.

On Succoth, or Simchat Torah, we would go from one synagogue to the next, queuing up for bags of sweets and fruit, often receiving a gift, then going to the back of the queue again.

Already, before I had even started school, the religious people tried to claim me, tried to make me go to the Hebrew classes, and the Hebrew teachers were far stricter than anyone I had met up till then. My mother agreed that I should go, perhaps to get me out of the way. So I went once or twice, to the *cheder* in Redmans Road. But the Hebrew symbols were meaningless to me, and the call of the streets was stronger than the call of God. So I played truant.

One day the Hebrew master was at the door, calling about my absence. I hid under the table. He came in and stood with his legs apart in a pompous pose: 'What about his Hebrew education, his Bar Mitzvah?'

'Would that butter his bread?' my father replied. 'A poor boy can't afford to be religious.'

The street door was open; so I rushed through the man's legs, and flew down the seven flights of stairs, four at a time, and into the streets.

A little while later I was not able to use my legs so freely. I developed rickets—and my legs went into irons. They stayed on for a month or so, but my mother wanted to take them off.

'If you do,' the doctor said at the Jewish hospital, 'his legs will fall away from under him.'

My mother took the irons off nevertheless; and I was soon running through the streets again. My mother trusted no-one and nothing, except her instinct.

I played outside in the park, with my brothers and sisters, and the Lever children, and on one Saturday morning there happened the first tragedy in my life. A man had been coming around regularly with a magnifying glass. He'd catch the rays of the sun and burn pieces of paper, and we'd all stand around to watch the flames. We were drawn to that man; even though time and time again we had been warned not to go near him. On this Saturday morning he burned the paper as usual, and touched us all, boys and girls, between the legs. The next moment a policeman was gripping hold of him and pulling him away. We followed him as he was being dragged along the green. I couldn't understand why the policeman was hurting him so much, all because of a magnifying glass and a few pieces of paper.

We played a lot in that park: hop-scotch and 'Poor Jenny is a-weeping'. My mother's name was Jenny, I thought they were connected. We were often too busy to go upstairs for food, and sometimes she would throw me down a crust of bread in a paper bag.

'Mum-eeee! Throw me down a ha'penn-eee!' I called up. And she would come to the railings and shake her head. A ha'penny was gold dust in those days.

I used to search the little streets for money, and remember thinking that if I walked on one side of the road I might miss it on the other side. But once I did find sixpence, and I flew up the stairs to give it to my mother. It was those stairs, those seven flights, that ruined her, that crippled her health and eventually led to her death. Those flights that she went up and down three or four times a day, stopping at each landing for several minutes to catch her breath, on her endless journeys to find a couple of shillings from somewhere or other.

'When I'm rich I'll take you to Torquay,' I used to say. I thought Torquay was somewhere in the tropics. But I never took her anywhere.

All my aunts and uncles and cousins were poor, except one uncle who won some money on the Irish Sweepstakes. He would drive up once a year in his Rolls Royce, all the kids of the area would surround the car, and the chauffeur would open the door, and my little uncle would trot up the stairs, puffing on his cigar. He would give my mother a kiss and a pound note, and we would line up for sixpence each. A yearly ceremony, where my mother would cry tears of gratitude, and off he'd trot again, down to his car.

My father was almost blind, and bad eyes don't improve with the sort of work he was doing. A clicker gets his name from the sound that the knife makes as it clicks around the pattern and into the leather. And when he did work, his face had been getting closer and closer to the bench, and his hands were getting slower and slower. I remember the day he cried. The sound of my father crying was one of the worst sounds in the world. He just lay on the floor and wept. Women's tears were easy to cope with; after all, I had four sisters. But we all stood around him, not knowing what to do.

Apparently the boss's son came to my father's workbench and

said, smiling, 'Mr Kops—you've worked very hard in your life, and we think it's about time you had a little rest.' My dad was delighted to hear this, thinking perhaps they were going to send him to some philanthropic clickers' convalescent home.

'So we're going to give you an extra week's money. And here are your unemployment cards.'

Then it dawned on the old man that he had just been given the sack, after thirteen years with the same firm.

'The toe-rag, the lousy rotten toe-rag!' my father moaned on the floor. 'Toe-rag' was the worst thing that he could call anyone.

Although I never felt close to him, I must admit that he was a tryer. Afterwards he went to race meetings, to sell lemonade and chocolate. And I journeyed out of the East End for the first time, went with him to Epsom to collect empty bottles to get the deposit money, and to scratch out the prices on the bars of chocolate for him to sell at a higher price. On the way home we'd buy food, returning in a sort of triumph, in those desperate times.

During the holidays we were all at home. All under my mother's feet, when she would sing, sardonically, 'How I wish it was Sunday every day'—or she'd say, 'That's all I'm short of. Some holiday I've got.' To get away I would sometimes go to the synagogue along the road, purely to drink from the goblet of wine. Not that I wasn't caught up in the ceremony, for whilst mouthing my fake Hebrew I found myself dovening, swaying backwards and forwards as my ancestors had done for thousands of years. I tried to stop but it was impossible so I gave myself up to it.

'Religion's a lot of tommy rot.' My father said time and time again, but I noticed that he loved being involved in the main ceremonies of birth, marriage and death. When my young cousin died I saw mourning close up for the first time. The family arriving with cakes and chocolate, trying to cheer up the immediate family who sat on cut-down chairs. The mirrors were covered, the men were unshaven and a woman walked round the room cutting the sleeves of the closest relatives with a razor blade.

'What's that for?' I asked my father.

'The rending of the garments.'

'Why do they sit so low down?'

'To be close to the earth. Shush!'

'Why the mirrors covered?'

'So that we don't see our own sorrow, to stop vanity. Now shut up!' Then he prayed with the others and just as fervently. My father was a strange atheist. Although very much bound up with the family and with life my parents were very much tied to the dead. My mother's constant expressions were, 'I swear by my mother in the grave'; 'may I drop dead on this spot if I'm not telling the truth'; 'may I get run over and smashed.' Sometimes if she was cold she would shudder and say, 'someone walked over my grave'.

About the time that my cousin died a bird flew from one of the trees onto our landing. It was injured and I took it inside but it escaped and fluttered away from me. It clung to the guard around the fireplace, and then it fell off—and I accidentally trod on it. It lay dead, and I cried. My mother told me to throw it down the lavatory. 'Where does it go to, the lavatory?' I asked.

'Why, to the river.' She replied, and my sadness gave way to wonder and I suddenly became aware that my house was attached to the river, and the river was attached to the world. That day a man came to fix the electricity in the house. We were all so excited —we switched the light on, hundreds of times, on and off. 'Let them get on with it, ma,' the man said, 'they'll soon get fed up with it.' And we did.

But though we used to play together we all had our different worlds. Marie was serious, went regularly to the Brady Street Girls' Club—Essie, the blonde little temptress, a little Mae West they used to call her, we had a photograph in sepia to prove it—and Jack, up in the bedroom being a Gentleman of Japan, rehearsing The Mikado for some local Operatic Society, before that he used to write monologues and practise them. There he was strangling himself with his hand clutching his throat and his tongue hanging out while we all watched with horror and pride. 'Why should I have to hang on the end of a rope, the rope! The Rope! AAAAhhhh!' Carroll Levis was King in those days, on Radio Luxembourg; Stardust would play and his soft Canadian voice would say 'The discoveries of today are the stars of tomorrow'. And every poor boy's dream was to be discovered and to escape and be good to his parents. Jack actually got an audition but nothing more was heard. A little later he stopped strangling himself and settled down.

Phoebe was slightly distant, in her moody brooding world— Dave, in the other bedroom, all alone being cricketer, bowler, referee, umpire and commentator all at the same time, and Rose, toddling around in that gooey, cooey world of babies. I used to love playing with candles and poking the fire, seeing cities and forests and people in the flames.

'You'll wet the bed.' My mother said. I don't know where my mother got her superstitions from—she was one of the most superstitious women alive. If one of us swallowed something and it went down the wrong hole, she'd say, 'Look up, and turn round three times.'—or 'spit out and go to the lavatory.'—or 'look down and close your eyes and count fifteen.' It usually worked. It must have come direct from the Middle Ages.

All the time I wanted to know about my parent's past—where our ancestors came from but I could never get much out of them except a few details about their grandparents, and that was that.

But whereas the others were quite content to accept those few details, and the world around them, I wanted to know how I fitted into the order of things, wanted to discover my roots and establish some sort of identity. I used to lie awake at night, long after everyone else had said good-night, and watch the progress of the bugs up the wall. Though I'd squash the fleas upon me, I could never crush the bugs, because the smell of them was even more repulsive than the sight of them. We were so ashamed of those bugs; yet one night I overcame my repulsion and looked at them as creatures, little miracles.

'Bern,' Phoebe would call over. 'You still awake?'

'Yes—what do you want?' I was miles away. Not in that room, not in the East End, not in England or even the world.

'What you thinking of?'

'Nothing,' I'd reply. 'What you thinking of?'

'Nothing also, Good-night.'

'Good-night.'

We were always close. Phoebe was always called a little mother, though once she did drop me down a flight of stairs when I wet her. Maybe that explains why I became so different.

The boats moaned on the river, sounding like prehistoric monsters at a feast. And the trains shunted endlessly through the night like giants pinioned in a prison cell, hitting their manacles with their manacles, filling the dark with hollow clangs. I would lie awake dreaming of travel, feeling sick when I thought of eternity, and cry myself to sleep thinking of death, of my death, my pillow wet with tears.

'When I die it's for ever and ever and ever and ever.'

Coats on the door would frighten me, and I'd pull the bedclothes right over my head. I've slept like that ever since.

But life was too funny and too serious for me to be entirely lost in dreaming; and most of the comedy and tragedy took place in the home, and then amongst my cousins and uncles and aunts. We were a very close, almost too close, family. Most of our cousins were double cousins, because the Kopses, those who came to England, the brothers and sisters, married their equivalent number amongst the Zetters. One whole family married another. The Kopses were a serious, moral, almost melancholy lot, who saw sorrow and despair everywhere, looked always on the black side of things. If you said, 'It's raining outside,' they'd reply, 'I suppose it will get much worse.' They were never happy unless they were miserable. But the Zetters were an entirely different kettle of fish: good-looking, tending to over-optimism and living beyond their means. They were mainly gamblers, either working as tic-tac men on the racetracks or as bookmakers at the Hackney Wick dog stadium. They were fast talkers and I always found them most attractive, especially when they excitedly described the events of each race meeting. For every racing day carried its own inquest. The Zetters were never lost for ideas and were always looking for an opportunity to make a few bob, such as going from door to door and buying old gold and flogging it in the street markets on Sunday.

One of my uncles, I forget from which side of the family, tried to commit suicide in Whitechapel Station. He drank a bottle of disinfectant in the lavatory. Fortunately for him a porter heard the bottle crash to the floor as my uncle crumpled up. And even more fortunately, the London hospital was opposite.

The Kopses were clean and practical, and liked food in their bellies. But the Zetters always seemed to dress smartly even though their bellies were empty. All sorts of dramas and intrigues were going on all the time at any family gathering. One could always see the women whispering across to each other or mouthing words across the room, and gasps of exasperation and surprise. I could never make out what it was all about.

I was a little older by the time another cousin died, a girl called Doris. She developed meningitis suddenly, a beautiful girl full of life, who used to sing, and she was singing right up till the last moment. Her voice belted out from the hospital ward, and was heard right across Stepney Green, singing, 'Si, si, si, that South American Joe.' My mother said she caught it washing her hair, so consequently we all stopped washing our hair for a long time.

I heard the word 'Hitler' one day, heard my mother and my aunt cursing him. At first I thought he was an uncle out of favour. But my father told me he was our enemy, in another country, who wanted to destroy us all. Every so often after reading the newspapers my mother and my aunt would have a session of cursing.

'A broch on his kishkas!'

'A crenk on his brain!'

'May he get run over and smashed!'

'May he lack salt!'

'May he lose more blood than sea in the ocean!'

'May all his teeth fall out except one, and may he have the most terrible toothache in that one!'

It became a regular slanging match to see who could curse the worst. But it didn't do any good. The newspapers contained pictures of Jews being held up to ridicule by a jeering crowd, or a Jewish child scrubbing a road. My mother cried. 'When I lost my daughter I cried enough tears to swim from here to America. I thought I had no tears left—and here I am crying again.'

I began to get afraid, and I brooded. All the other children seemed to be springing up, and I was the smallest, reaching no higher than the table. When we ate we were not all served together: my father and the baby came first, and then the children, from the eldest downwards. I watched the cabbage and the potatoes disappearing in the pot, and practically panicked that it would all be gone before it was my turn. I stood next to my mother at the gas stove, trying to pinch the food as it was being cooked. Sometimes now I wonder whether the artist or the clown doesn't in fact emerge out of fear and sadness, out of trying to prove something to someone, or himself, out of the desire to be noticed. 'Hey! Save some potatoes for me!' I never remembered my mother eating—though her weight never decreased.

I remember going with her along the river. It was Bank Holiday, and we were off to the Downs at Purley. Under the Rotherhithe Tunnel I clutched her and screwed up my eyes. 'If you don't worry, I won't worry,' I said to her. But I was terribly worried—and in a way I think she liked my fear, and I resented that, and felt guilty because I did. I used to love to smell her hair.

She was an ordinary woman who was extraordinary to me. When words got too much for her she'd just sit down and sigh or cry or sing, all the old songs: 'When your hair has turned to silver, I will love you just the same,' or 'You die if you worry, you die if you don't, so why worry at all, it's only worry that killed the cat, anybody can tell you that.' But this didn't stop her from worrying. She had a most terrible fear of the elements—if it started to rain she'd scream for us to come home, and if it thundered she'd unplug the wireless, hide the knives and forks and take all seven of us into the dark passage underneath the stairs. She told us we must always beware of strange people in the streets: 'People will try to take you away,' she warned us constantly. I would often wander out in the hope that they would.

In those strange rationalizations of Jewish people, she always expected things to turn out for the best, though experience proved to her time and time again that they didn't. To her, rich people were poor people with money, whereas her riches were seven children.

I played in the playground of the Buildings, and heard the children next door at the Jewish school singing Hebrew hymns, and reciting their multiplication tables. I knew my time was approaching and I dreaded the day. I was still bed-wetting, but somehow being so small and not going to school still gave me some excuse for doing that. Meanwhile, I organized the kids of my own age in that grey rectangle of stone that we called a playground, and under the stairs I played with Sarah and Anita from 'B' block, nearly always at hospitals. One day the girl downstairs said, 'I'll show you mine if you show me yours.' I undid my flies for her to see, but she didn't reciprocate—and I hated her, and didn't speak to her ever again.

With Sarah it was more idyllic. We lay on the floor together, behind the settee in her house, me pouring water into her vagina, or poking matchsticks into it, and she instinctively touching the thing I had only used for peeing with. She turned on me, however, and downstairs in the park told a gathering of children what I had done to her. I felt so ashamed, my whole world collapsed. Of course I denied it completely—I think she never forgave me for that. Everyone always said that we would get married, but I haven't seen her for almost twenty years.

About that time I played a lot with my cousin Derek. One day for no reason we took a goldfish out of a bowl and cut it in half with the scissors. This led to other excesses. I used to sit on the lavatory sometimes for half an hour.

'Have you fallen down the hole?' Various members of my family would call out at odd intervals. And I'd pretend to be straining. But I was catching flies with my hand and throwing them into a spider's web. I used to like to see the fly struggling and kicking, and the spider close in and surround it with silver thread. Other times I would hit flies with newspapers until I thought they were dead, then I'd pour a mound of salt over them and watch them come to life again.

But I wasn't only cruel. From off the mulberry leaves near the Buildings I collected silkworms, kept them, or I'd look for hairy caterpillars in front of the park and nest them in match-boxes. And I became very worried about the children in Duckett Street and Paragon Mansions, for they were in a far worse state than we were, with no shoes or socks, running sores on their faces, staring through the railings or standing on their stinking stairs. I became aware of a world far worse off than my own.

Every Sabbath my mother got out the only linen, and we'd manage to have some lochshen soup, and then we'd all play cards or have a sing-song. But I would sit by the window more often now, counting the church spires and watching Tower Bridge.

My mother hardly ever went out but I well remember the night she did go. There was an election going on, and the voting vans were going through the streets, the microphones promising God knows what, we who never had it, hadn't got it, and were never likely to get it. I could hear, 'Vote for Doctor O'Donovan, for better conditions!' I jumped up at the window, and when I jumped down again the sewing machine collapsed on my head. Afraid that I might get told off, I jumped under the table. My sister Essie, delegated to look after us, pulled me out and rubbing my head, found that her hand was covered with blood. I was rushed to the Jewish hospital where I received seven stitches in my scalp, and a penny from the doctor for not crying.

When my mother came home that night it was so quiet she knew something was wrong. Six white faces stood there, and then she realized I was missing.

'Where's my Bernie? Where's my Bernie?'

She rushed to the bedroom where I, with an even whiter face, was sitting propped up, very proud of myself, my head swathed in bandages, building castles with playing cards.

'I'm never going out again,' she said. 'The one time I go out and look what happens! I'm never going out again.' And I don't think she did, not by herself. She just stayed with her family, watching and worrying.

When I recovered, I started school.

2

Boy in the World

I hated school. Every morning for more than a year I think I cried—and when I saw that crying wouldn't work, I pretended to be ill. I worked through every illness that I knew about, mostly protesting that I had a sore throat. One morning I pretended that I had lost my voice, and put up such an act that my mother believed me. And when the school had gone in, I smiled smugly, and snuggled in bed as I heard the children in the hall of the school singing the usual patriotic song. But to my horror my mother schlapped me to the hospital. To my amazement they found that I had tonsilitis. I don't think I pretended after that.

Each dawn brought an empty feeling of dread and I dragged myself unwillingly towards the infants' class. The Hebrew and everything else that they taught me went through one ear and out the other. All I longed for was the bell, to rush into the streets, back into the world. For I, being rejected by my brother and his gang, had now accumulated a gang of my own. There was Angel, and Gerald Lever, and Maxie Dyas. We had our own secret calls, our own secret code, and our own secret signs and our own invisible ink made of lemon juice. We played hide-and-seek or whizzed round the streets on our home-made scooters, chasing through the foggy nights, only returning to the base when we heard the call: 'Allee in, we ain't a-playing!'

My brother, seeing that I had made a success of my own gang, now condescended to let me join his, which I did with considerable pleasure, and apparent indifference. Dave and I would now often play together, tying people's legs together under the table or unwinding a reel of cotton all round the floor. Sometimes we'd go to the sweet shop opposite, where he would engage Mr Lindsberg in conversation while I tried to pinch little cubes of chocolate. My mother found out, and I thought she would knock me across the room, but she didn't. She only shook her head and wept a little. We promised not to do it again, and we didn't.

Outside the Stepney Jewish school stood Esther the sweet woman, who I think did more business than Mr Lindsberg. She was an excitable widow who never used one word when twelve would do and she sold sweets from a battered pram, and stuck lollipops and lucky bags into the park railings. She was the Queen, the fearsome Empress, and most of our fantasies and dreams revolved around her pram. She chastised us as if she was doing us a big favour in serving us. Oh, the magic of that pram—the almond whirls and the sugar twirls, the chocolate kisses and sherbet fountains, the liquorice sticks and the hundreds and thousands, the stick-jaws and the gob-stoppers, the aniseed balls and the bulls-eyes.

One day when school was out, and she was pushing the pram away, I and my friends taunted her. 'Why ain't you got a baby, Esther, in that pram?' She turned and chased us.

The East End was full of characters, full of people crying their wares—the Indian toffee-man: 'Indian toffee, good for the belly, ask your mummy for a penny, and buy some Indian toffee!' Even if I had a penny my mother wouldn't let me buy any—she said it was poisoned. 'That's the way they carry children off to India!' But I used to love to watch him smiling with gold teeth and throwing the coloured sugar into the whirring silver bowl, and see the pink floss being spun onto the wooden sticks. And the toffee-apple man, with I swear five hundred toffee apples attached to a contraption on his head. And the muffin man with his bell, and the woman selling lavender: 'Who will buy my sweet scented lavender? Sixteen branches for only one penny.'

Not so long ago, yet gone forever.

The man who came with a small roundabout, painted the colours of the rainbow, and for some old clothes he'd give you a ride. I once offered him my socks, but he told me not to be so daft. And those men who came around the streets calling for old iron and lumber, who came with goldfish for old clothes. Why did they want old clothes, I thought. Who'd want the old clothes that we'd throw away? Even though I never remembered my mother throwing anything away.

People used to go into the streets in those days—both during the day and in the evenings. The Mile End Waste was always crowded with people looking for bargains, and I liked to watch the people looking for bargains. The women were looking for bargains of food, the men looking for bargains of razor blades and shaving soap, the children looking for bargains of sweets, and the young men looking for bargains amongst the girls. I ventured away from the gang, and out of Stepney Green, and I wandered along the main Mile End Road, asking people for cigarette cards. And I'd forget that I was drifting, being so entirely caught up in the world around me: the old Bubayachnas, jawing on the doorsteps, talking about the price of fish, reading letters from relatives in Russia, often crying; talking their strange mixture of Yiddish and Cockney. They would say what they had to in Yiddish, and then completely repeat it in Cockney pidgin English. But some of the old women, including Mrs Marovitz from another block, had been in England more than forty years, and still she could speak no more than three words of English.

I dawdled through the street markets, watching jewellery being haggled over, and thousands of herrings being pulled from their barrels and sliced by men whose fingers looked just like herrings. The streets behind Whitechapel fed me with a new sustenance: Old Montague Street, and Black Lion Yard, where the out-of-work tailors congregated on the corners, discussing politics, religion, money and politics, until someone would rush up: 'I've got work for two men for two days!' Everyone would crowd forward, the men would be chosen, and the remainder would return to the discussion of politics.

Old men with beards, sitting outside Whitechapel church, eternally reliving the Russian revolution. Men stood around everywhere, anywhere, outside the Kosher restaurant or the Turkish bath, or the Labour Exchange. Arguing was their occupation and you would have thought that they would soon be hitting each other—but instead they'd pat each other on the back and most reluctantly tear themselves away when midnight approached.

I caught snatches of their conversation as I stood near, trying to squeeze myself into the wall, so that I shouldn't be seen.

'Now Trotsky said to Lenin . . .' They'd speak as if they had the whole inside story. 'And I said to Kropotkin . . .

'Gorky said to me . . .'

'But Trotsky was a nudnik.'

'Tenk God for communism!'

'Then why did you run away from Russia, Mr Gold?'

'To get away from my wife. But I have infinite faith in Stalin. He said this as if that was all the Russian dictator needed.

But across the road the scene wasn't so attractive. In Fieldgate Street there was an endless queue of ragged, expressionless men outside the Labour Exchange.

'Beigels! Beigels!' the old woman called from the corner of Brick Lane, with her dim, fat daughter sitting on the opposite corner. She shrieked incessantly, oblivious to everything around her. Along the Waste in the evenings the naphtha flares lit up the stalls, and sometimes a trader would hand me a blood orange or an over-ripe banana. And even though my mother had warned me, 'Don't take nothing from no-one,' the temptation was usually too great.

There was a sense of security in those days, despite the poverty. The communal feeling brought out the very best in the people of the East End. There was no question of keeping up with the Cohens, and there was no chase for gadgets. We were all in the same boat, children of the same onion boat. And I cannot remember the excitable neurosis that pervades bourgeois Jewish communities today. There were girls and the boys, flirting along Whitechapel High Street, fabulous girls with black eyes, eyes so beautiful, so alive, that one didn't notice the patched clothes. And the boys, larking about, running in and out of them, the girls giggling—and all of them queueing outside John Isaac's for chips.

There was a much wider use of language, a far more clever gift of the gab heard in those streets, when people were thrown onto themselves and each other. People talked to each other. Perhaps it was because they came from families, large families, where they were not fed on predigested stodge. The struggle had an exciting side—each day, when a mother could put her children to bed with a little supper in their bellies, was a fresh achievement.

A light came into our lives, a young man by the name of Ivor, who wore plus fours, a perpetual smile, and courted my sister Essie. My mother made us all leave the living room, and we'd all be whispering around in the passages or on the stairs while they cuddled on the settee. He came from Jubilee Street, from a well-off Russian Jewish family. His father was a cooper. Ivor was a god to me. He brought fruit to the house—fruit! We who couldn't afford potatoes were suddenly eating pears and oranges.

The children all lived, talked and dreamed about him. He used to throw me up in the air, and tell me stories, including the facts of life, which embarrassed me more than him.

We were all warned by my mother not to stop this romance flourishing, not that we needed such advice. Phoebe was away at convalescent home when he entered the family; we all told her so much about him, and when she came home she wasn't disappointed. He shook hands with her the first time they met, flashed her a secretive glance, and when he left she found a sixpence in her palm. She never got over that, and was hooked like the rest of us.

However, gods have to tumble, and Ivor was no exception, though then I didn't know why he had tumbled in my mind. He would come and sit on the settee, and I would encourage him to sit back and make himself comfortable—a practice I was following with almost every visitor now—for in this way I hoped he would drop some coppers or even sixpence down the back of it. And after he'd gone, and when nobody was in the room, I'd turn the settee upside down to get the money out. I ruined the furniture that way—but I just had to go to the pictures, for the world of Gary Cooper, Marco Polo, of The Mark of Zorro and Sanders of the River, was calling me.

Somehow now I always managed to go to the pictures every day. I'd go round to all my aunts and ask them for old clothes and rags, they, I suppose, thought I needed them for the family. Then I'd get jam jars and take them to the rag shop. And every time someone came to the house I'd ask them to lend me a farthing. By hook or by crook I'd manage it. I remember my mother saying, 'Whatever that boy wants, he gets. You'll see—bit by bit, whatever he wants he'll get.'

I began to draw distant from the family, the house, and the

games, and the playground had much less hold on me. I wanted to be on my own. One day my father punished me for being cheeky, and in his usual extreme tantrum he kicked me, though he kicked the air more. I ran out of the house and crept back in when no-one was looking and hid behind the sideboard. Hours passed, and I heard my mother crying, and I was so pleased that I, alone, could have this effect on someone.

'If only he'd come home!' she said to the others.

Well, I thought magnanimously, she's had enough punishment, so I came out—and she sloshed me round the room.

I became more aware of London, and of England. Instead of the cinema I would walk around the riverside, or get a sixpenny all-day ticket on the trams, and I'd travel past the Elephant and Castle, and sometimes even as far as New Cross or Greenwich. How beautiful Greenwich was! I could hardly believe it, and I'd stay away all day. My greatest delight was sitting upstairs on a tram, right in the front, seeing the silver lines in front of me, shooting along in the middle of the road, pretending that I was driving.

Certain things scared me on the way back to my home: for instance, I'd hate to go near a church, perhaps because my mother would always rush by if I was with her. But on my own I was even more scared, thinking that the grey sickly mass of stone would fall on top of me. This was my greatest fear as a child. And nuns were too—though this fear was shared with other Jewish children, who often saw their parents spitting seven times through their held-up fingers. I hated to see a crucifix outside a church. Why did they have a statue of a dead man outside a church? The agony and the ugliness made me close my eyes until I had passed.

Each time I would return to my house, to a terrible telling-off and a cuddle. I was getting a reputation in the family, for being a wanderer—I didn't mind at all. It seemed to make Kosher the way I wanted to go, although I was completely unaware of my journey and my destination.

Some of my relatives came from Holland for the first time, and there was great excitement in the family. A great favourite of mine was a cousin, who was then quite a famous dance band leader over there. Joe Kops and his Hot Shots. He gave me something that I was hungry for: some details about the past. My family had not always been clickers and bookmakers; there were some artists in the family, and one of my uncles had been one of the most famous socialist poets some years before. This was the first time I had heard the word 'socialist' mentioned.

He told the family that we were crazy to stay in England, that we should all pack up and go back to Amsterdam, for it looked like war was coming, and Holland would be neutral. Through him I was able to find that some of my family had come from Eastern Europe, and some had come from Spain and Portugal.

Fate is a weird bitch—for my father, who came here to escape poverty, also escaped the gas chambers; and those who were well off, and stayed in Amsterdam, perished in Auschwitz.

'War.' That word kept creeping more and more into talk. But 'Uncle' Leo, cousin Joe's friend, assured us that everything was going to be all right. He was a non-Jew from Germany, and he told us that Hitler's measures were temporary ones. My sisters didn't like him very much; one day I saw him touching Phoebe on her breast, and when she got angry I also took a dislike to him. We learned later that on returning to Germany he joined the Nazi party, and I believe he did quite well in the organization.

Anyway, my father decided that England was his home. Besides, the girls were working, and we were just managing. Essie and Marie were now going to dances. One evening I remember them trying on their blue and yellow dresses that they had just made. It was such a big event in their lives—and the rest of the family leaned over the balcony to watch them walk along Stepney Green proudly showing off their gowns.

Phoebe earned six shillings a week as a felling hand—and one day I went to her factory, where hundreds of girls were slaving away in a hall crammed with sewing machines. Here the clothes for Savile Row and Regent Street were being made, where rats and mice scampered along the rafters, where the girls couldn't walk past the boss without getting their behinds pinched, where my sisters were continuously being offered silk underwear by the boss, for you-know-what. My sisters never accepted, but some girls did—and it wasn't only the silk underwear, but also the flattery of being wanted by the boss. The language those girls used certainly made a ten-year-old blush. They worked from eight till six, slaving away in those places, definitively called sweat shops. And how many times my sisters would come home crying, for either the boss was trying to get fresh with them, or a needle had gone right through their finger. I wanted to know what getting fresh meant. 'Don't ask too many questions,' my mother said. In those days I never stopped asking questions.

If my sisters came home from work more than five minutes late, my mother was already tearing her white hair with anguish, and sending one of us to look for them. 'But be careful—don't talk to no-one!'

Once I was sent to meet Phoebe in the fog, and a woman came up to us; we both screamed so much that half the street came out. The poor woman was only asking the way.

Tall stories abounded in Stepney, stories of children being burnt instead of the guy on Guy Fawkes' Night; or the child that had swallowed an octopus egg, which had grown inside her until it killed her. This was the spawning ground of the underprivileged, of the boys with the gift of the gab, who had no knowledge of their roots, who dreamed of fame because fame brought money and money bought escape. We wanted to prove something to ourselves, to run twice as fast as the Christian world in order to keep up with it. I became aware of the Christian world, one terrifying day, when Eddie Cantor, the fabulous Jewish boy, the star of our dreams came to a restaurant in Whitechapel Road. Thousands of people came to cheer him.

'Bloody Jew-boy!' I heard a woman next to me mutter to herself.

She was talking about the star of 'Whoopee' and 'Roman Scandals'—and I pulled her coat. 'But that's Eddie Cantor!' I said.

'Shut your yap, you little yid!' said a little woman, with threadbare clothes. I didn't hate her—I was just afraid. A little later I was standing outside the Troxy, the fabulous and 'biggest cinema in the world'. We were waiting to see Sophie Tucker come out, and when she came, men started to throw stones at her, and we all screamed and rushed home.

'They were lousy Blackshirts,' my father said. 'It's all because she sang Yiddisher Momma,' my mother added.

And in Itchy Park, and in Victoria Park, we weren't all playing together anymore. A group of little boys screamed at us, 'The Yids! The Yids! We've got to get rid of the Yids!' I recognized a young mate amongst them, I waved, and he waved back.

So now we had slanging matches. For they would sing, 'Archibald, the King of the Jews, bought his wife a pair of shoes, when the shoes began to wear, Archibald began to swear.' We all took that as a colossal insult, and I don't know why. I mean, buying your wife a pair of shoes is a perfectly normal thing to do. Anyway, we yelled back: 'Archibald, King of the Yoks, bought his wife a pair of socks—when the socks began to wear, Archibald began to swear.' The only difference between us, it seems, was between shoes and socks.

But the Jubilee came, to take our mind off things. The Jubilee of King George V and his wife. I stood in Mile End Road with the kids from the school waving a Union Jack. The white-faced queen waved her fingers back at us, and I remember thinking, she's really dead. They've just stuffed her and put clockwork inside her. The king also. That was that. From that moment on the King and Queen were made of clockwork. And all those people who I heard screaming against royalty, the tailors and the pressers and the felling hands, many calling themselves red-hot Communists—they were all there with their Seebackroscopes, wildly waving Union Jacks at the passing parade.

But my dad was having none of that. 'Think of all them rooms in Buckingham Palace. Empty while people are starving!' For the life of me I couldn't see how people could eat rooms. But I was now a little closer to my father. Everyone would take the rise out of him for liking classical music, because the rage in those days was the Tango, Roy Fox, Geraldo, Joe Loss and Billy Cotton. We used to fight over the wireless, but Radio Luxembourg usually won. But to stake my difference, and my independence of dance music, I decided to go with my father to see an opera, much to his surprise. So I saw my first theatrical performance—*Aida*, done at the York Hall Swimming Baths. Even though I fell asleep, the sheer experience of sitting amongst dressed-up people was magnificent. I loved the entombment scene—but when everybody else started crying,

I couldn't understand why, and I sat forward, laughing, with the sheer delight of it all.

So I started going with him, once even to the Sadlers' Wells in Islington, where we queued for three hours and didn't get in. *Faust* was my favourite of all, and Mephistopheles was the hero, whom I couldn't bear to look at.

Infant school was over, and I started going to a Christian school at the other end of Stepney Green. I used to pass a blacksmith on the way, and I was nearly always late, being intrigued by the horse-shoes being made red-hot, and seeing them sizzle on the horse's hooves. I loved the smell. My sister hated it.

At that school I had to learn to defend myself the hard way. I hated every teacher. Figures and numbers and words were pushed into my ears, and poems were pulverized and shoved down my throat. Once we read *The Tempest*—not bad, I remember telling a friend, but I cried when I read *The Forsaken Merman*.

One morning at prayers we were singing 'All things bright and beautiful, all creatures great and small', and the boy behind me shouted out, 'Kops has got a bug crawling up his coat!' That hall could have opened up to swallow me, I was so ashamed. I used to inspect my clothing every morning before I left my house, but there was always one that seemed to elude the search. And the other horror were the nits and the woppers we found in our hair—even though we constantly went through it with a tooth-comb, we never seemed to get rid of them. Yet it was quite a thrill finding them, and squashing them between two thumb nails. Mind you, the black day of the soul was when the nurse came to inspect us in class. She'd sit in the front on her chair, and we'd line up, and one by one tremble under her scrutiny. More than once I had to go to the cleansing station, and on one occasion I was jeered at by some boys in the playground, boys who had also been to the same place at other times. One hit me on the nose. 'Dirty git! You killed our Lord!' Through my tears I cried, 'I never killed no one!'

'I mean Jesus!'

'That was a long time ago—and I didn't have nothing to do with it.

In those days I always thought that Christ had been a traitor, the Yiddisher boy who fell amongst goyim. Anyway, I fought over it, and later got rapped on the bum by a master for making a lot of noise.

My mother came up to the school. She always did on these occasions, and I heard her as I was sitting in the class, and then I'd see her burst into the classroom, five feet tall and four feet across, shouting, 'Where's that master who hit my boy? I want to see the headmaster!' She always came up to school, even though we always tried to keep it from her or beg her not to come, and even though she promised she wouldn't, she always did.

Later, discussing Christ and schicksers and goys, my father told me there were two sorts of people in the world: Jews and Jew-haters. And as a Jew I had to hate the haters.

Now the fights began in earnest, especially when I went to the penny pictures with my brother in the Commercial Road, a place designed to keep us out of mischief and off the streets—but the mischief that went on in that Mission Hall, no tongue can tell. The fights before the show began, in the aisle, between the Jews and the Christians—and Mr Walker, the cripple with his dog-collar, innocently preaching brotherly love, before the Flash Gordon serial. Or those horrors about the destruction of the Red Indian, when our fights were forgotten, and the world was divided simply between good 'uns and bad 'uns. And like the rest of the audience I jumped up and down with delight whenever an Indian fell off his horse.

The name Hitler crept more and more into the conversation at home. Now I knew he was definitely not in the family, but was out to get every one of us. And every Sunday morning a new show was being enacted in Stepney Green, a frightening horrible show run by a man called Mosley, who looked like a Jew, who some said was even partly Jewish. That explained it. 'Explained what?' I asked. Grown-ups were too busy to answer a boy who asked too many questions; but events gave me the answer.

The first person to get a pitch in Stepney Green held the meeting on Sunday morning. The Communists and Blackshirts and Blue and White Shirts used to try to outdo each other by arriving earliest, until in the end they began to arrive late Saturday night. My mother would lie awake, staring out of the window, to see who got the pitch. If it was the Blue and White Shirts, or the Commu-

nists, she'd go to sleep relieved. But if it was the Blackshirts she'd
stay awake all night, and there was a terrible tension Sunday morning. But mostly on Sunday morning, those men in their shiny black
uniforms, with their great black vans and loud-speakers, would
hold the meeting. I knew they must have very rich friends—because who else could afford uniforms in those days? Especially
some of those men whom I recognized from the Labour Exchange,
or Duckett Street, who used to wear rags. The lightning flash was
the dreaded symbol, especially since I was afraid of lightning.

Then the big boss would arrive, and the whole of Stepney Green
was black with people. Sir Oswald Mosley would try to speak.

But we had not been idle in the early morning, and had been
going from door to door to collect pennies. Then we'd rush to buy
whistles and blowers, and collect sauce-pan lids, and we'd stand
on the landings banging the lids and the kettles and the sauce-
pans together. The police could do nothing about it because we
were on private property. Mosley wanted the publicity—he came
in to the heart of the Jewish area to provoke us. But we certainly
stopped him speaking in Stepney Green by kicking up the most
hellish noise.

Sometimes I ventured into the street, and I saw the policemen
on their horses, protecting the Blackshirts, and swinging wildly
at the people I knew. I saw my own brother, an onlooker, hit over
the head with a truncheon, and he fell to the ground. But one of
my big cousins saw it also. A few weeks later he and his three
brothers waited in a doorway in Jubilee Street, and when the
policeman passed they did him up good and proper. They had
remembered his number, and shadowed him.

We in the East End had no doubt that the police were loaded
against us. So you see I grew up with a healthy hatred for the law,
a hatred and a knowledge that has given me a wonderful sense of
security, and placed me in a good position for the rest of my life.
After all, it's good to know where you stand, it's good to know who
are the enemy. And it's excellent, at an early age, to differentiate
between the police force and justice.

Everyone seemed to be wearing shirts in those days. They'd swing
through with their bands playing, the Greenshirts, the Orange-
shirts, the Blackshirts and the Blue and White Shirts. I joined the

junior Blue and White Shirts, and though I didn't know what they
stood for, I knew that they stood against Fascism. I used to run
messages for them, usually given to me by a man called Mr Prit-
chard, who later got killed in Spain. The balloon was going up in
Stepney—there were people out to get us, and we didn't wander
the streets so freely any more. Mothers called their children home
earlier.

The climax came one day when I was passing Aldgate with my
father. There were barricades, and thousands of mounted police.

'What's happening?' I asked.

'The Blackshirts are trying to march through,' he replied.

From my small height I could see marbles being thrown under
the hooves of the horses, and horses going over, and I could hear
people screaming and shouting, and the terrible urgency of fire
engines and ambulances.

'They shall not pass! Mosley shall not pass!'

'The Yids! The Yids! We've got to get rid of the Yids!'

'They shall not pass! They shall not pass!' Over and over again.

And they did not pass. That was the beginning of the end of
Sir Oswald Mosley and his under-privileged boys.

'But who stopped them? Who stopped them?' I kept asking my
father on the way home.

'The dockers did,' he replied proudly. 'It was the dockers.'

I had seen many dockers on my walks, past St George's Docks
and East India Docks.

'But dockers aren't Jewish, dad, are they? I mean, Jews are
tailors and furriers, aren't they?'

My father agreed.

'But I thought you said the world was divided between Jews
and Jew-haters?'

I asked the question twice, and he seemed confused. I felt sorry
for him—and very, very pleased with myself. Not for my question,
but because of the events of that day.

We hurried back to my home, and we all had supper.

3

So they're also Human

Suddenly everybody started reading newspapers. The Zetters, my racing cousins, always did read the back page but suddenly the Kopses started reading the front page. This was ominous. The headlines got bigger and bigger and blacker and blacker. You didn't need to be a prophet to know which way the wind was blowing.

My father flung down the *Daily Mail* and stamped on it, 'Look, they'd welcome that bastard Hitler.' My mother, shaking her head between her hands, said, 'So they're also human, it'll all blow over.' And my racing cousins added to my mother's optimism, 'Bet you half a nicker nothing will come of it.' Anything for a bet. If the world was coming to an end they would be betting each other on the exact time of day.

It got dark very early one particular day and my young sister Rose followed my mother around the house constantly clutching at her dress. 'She's driving me mad,' my mother said.

It poured with rain and all the children looked like doom and Rose became hysterical, screaming that the rain would drown everybody in the world.

I just had to get out of the house. So, taking advantage of her anxiety, I asked my mother for sixpence. She gave it to me without knowing what she was doing. 'They're all driving me mad,' I could hear her repeating as I ran down the stairs.

There I was, eleven years old, striding up Stepney Green, saying to myself, 'All right, even if the earth is going to get blown to pieces, that isn't the end of the world.'

Near the top of Stepney Green I met Mr Green. 'Where you off to?'

'Dunno, for a ride. Is there going to be a war?'

'Without a shadow of doubt, I can feel it in my water. I'm never wrong.' He spoke as though he had lived through a thousand wars.

And he had in a way, with his wife. Mind you I liked her more than him.

'So they're also human.' My mother's words echoed through my head as I sat on the 25 bus. 'They've also got children.' The bus raced towards the West End. I wanted to believe my mother but I knew her too well. If we were all on a raft starving, surrounded by sharks she'd probably say 'Thank God we've got our health and strength'. How often had I fallen down, grazed my knees and cut my forehead, sprained a finger and she'd rub the afflicted part and say, 'Good, good, you might have broken your legs.'

But this was my first journey Up West and I was much too excited to worry about the world situation any more. Head averted, eyes staring wide, I stood in the marble palace of Lyons Corner House and heard a few strains of the gypsy band. Then it occurred to me that probably my mother had never been to the West End in all her life. People looked so happy. I wandered round the streets drawn to the bright lights of the windows, banging my head against the glass windows, like a moth, pressing my nose close to the confectionery shops.

And there was one shop in particular behind Tottenham Court Road. It had a Jewish sounding name. It was full of sausages and fat people eating, dressed in beautiful clothes. I pressed my face against that window too, my mouth watering. Then I got the most terrible fright. On the wall was a photograph of Hitler, a Union Jack and a swastika on either side. I was terrified, afraid that they would pull me inside and kill me and I rushed home in panic. 'That's how they make their sausages.'

'So they're also human,' my mother repeated, trying to allay my fears. But from that moment on, I knew for certain that the war was coming.

This statement 'So they're also human' was one my mother applied to any people who were not Jewish. For instance, one day a boy I knew got knocked over by a car. I told my mother later.

'Yiddisher boy?' she enquired.

'No,' I replied, 'he's a Christian.'

'So they're also human.'

A terrible attitude yet, in a way, understandable in a tight-knit community where universal truths could only be expressed through the specific. Besides, Jewish people didn't only have this attitude to non-Jews. They ridiculed Jews from other communities, denigrated each other mercilessly. Humorously, perhaps, but nevertheless denigration.

My father would often say, 'What can you expect of a Polak,' or 'Lousy Germans'. And the Polaks would say, 'What can you expect from a Litvak' or 'Bloody Chutz'. My father's worst insult to a fellow Jew was, 'He's a lousy Peruvian'. God knows why this was an insult, and what was a Peruvian anyway? Surely someone who came from Peru. Not to my father. The Jews from Holland, they were wonderful; the Spanish Jews? At least they were reserved. But all the others? You could keep them. Even the Bulgarian Yidden. But it was the Peruvians, the unclassified Jews who made him go really red in the face.

How often the woman next door said in her thickest Russian Yiddish, 'The trouble with this country is there are too many bloody foreigners.'

But joking, like the broken glass, can't hold up the weather. People may have been smiling and stuffing themselves in the West End but in Eastern Europe states were being carved up and now letters were arriving constantly from Holland imploring us to leave England and go there.

My mother's health got worse and she coughed most of the time. How I hated her coughing. The more she gasped for breath the more I wanted to get away. And I did. But in a way that I didn't expect. For months I had been having terrible pains in my body. So much so, that the world situation became a rather second-rate fear. Believe me, I had troubles enough of my own.

I was afraid to tell my mother in case she would take me to the hospital and they would tell her that I was going to die. Or they might keep me in. To be 'kept in hospital' was a terrible phrase in the East End. For when children were schlapped away from their parents and taken up to the wards, it was a major tragedy for both parent and child, no matter how minor the illness was. No subtle psychological softening-up processes. Anyway, the pain started attacking my fingers and legs. One day she saw the pain from my expression.

'What's the matter, what's the matter?' She was always like that, eagle-eyed in anticipation of appendicitis or a sore throat. Anyway, it all came out. It always did in the end. You can't hide anything in a Jewish family. I was rushed to the hospital there and then, even though I had been walking around with it for two months.

It was nothing romantic or dramatic like a sudden operation needed for peritonitis, or too much blood or not enough. It was merely severe rheumatism. Not even anything to do with my earlier illness of rickets which, despite its name, had a certain distinction. But I had to be kept in, nevertheless, and despite my tears a great part of me enjoyed the drama. Or at least part of me was outside, watching myself crying as I was torn away from my mother's skirt. The nurse reassured me there was nothing to worry about. So did my mother, tears rolling down her face as she did so.

For a few days I was kept at the London Jewish Hospital, building castles with cards, and happy with the men and sinking down in my bed with a white face at visiting times. And my locker filling with chocolates and oranges but never flowers. Jewish people rarely used to take flowers when they visited an invalid. After all you can't eat flowers, and they die so quickly. Besides, flowers have a kind of personality and four visitors around the bed all competing for attention cannot afford such a colourful rival.

I fell for a nurse. A white-gowned probationer.

'Angels of mercy,' my mother said. 'They're all Yiddisher girls too.' We were all so proud that everything in the Jewish Hospital was Jewish. Even the X-ray machines. Goyim also used to come to that hospital for treatment. It gave me a wonderful sense of satisfaction to see Christians in the out-patients. Maybe they won't hate us so much, I thought.

In the London Jewish Hospital they were very kind and it was a blow to hear that I was being moved to a special children's hospital, somewhere in the country.

'The country?' my mother said. 'What's wrong with London, why do they have to move him miles away? What's so good in the country?' I, who needed soothing, tried to soothe her. This soothed me, besides, the thought of leaving Stepney Green excited me. 'But it's not a Yiddisher hospital,' my mother said.

A fat lot I cared. A hospital is a hospital, with nurses always waking you up at five in the morning to give you a blanket bath

and pour horrible medicine down your throat. And the smell of
disinfectant and polish and someone always moaning in the night.
So I was moved.

As soon as I saw the building I knew I was going to hate it. I
started to retch. I don't know why. And though the hospital was
surrounded by trees I felt very afraid. It seemed endless, to go on
and on for ever. As the ambulance men carried me into the ward
something died within me. A part of my life was over and all excitement left me. I was terribly alone. They could come and visit
me twice a week but I was on my own, away from the world of
Stepney Green.

My bed was on a balcony. An open balcony attached to the ward.
A strange place I would have thought for a child suffering from
rheumatism. 'Still, they know best,' I tried comforting myself with
the comfortable language of grown-ups. My first day was made
bearable by the boy in the next bed who suddenly used the longest
word I had ever heard. 'Contradiction.' 'What a beautiful word,' I
thought as I repeated it syllable by syllable.

The food was terrible. And then, of all things, when the night
threatened all the children started to sing a hymn.

'Now the day is over and night is drawing nigh, shadows of the
evening steal across the sky.' It made me feel sick. I was so lonely
and cold I cried myself to sleep.

I woke in the night. Everyone was asleep and everything was
dark except for the blue light of the night nurse, and the branches
of the trees were tearing at the moon. For the first time in my life
I was really afraid; not even Mosley or the Police had made me feel
so low—willingly I would have walked out of that hospital and
got back to Stepney Green somehow. I thought about it, saw myself
on the main road in my pyjamas. But you know how it is, you never
do under these circumstances.

Within a few days it became like a prison to me. I felt I was in
there for some sort of punishment.

I asked the boy in the next bed if he knew what was happening
in the world, if he had any idea what the latest news was. He
looked at me as if I was mad. I didn't want to ask the nurse in case
she told me the worst. But then what was world war compared to

the night nurse who was a rotten old bitch who looked like a witch?
And that was her nickname—'Witch'.

Away from the family for the first time the wind was taken right
out of my sails. I started wetting the bed regularly. The shame of
it. The night nurse in the morning would hold up the sheet for the
children to see and they would laugh, but not the kid in the next
bed. But the more they ridiculed me the more I wet the bed.

'We'll have to give you a rubber sheet, like a baby of two,' the
night nurse said. And they did. 'Angels of Mercy?' Bitterness
entered my life.

I tried everything I knew to stop wetting that bed. Almost
stopped drinking but that didn't work. The puddles and the
patches on the sheet got larger. Stark fear overcame me. I even
considered tying up my penis with string. Then I tried keeping
awake all night. I once managed to keep awake until dawn but
then I fell asleep between four and six and when I awoke I was
soaked in urine. The other children wouldn't talk to me, even
though some of them wet the bed. I was older, was expected to
know better. My whole life centred around this. When my parents
came to visit me I must have looked twice as bad as when I was
admitted. I refused to tell them what was wrong.

At nights now I tried other tactics. In secret, when everyone else
was asleep, I would strip the sheets off the bed and lay on the
rubber and when that didn't work I tried to move the mattress
slightly to one side and lay on the spring. Then in the morning
early I would mop up with my pyjama jacket. But then there was
the problem of what to do with the pyjama jacket. Anyway the
spring was cutting too much into my body so I again lay on the
sheets. One night, having got water from the nurse for supposed
thirst, I tried to wash the sheet out and hang it over the balcony.
She caught me and smacked me. If I wet on the mattress I would
turn it over while all the others slept. But I was always discovered
by the morning nurses making the beds. It was no joke, they rubbed
my nose in it.

The climax to my nightmare came one lunch time. Eating my
lunch I found I couldn't swallow the cabbage stalks or the gluey
tapioca. By now the nurses couldn't stand me and one of them

forced it all down my throat and when I was sick they made me eat my sick.

'The Yiddified bastards,' my mother said. And I think she wanted to take me home, but there was a sort of mystical attitude towards the hospital. After all, they were trying to get me better. I screamed when she left. But a few days later when my sister Phoebe came to visit me I was very quiet. I didn't need to say anything. She went straight home and told my mother that they had to get me out immediately. And they did. They came with my clothes there and then and I dressed and sang the song I had learned there:

> *'I'm off to London next Sunday morning.*
> *I'm off to London half past eight.*
> *Give my love to the dear old doctor,*
> *Tell him I can't stay here any longer.'*

Only I didn't give my love to the dear old doctor and my mother and Phoebe swept me out of the hospital gates and on to a Green Line coach, back to the East End.

'The momsers,' my mother said angrily. But I wasn't angry because I was so happy and so grateful to Phoebe, whom I have loved dearly ever since.

I must have looked very, very ill when I returned home, because they all just stared at me and quickly upholstered smiles. They spoiled me for over a week. It was wonderful.

In a Jewish household nothing heals quicker than sadness—they simply wouldn't let me be withdrawn. Besides there was also the compensation of Munich. Though looking back, some compensation.

The woman next door came running in with a newspaper. It sounded as if she was shouting, 'Piss in our time'. I wondered what on earth she was talking about.

The house became crowded with relatives and friends. Oh, I loved the look of Mr Chamberlain. My mother said, 'I knew it, God is good.'

Rumours were flying thick and fast. 'Somebody said he's partly a Yiddisher feller,' someone said. Anybody we revered had Jewish blood somewhere. But the *Jewish Chronicle* hadn't claimed him so he couldn't have been, but my brother fingered his photograph in the newspaper. 'He's got a moustache just like dad.'

'So's Hitler,' I chimed in.

'Is it good for the Yiddisher people?' my Aunt Betsie asked. 'Of course it is,' Mr Lever replied.

'What about the Yids in Czechoslovakia,' my father asked. 'Anyway if there's war there'll be plenty of work.' Nobody replied to him. 'God is good,' my mother repeated.

'It had nothing to do with God,' said Mr Zuman who surprisingly came out of his almost trappist vow of silence. Up to then all I had ever heard him say was to sigh every half-hour, 'Oy vayz meer.'

But we pored over the newspapers and savoured every word. Suddenly even Hitler looked nice. The Jeremiah from next door said, 'Didn't I tell you all along everything would be all right? I study these things.'

But my mother wondered what it meant, 'peace in our time'. Did it mean war some other time? How long is 'our time'?

Adults may have been taken in, but I don't think the children were. After all, a few weeks later they started practising with barrage balloons and searchlights in the sky. And there was talk of us all getting gas masks. A strange prelude to peace.

A letter came telling that I was being sent convalescent to Hove.

'It's a Yiddisher convalescent home, so you'll be all right there,' my mother said. Besides, the Jewish Board of Guardians had arranged it. This title had always summoned up a picture of kind old Jewish gentlemen with long beards.

So I saw the sea for the first time and this time they were kind to me. And even though the bed-wetting continued no-one ever mentioned it. I think it cleared up soon after that.

It was the first time I had been thrown together with religious Jews and, though I couldn't read or take to the prayers I mumbled gibberish and they all thought I could pray. The fried fish was out of this world. It was almost worth being ill to have such fried fish. I wrote home about it.

The sea fascinated but frightened me, for I remembered the warnings of my mother. 'Take care you only paddle, and only up to the ankles.' And when I did paddle I always faced the beach and never looked out to sea.

Brighton beach was crowded and I strolled in the sun, and though I envied the kids of holiday-makers noshing ice-cream, it was still paradise. One day I saw Lobby Lud. He was the man from the *News Chronicle*. You had to present him with the *News Chronicle* and say exactly, 'You are Mr Lobby Lud and I claim the *News Chronicle* prize.' I chased him but I didn't catch him. Anyway, I never had a *News Chronicle*.

On the beach, the *Daily Mirror* Eight were exercising. Lovely girls dressed all in white, moving rhythmically to music, surrounded by thousands of people.

My mother had warned me also not to go into the water too often because of my rheumatism, implored me always to dress up warm and do up my neck.

Every opportunity I got I was paddling in the water in an open-necked shirt. And after several weeks I felt marvellous. But paradise became boring and I was homesick again and wasn't sorry to be discharged and to return to Stepney Green.

Besides, there were weddings soon. Meanwhile, I returned to my dreary school, where Mr Swaffer suddenly announced that we were going to study algebra. I was bad enough at almost everything, but at algebra I was catastrophic. Everyone in the class seemed to understand what he was talking about and I could add up and take away with the best of them, or the worst of them, but algebra was completely beyond me.

To add insult to ignominy the algebra teacher was also the sports master. I think I stood a better chance of living in Park Lane than kicking a football, even if the ball was right in front of my foot. Anyway, one day at cricket I was wicket-keeper, and slightly proud of my position. The batsman missed the ball, the ball hit me on the nose and the bat hit me in the temple. The playground seemed to coagulate around me—mild concussion.

When I returned to school we sat for exams and everybody asked everybody else what they would do in a year's time when they finished school. I didn't have the slightest idea. Most of the others were very sure of themselves.

Essie got married and my mother cried for joy. Jewish mothers always cry for something. Ivor paid for the wedding and my father never stopped telling everyone about it. We celebrated on the seventh flight of Stepney Green Buildings. Two houses were thrown wide open and tables were put together to make one long table going from the bedroom of our house over the landing and into the bedroom of the neighbour's house. There were several sittings to dinner and did we fress? Ivor was once more resurrected in my imagination. He had a way of winning hearts with a wink. All the neighbours stood around as we sat eating and talking and singing and jabbering, and eating and drinking and talking.

'What do you think of it eh?' my father kept saying. 'He's very well off.'

'I'm the luckiest woman in the world,' my sister said to my other sister.

'My daughters have really done well for themselves. And why shouldn't they, they're good girls,' my mother told Aunt Liddy.

Essie and Ivor got a little flat in Bow and she stopped going to work. He gave her a shilling a day for lunch and she came to our house to eat with us. I would meet her along the Green, grab the coin, dash to get potatoes and eggs, and out of her shilling all of us would have egg and chips for lunch.

I remember how my father moaned around that time. 'Just when they grow up and earn a bit of cash they get married and leave you.'

By now my parents were hypnotizing me into my future work. Either I had to go into the same thing as my father or become a chef. I couldn't argue with them because it all didn't mean very much to me. I wasn't ambitious but my father was always saying, 'A poor Yiddisher boy can't afford to be ambitious'. I wondered what 'ambitious' meant. He put the word into my head. So I enquired and found out what it meant.

This attitude of my father's wasn't typical. Rather incredible when you consider how he suffered in the leather factories. Still, he did say I could become a chef and this did appeal to me. Maybe it was the thought of having lovely food and those white hats made you look so tall. No-one knew how you set about becoming a chef, and nobody enquired.

By now everybody except Rose and myself were working but we were still badly off. All the money was spent on food, for we were seven growing children with insatiable stomachs.

My brothers were flexing their muscles, becoming more proud and particular, and Jack even bought a new suit. I used to look at it with love and envy and brush the lapels with my fingers, especially when I was taking it to the pawn shop. And now I was going there alone because the stairs were getting too much for my mother.

The suit was being pawned without Jack's knowledge. He'd wear it on a week-end and I'd pawn it on Monday, then on Friday evening, when he brought his wages home, my mother would divert him, engage him in conversation while she'd slip me some money. I'd rush to the pawn shop, bring the suit back and get it into his room somehow without him seeing. It always worked smoothly except once, and then it was murder. But the suit continued to be pawned.

Marie got married. She was my oldest sister and we were all relieved, because she was no little Mae West like Essie, but rather homely and serious. Her boy-friend, Mick, the complete opposite to Ivor, was quiet and small and muttered few words. Born in Kiev, he came from 'a good family'. His parents had a grocery shop. This impressed us very much and on top of that he had a good trade. A cabinet-maker; he was making a good living.

The wedding was held at the Grand Palais in Commericial Road where the Yiddish Theatre used to be housed. Those actors who over-acted magnificently would have been hard put to have equalled the performance of my assembled family that evening. And there was a band also, playing right through dinner. For weeks before I boasted to everyone there was going to be an orchestra. Well, all right, three musicians can be called an orchestra. Anyway I called it one.

Mick's family paid for the wedding. And my mother cried her usual tears of joy, 'What do you think of it? His family paid for everything.' The only dowry he inherited was the Kops family.

What a dinner! Dave, Phoebe and myself put chicken legs into our pockets. Not because we couldn't cope, but because we were thinking of tomorrow. And my father wore a top hat. He was drunk, laughing and singing.

'I feel like a millionaire,' he said, puffing a disintegrating cigar, ash smeared all down his lapels. We all stood around him, pointing and laughing, and he danced with us. And Ivor did the Chuzutska and the young cousins joined in. I realized then that the veneer of England and Europe was very thin upon us. 'Oy-yoy Shiker is a goy.' We sang and danced until we collapsed and then we got up again and ate ice-cream until we burst and then we ate some more.

The older men played cards, serious and quiet, oblivious to everything under a cloud of cigar smoke. The children were running around and playing, the old women were yachnering, the young girls giggling and the young men feeling each other's cloth and comparing their new ties.

Dave and I were so proud showing off our new suits, the first new suits we ever had. With long trousers and Eton collars.

The wedding finished at two o'clock in the morning and Mick got a taxi to take us home. My first taxi ride, and I enjoyed that even more than the wedding. All of us singing through the night streets of the East End. 'Bei mir bis du schein—on Hitler's broch on der brain.' But as we wound up the stairs to the top my mother tried to shut us up in case we woke the neighbours.

Came the dawn and the reckoning. Each of us nibbling the remains of our chicken legs and stuffing ourselves with liquorice all-sorts. I wanted to keep my suit on all day but my mother wouldn't let me. I saw her brushing it on the table. I knew why.

'Please don't pawn it,' I begged.

'I'm not making no promises.' She sighed and I cried. But she pawned the suits later in the day. Well, you can't eat cloth, I argued philosophically with myself. But I implored her time and again, 'Please don't leave it there. Get it out soon.'

She promised. And she meant to, but we never saw those suits again. I thought about that lost suit so often in my life.

Peace in our time was a beautiful but empty expression. 'I told you so,' one of my betting cousins said. I didn't remind him that he never stopped saying that there'd never be a war ever again. The talk of war started again as Hitler started to move. This was it. And I, looking over Stepney Green, felt unsafe, so vulnerable, watching the barrage balloons hanging low in the sky.

'Where can I run?' I thought. 'Where can I hide?' I knew there was nowhere.

At school, much to my surprise, I had done well in the exam. The boys and the teacher couldn't believe the results. Neither could I. But I had won a scholarship. I thought there must have been some mistake but I wasn't going to question it, because in the hall, before the assembled school, the headmaster announced the result and told us we were all getting a half-day holiday because of my, and a few others' endeavours.

'Good old Kopsy.'

I had put down to go to a catering school, so it looked as if I was going to get my tall white hat after all.

But Hitler had other ideas.

And any celebration in the family on my behalf was lost in the terrible news and the certainty of the coming war and the fact that we were to be evacuated.

My mother said, 'Just when things start going well for us, that Momser has to spoil everything.'

All children of school age were to be moved from London. That meant just Rose and me alone out of the family. We kept it from Rose until the last moment.

'But we're all going to get killed,' she cried. My mother's optimism had subsided, yet still she clung to a strand. 'Even if there is a war, they won't bomb innocent people. They're also human.'

'I want to stop with you. I want to get killed with you,' Rose screamed as we assembled in the playground with our gas masks and labels tied to our coats. And then we all moved away, all the children and all the parents crying. And again, for me the fear and the excitement. I know that for my mother the separation from us was even worse than the thought of war.

We marched away in crocodile fashion and I looked back at Stepney Green. The leaves so green in the September sunlight. This was the place where we were born, where we grew up, where we played and sang, laughed and cried. And now all the grey faces as we passed were weeping. It was strangely quiet. Only the birds in the trees were singing now. They didn't know about the crisis. They didn't know what man was bringing to the earth.

In the train I could hardly contain myself with excitement when it moved out of the station. I jumped from window to window. But then I came back to earth with a clunk when I looked at my terrible responsibility, my crying snotty-nosed red-eyed little sister. I had promised to look after her and not to be separated from her.

'But where will we be tonight,' she appealed to me. And I shrugged, 'Your guess is as good as mine.'

'But we'll be with strangers.' Rose had never been away from home, never been more than six inches away from my mother and now she was clinging on to me and the other children were watching us, 'Will we be with Christians?'

I reassured her, 'So, they're also human.'

4

I hear Sirens

Nearly thirteen years old, when I should have been studying and practising for my Bar Mitzvah, I found myself in Buckinghamshire in a church hall at that. A picture of Christ on the wall, and my young sister sitting beside me hiding her eyes.

I thought that we had travelled to the other end of the earth, yet when I asked one white-haired old lady where we were, she replied, 'Denham dearie, where the film studios are.' But my mind wasn't on film stars. 'Where's that?' I asked. I was told that it was only twenty miles from London, and as a matter of fact two miles away at Uxbridge you could get a tube train on the Central Line to Liverpool Street Station. I kept that in mind.

My sister perked up when I told her how close we were to home. So there we were, September the First 1939, Friday night, when we should have been having lockshen soup, waiting to be billeted on a family who wanted us about as much as we wanted them.

But later we really did want them because, owing to the fact that my sister and I wouldn't be separated, the billeting officer had a very hard time trying to get us off his hands. We were the last ones left in that church hall.

'But won't you be separated—you'll be awfully near each other, Denham's such a small place.'

Rose shook her head about twenty times and clutched me tighter. 'No,' she replied, 'I promised my mum.'

Near to midnight the billeting officer was getting quite desperate. Then he drove us around in a car from house to house trying to sell us. His desperation must have eventually made him a better salesman, because a young woman and an old woman, standing at the door, nodded their heads up and down. We were in. And no sooner in than whisked straight upstairs to the bedroom, Rose practically walking in her sleep.

53

'Poor mites,' I heard the woman say. And no sooner did I sit on the bed when morning came.

Rose whispered. She whispered for days. Everything was so clean in the room. We were even given flannels and toothbrushes. We'd never cleaned our teeth up till then. And hot water came from the tap. And there was a lavatory upstairs. And carpets. And something called an eiderdown. And clean sheets. This was all very odd. And rather scaring.

Now I had become the mother. Rose wouldn't let go of me. I thought for one dreadful moment that I would have to go to the lavatory with her.

Mr and Mrs Thompson were very kind and her mother, Mrs Patmore, had white clicking teeth. Mrs Thompson had a sister called Aunt Mabel who had two dogs and a perpetual smile. I don't think I heard her utter more than a few words all the months I was there.

I felt it my duty, on the very first morning, to tell Mrs Thompson we were Jewish. She told us she knew, for it was already all around the village that Stepney Jewish schoolchildren had been inflicted upon them.

'Mind you, they're terribly well-behaved,' I heard her telling the woman next door. Then we sat down to eat our breakfast. We never had breakfast in Stepney Green, just a cup of tea and a slice of bread. There we were, in a shining little room that smelled of polish, and a table all set out with knives and forks and marmalade. And we were eating soft-boiled eggs. Well, if this was evacuation I was all for it.

Next day our teachers called us together, told us that we were the representatives of the Jewish people and they expected us to be well behaved. There were two masters, a young one, Mr Lipschitz, and an old one, Mr De Haan. I was drawn towards the older one.

The people I was staying with were quite kind, but I very much envied some of the other boys who were billeted on the actor Conrad Veidt, 'Cor we have servants waiting on us and the same food as him.'

My sister started crying 'I want to go home'. One day away and already she wanted to go home. I decided to be short with her.

'Shut up,' I said, thinking that ought to do the trick. She wept more bitterly, so I had to be kind. But I must say she got much happier after a few days and colour came to her cheeks.

I couldn't understand the Thompson family for no-one had yet mentioned the coming war. During that day I kept on asking, 'What's the news? What's the news?' They looked at me incredulously and said to each other things like 'Don't forget to pick up the seeds', or 'The hens are a bit off today'. They were living in a different world. I suppose most of the people in England were rather like that. Maybe that was their strength. A sort of noble, stupid strength. Why don't they curse the Germans? Why can't they see the enemy? I boiled inside.

Over tea I tried to tell them about my family in Amsterdam. Told them that to be Jewish meant to be persecuted. Mrs Thompson sliced up a tomato, put some salt on it and said, 'Don't you worry your head about that.'

The next day was memorable enough. September the Third. A beautiful day. We went blackberry picking. Memorable because we had our first sight of open fields. Memorable because of our delight in rolling over in the grass and seeing baby rabbits scampering for the hedges.

All at once I saw life in a different way. For now I realized that the world was an open place of light, air and clouds. A tree was a miracle. How strange! It poked through the earth and stood there waving. Trees were alive and so was grass and earth and everything. Here I could see the sky but London was a maze of stones. Here things were growing and there, beyond Uxbridge, was an artificially created world of brick. A world that was about to blow itself to smithereens, as if we hated our trap and wanted to destroy it to start again. The trouble was we might kill ourselves in the process.

Doubt entered my mind that sunny day. Doubt and conflict. For though I lay in the sunshine chewing grass and watching the birds swoop, I loved that trap. I was part of that world and I knew that I would soon tire of this one. I was not cut out for country.

We ran across the fields laughing and shouting our heads off, and we both got stung by nettles which we plucked, thinking they were ordinary leaves.

Mrs Thompson had warned us not to be late for lunch, but when we came across a whole hedge of blackberries we just went mad. Soon our mouths, our legs and our hands were completely stained purple.

I was stooping towards the ground when I heard sirens. 'What's that?' Rose said.

'Sirens, they're practising.

She said she was scared and I told her there was nothing to worry about but, nevertheless, we walked across the fields towards our foster home. The sirens went right through me, touched something deep within me. But the day was too lovely to worry about war or death. The grown-ups knew what they were doing, didn't they?

Walking across those fields I heard more than sirens. Or rather, deeper sirens pulling me towards the rocks, tugging me inland, into myself, where doubt and fear were the only certain signposts in that city of my confused thoughts.

Sirens that called to me from within the maze of myself.

That day was memorable because of the war that had come to the world, but on that day my war also started. A war that had nothing to do with the crossing of frontiers and the destruction of cities, at least not directly.

When we reached the main road a policeman shouted at us. 'What are you kids doing out, don't you know there's a war on?' His words left me cold and I noticed he had a tin helmet on. We started running towards the house, but by the time we reached the gate the all-clear was sounding. We rushed into the house. 'There's a war on! It's war isn't it? It's war!' My sister's words got jumbled up with mine then quietly I said, 'Is it war?' Mrs Thompson's mother nodded. She was laying up for lunch and she was polishing up the plates. We all sat down quietly to eat lunch. This was the first real, square, ordinary meal I had ever sat down to at a laid-up table.

'Horse-radish sauce?'

Now the Stukas were diving on Polish towns and the Nazis were goosestepping through frightened villages and we were eating roast beef and Yorkshire Pudding.

But I certainly enjoyed the food.

They wouldn't talk about the war. 'What do you think will

happen?' I kept asking. 'What about my mum and dad?' 'Will they bomb the cities?'

Events, and not the Thompsons, gave me the answer. For nothing happened at first and we settled down in Denham and became more familiar with the ways of ordinary English people. And we realized how different we were from them. We spoke the same language but meant different things.

There were a few books in the house. Books of quotations, a Home Doctor and Gems of English Poetry.

The leaves fell and as the nights drew in and I sat poking the fire and stroking the cat and reading the poems of Robert Burns and the sonnets of Shakespeare. There was one poem in particular, 'My mother bore me in the southern wild and I am black but O my soul is white. . . .'

And another one by that same poet called William Blake, 'Piping down the valleys wild'. I used to wander in the garden reading the first four lines over and over again until I learnt them by heart. I heard the sirens of poetry that autumn. Vera Lynn sang on the radio, 'Yours till the stars lose their glory—' and everyone said that the war would be over very shortly.

When Christmas came they bought us toys. They didn't seem to understand that Christmas wasn't our festival.

'Don't tell 'em,' I said to my sister.

But we became more intensely Jewish that December and I tried to tell them about our Chanucah. 'Do you know why there wasn't room at the inn?' I said, 'Why Christ was born in a manger?' They all shook their heads. 'Because everywhere was full up for Chanucah,' I said. I don't know if this was a fact, but it certainly impressed them. I realized then you could invent stories and people would believe you.

Christmas morning and our room was full of toys, sweets and fruit. Later, laughing, they told us they had fitted up a microphone under the bed to hear our reaction to the presents. At first I worried. What had I said about them? Then I was furious. 'Bloody nerve, spying on us.'

We had a wonderful time that Christmas, even Auntie Mabel spoke, but I searched that bedroom thoroughly ever after.

And at night now I used to pray. 'Oh God, I don't believe in you but I'm not taking any chances. Let the war end soon.'

Fishing in the stream, learning to ride the bicycle and taking my first part in a theatrical production. These were the memorable incidents of early 1940.

The play was called *Our Black Brothers*. With burnt cork on my face and a tea cosy on my head I made people laugh and it made me feel very good. So I departed from the text and clowned around and made everyone laugh more. I felt very pleased with myself and expected the master to congratulate me. He was furious and I was astonished and hurt but still pleased with myself. I still remember the message of that dreary little play. Black people could be almost human, and friendly, provided you treated them in the right way.

Mr and Mrs Thompson enjoyed it immensely and I dressed up very often after that in hats and coats and false moustaches and they would pretend they didn't know who it was and I knew they were pretending. But they didn't know that I knew.

The family came to visit us and brought us Yiddisher food. The Thompsons said, when the family had departed, that they were delighted to find they were nice people. We were very pleased.

Very nice people are all very well but I was getting a little tired of the gentility. And there was no life in the streets of Denham. People curled up and died at seven o'clock every evening. And one had to creep around the house. I was getting a bit fed up with Aunt Mabel's enigmatic smiles and Mrs Thompson's mother's clicking teeth. And besides, never once did Mr Thompson put his arm around Mrs Thompson or squeeze her or pinch her cheek. Could they have not been married? I doubt it.

Mind you, there was certainly activity at the Jewish School in exile. Talk about a little bit of Asia in Buckinghamshire.

Mr Lipschitz, our younger master, with liberal ideas, started a Habonim group—a Zionist youth organization rather like co-educational kosher boy scouts, where you sang lusty songs and danced vigorous dances all about building up Galilee. I didn't go for that stuff at all.

I think I started to become disillusioned with Habonim when I learned that the intention was ultimately to go to Israel. The only place I wanted to go was the East End. But I didn't. I went to Brighton.

I had orders to join the Westminster Technical Institute to take up my catering scholarship so I said so-long to my sister Rose who now, by the way, was chubby and rosy and happy. I bade farewell to Mr and Mrs Solemn Thompson, Aunt Smiling Mabel, Mrs Thompson's Clicking Mother, to the Zionist lusty boys and girls, to Mr Lipschitz with his 'No caps on heads when you pray', and goodbye to Mr De Haan with his fierce traditions. Goodbye, goodbye, to Denham, which is in Buckinghamshire, where the film studios are and where four of my pals had the same butler and food as Conrad Veidt.

Brighton was so different from the time I was there before. Just barbed wire on the beach which was once so crowded with the *Daily Mirror* Eight. No Mr Lobby Lud, no ice cream. It was so grey and desolate, and the front was deserted. I walked alone with only the boom of the waves and the shriek of the gulls. It was frightening.

At the Westminster Technical Institute they told me I wasn't going to be a chef after all. I was going to learn to be a waiter. I told them it was all a mistake but who was I to stand up against the catering educational hierarchy? The head-master pointed to the papers in front of him. 'There's no mistake, it's here in black and white.'

'Three years to learn to become a waiter? All you've got to do is put plates on the table,' I said, but they scoffed, told me it was a delicate art. I didn't like it at all, but later, putting on my waiter's suit, I convinced myself it looked much better than a chef's outfit. Mind you, I would have loved a white hat.

We cooked and served dinners and learned the intricacies of waiting on tables. My, you have no idea how fascinating it was. Often I would think 'Here we are at war, in the middle of a life and death struggle and I am learning how to hold three soup plates in one hand.'

The only compensation was the few pounds I got from the government. The first money of my own in my own post office book. When it came once a month I'd spend it all on sweets when I should have been buying books and pencils. At night the wind howled and I felt empty and saw no future in it.

'Stand out all the boys who can't swim,' the games master said, and three or four of us stood on the edge of the swimming pool. He said he was going to teach us how and gave us a sharp shove into the water. It was only the shallow end but I slipped and my head got covered. I struggled under the water. When I came to the surface I screamed and screamed. I could hear my voice echoing through the baths and I saw all the boys staring at me. To this day I have never got over my fear of water. I even hate crossing it in a boat.

But I used to stare at the sea every day and became obsessed by it. The sea surrounded us and at any time she might pounce and reclaim her lost continents.

The school moved inland when the phoney war ended and I wasn't sorry.

At Dorking in Surrey I was billeted on a colonel's estate with several other boys. A maid waited on us and one day asked me to touch her breasts. It was the first time I had touched full-blown breasts. They were beautiful. Whenever she referred to sex and having babies she called her womb her wound.

I still didn't know what I wanted to be but I knew what I didn't want to be. And that was a waiter. How I hated those stiff collars. All the time I was now thinking of going back to London and throwing it all up. 'How? How?' I racked my brain for an excuse to escape and my opportunity came soon enough for German planes were now crossing the coast daily. Now I was hearing sirens all the time.

That day of days, more Heinkels than usual crossed over Surrey. I crouched in the shelter with the other boys and masters and everything shook with the guns, and I shook with fright, unable to stop my teeth chattering and I was ashamed to appear afraid. There was a tremendously loud explosion and later, after the all-clear, we heard that a Heinkel bomber, full of bombs, had crashed in a field about a mile away. That afternoon there was confusion and I got the urge to visit my family, so I just left the school and got a Green Line coach to London.

London looked magnificent and I got off the coach at Aldgate, stood by Petticoat Lane, walked along Whitechapel Road, whistling a favourite song and in my head recalling the words, 'I went down the lane to buy a penny whistle. A copper came behind and took away my whistle. I asked him for it back, he said I haven't got it, Hi, Hi! Curly wig, you've got it in your pocket'.

When I reached the Buildings I scooted up those seven flights to my home.

'What's the matter, what's the matter,' my mother said, seeing me.

'Why have you left the school?' my father said, he being much more concerned with the prospects of me making a living.

I felt I had to dramatize the situation in order to stop being a waiter for the rest of my life.

'A bomber, German, full of bombs,' I spoke very slowly and all the family hung on my words. 'Full of bombs,' I repeated, 'was shot down and crashed on the school and exploded and destroyed the school. Two masters were killed and five boys, and I'm all bruised.'

'Where, where?' My mother rushed towards me anxious to know the afflicted part in order to rub it.

'I'm afraid I can't show you the exact spot.' That impressed them.

'You mean to say you can't go back to school again?' my Dad moaned.

'How can I if it's not there?' I replied.

'What's the matter with you Johnny? The boy's injured.' My mother pulled me close and quickly poured me some soup.

And from that moment on I believed that story myself. It was only years later I realized it was a complete fabrication.

When Holland was invaded the war really hit us and my mother sobbed. For weeks we worried about the family over there. But she cheered herself up with 'Maybe they won't treat them so bad'. But I, who had managed to read a copy of *Mein Kampf*, lent me in secret by my cousin, was under no illusions. For there it all was, in black and white, what Hitler intended to do with all of us. I read the book in horror and fascination. Strange to think it was one of the first books I ever read. I think I gave up the family in Holland there and then but I never ever contradicted my mother, and agreed that they probably were in an internment camp.

Dunkirk! The war became more than real, became a nightmare, but these English people, people like the Thompsons, were now showing the other side of their coin and I was so grateful that I had been born in England, and Churchill's name was probably being blessed in every synagogue in the world. And in every Jewish home and Jewish heart, except, of course, those who couldn't forget the class war.

'But he's a bloody Conservative,' one of my uncles said. There we were locked in the middle of a life and death struggle, and planes darting closer every day to London, and my uncle was still talking about that traitor Ramsay MacDonald and the stinking Conservative party.

The sirens went nearly every day and my mother, all sixteen stone of her, would be the first downstairs and into my Aunt Katie's house on the ground floor. She was the first one there, and I was always the second. My mother heard sirens before they even began but then she was hearing sirens all the time by now.

I remember her rushing down seven flights, her shoes falling off on the way, and she continued running in her bare feet and I was too scared to pick up the shoes. I was very ashamed of being so scared, especially on September the fifth, when I even managed to catch up with my mother and somehow overtake her. As she ran down she knocked on the window of every flat 'Air raid, air raid, air raid,' as if they hadn't heard.

Down in Aunt Katie's flat, the entire Kops and Zetter families sought refuge. Every room was crammed with the dreary Kopses and the excitable Zetters. The Zetters feeling rather restless because the war had interfered with horse-racing. But now the Kopses had something to really worry about and they came into their own. Crisis and cataclysm took the place of family quarrels.

Two days before the blitz started, three bombs dropped on Stepney Green, one in the park just in front of the Buildings, smack in front of our block.

'It's always the poor who suffer,' my father said. 'Why don't they drop them on Park Lane?'

'Was it a bomb?' one of my dazed aunts yelled. 'Well, it wasn't a firework,' I replied. 'We're finished! We're finished!' a girl cousin cried.

'It's the same the whole world over, it's the poor what gets the blame.' My Uncle Hymie sang and made all of us laugh, but a kind of hollow laughter for we were waiting for the all-clear to see what the damage was.

When it came we realized that it was our house that had copped it. It wasn't destroyed but the blast had made it uninhabitable. We rushed upstairs to investigate but it was getting dark and we brought down a bundle each and that was that. We left everything else behind. That was the end of 23 Stepney Green Buildings. And for the next few days we all lived communally in Aunty Katie's place.

On September the Seventh, the bombers came early. That day stands out like a flaming wound in my memory. Imagine a ground floor flat, crowded with hysterical women, crying babies and great crashes in the sky and the whole earth shaking. Someone rushed in 'The docks are alight. All the docks are alight.' I could smell burning.

'Trust the poor to get it in the neck, why don't they sort out the rich?'

The men started to play cards and the women tried a little sing-song, singing 'I saw the old homestead and faces I loved' or 'Don't go down in the mines dad, dreams very often come true' or 'Yiddle mit his fiddle', But every so often twenty women's fists shook at the ceiling, cursing the explosions, Germany, Hitler.

'May he die from a lingering tumour,' my mother wailed. 'That's too good for him,' Aunt Sarah said. They sat around, those old people. About thirty of them, with a collective age of roughly one thousand and five hundred years. And on their faces was an accumulation of suffering and dread and hope and fear. Revealing the story of our people since we wandered over the face of the world.

Yes, cursing got my mother and my aunts through those early days. I sat under the table where above the men were playing cards, screwing my eyes up and covering my ears, counting the explosions.

'We're all gonna be killed, we're finished,' one of my aunts became hysterical.

'Churchill will get us through, he's a friend of the Yiddisher people.' With these words she was soothed.

This time all my uncles nodded agreement, even the Marxist playing solo.

The all-clear sounded a beautiful symphony in my ears, and everyone relaxed, the men arguing politics, and the women talking about food. But the younger people wandered out to see the fires and I went with them, towards the Commercial Road. The closer I got the more black and red it became, with flames shooting higher than the cranes along the dockside. Sparks were spitting everywhere and tongues of fire consumed the great warehouses along the black and orange water of the Thames. Everything was chaos except the fire which was like a living monster with an insatiable appetite. And I was afraid of being devoured, besides I hated to watch the firemen working so hard so I left by myself and wandered back towards Stepney Green where black smoke covered the sky.

Yet, with all this, there was still a feeling of unreality. I couldn't believe it, it was like a film being shown before my eyes. Men were rushing around selling newspapers, screaming about the amount of German planes that were brought down, and there had been a family wiped out where I had just been standing. A boy from Redmans Road rushed up to me, excited, 'Did yer hear about the German pilot wot was shot down. Came down by parachute and was wearing women's underclothes. People tore him to pieces.' He claimed he saw it with his own eyes but I didn't believe him. I could believe the tearing to pieces part, but why should a pilot wear a woman's underclothes? That was too much to swallow.

The smoke made my eyes smart and water. A policeman standing near told me not to cry. 'Don't worry sonny, we're going to beat the hell out of those Germans.' His words, however, gave me no comfort. On the contrary, I couldn't cope with a kind policeman, not after my views about the law. It just gave me new problems.

When I got near the Buildings I could see my mother standing there screaming out for her children. 'My children, my children! Where are my children?' She was so relieved to see me she chastised me.

'They're coming tonight. Quick! Quick!' She schlapped me into

Aunt Katie's, where a nucleus of relatives were sitting bent round the radio listening to Lord Haw-Haw.

'Today the Jews of London are shaking in their shoes, but tonight there will be no more Jews.'

I looked out of the window and watched the darkening sky. But the flames took over from the daylight and the whole world was red. The family inquest reached only one conclusion. The Germans had set fire to the docks in order to have a beacon for the coming night of terror. We knew we were in for it. 'So it's the poor Jews who will have to suffer,' my father said, shaking his head up and down, as Jews had done for two thousand years before him.

'God is good, we'll get over it.' My mother's faith must have been lined with asbestos. But I couldn't think of getting over it and lived purely in the present, nervously talking to myself, playing the fool, or going to the lavatory several times over. When the siren wailed the bombers were on its tail.

'Tell me Mum, how you make plava cake.' I wanted to engage her in conversation, not only for her sake. Besides I thought these recipes had never been written down. I was sure my mother had her own special way of cooking that had never been used by anyone else.

'Don't drive me mad.'

'No seriously, how do you make it?'

'Look, you take a bit of sugar and a bit of flour and some eggs. A bit of this and a bit of that.'

Above the Buildings the planes were diving and inside I was dying. And she was holding on to me to keep herself straight and to comfort me.

'What do you mean, a bit of this and that? What are the quantities?'

'How should I know? What do you want of my life?'

My uncles were cracking dirty stories in the corner, the long drawn-out dramatic episodes only punctuated by the bombs. And my mother lost herself in the crowd of aunts, who were eating nervously. The air in the room was stale with smoke. Smoke from the fires outside and the cigarettes inside.

I got a strange feeling of loneliness, of being cut off in that

3

lighted room, cut off from all existence. Most of the kids had dropped off to sleep but I lay outstretched on the floor counting the explosions. Someone prayed.

'A fat lot of good that'll do you,' a Zetter said.

How long is a night of terror?

I collared my mother again, 'How do you make gefilte fish?'

But the all-clear went and I never learnt how to make gefilte fish. And now I have to buy it in jars. A very third-rate substitute for that most wonderful dish of my mother's, brought about somehow by adding a little bit of this with a little bit of that and adding just a bit of this and that and that.

'Oh, I've got such a pain,' I said to my mother.

'Go to the lavatory then.'

'I've been three times.'

'Go again, it's good for you.'

I left Aunt Kate about seven in the morning and wandered around the streets. The war had come home to roost.

Part of Stepney Green was destroyed. Single walls stood where houses had once enclosed a family. Beams of wood jutted out at crazy angles.

People were poking about the ruins, pulling out a few precious belongings. Those big black bombers had dropped eggs of death from their bellies. But I didn't have much time to reflect on life and death for a new game was in progress.

The boys of Stepney Green were scrubbing around in the debris near the clocktower for pieces of shrapnel. This caught my imagination and immediately I set to it. I found lots of pieces of blue and grey metal and proudly I showed them to another kid. 'That bit's no good, it's from an ack-ack gun, but that's all right. That's from a German bomb.' I wondered who made the rules but I played the game. I was very pleased with my shrapnel and I rushed home to show my family who were eating and cleaning up and washing and discussing and arguing and I went out again after breakfast, round to Redmans Road to look for some more. In front of me was a space, where once had been the house of a boy I knew. Not a very close friend, just someone I played with occasionally.

'What happened?' I asked a warden.

'They all got killed.'

Funny, I thought, I had seen him only the day before and now he was no more.

When I went home for lunch my father was sitting with his ear against the radio set, twisting the knob around the world until he settled on Germany.

'The Jews of England are either dead or hiding in their holes,' a sickening voice snarled over the air.

'That's what you think,' my father shouted back.

He still went on about the class war. That the West End hadn't been touched. I asked him why we didn't move there. He dismissed this with 'If we had money we'd be all right. Trust the rich.'

'It's the same the whole world over, it's the Yids wot get the blame,' Uncle Hymie sang. And then, rather incongruously, my father went on about how people always said there was no such thing as a poor Jew, and here in the East End there were over 200,000, all poor and all Jewish. 'If only the English people listened to us, had learned from the Yidden, they would have been all right.' He went on and on lamenting. But he saw a little ray of hope. After all we have the same enemy, at least Mosley's in prison, so they're waking up at last.

After the terror of that night people started to flock towards the tube. They wanted to get underground. Thousands upon thousands the next evening pushed their way into Liverpool Street Station, demanded to be let down to shelter. At first the authorities wouldn't agree to it and they called out the soldiers to bar the way. I stood there in the thick of the crowd with my mother and father and brothers and sisters thinking that there would be a panic and we would all be crushed to death.

It was the worst experience I had up until then and I wanted to rush out of that crowd, but I was jammed tight. I would have preferred to take my chances in the street with the bombs. Anything was preferable to that crush. I shouted my head off, went limp and was carried along by the surging masses, trying to hold on to my slipping identity. The people would not give up and would not disperse, would not take no for an answer. A great yell went up and the gates were opened and my mother threw her hands together and clutched them towards the sky. 'Thank God. He heard me.' As if she had a special line through to Him and He had intervened with the Government on behalf of the Kops family.

'It's a great victory for the working class,' a man said, 'One of our big victories.'

And though I felt ill and my heart was beating over-fast, all the family were thrilled to know that people had taken over the underground and made the government acquiesce.

So I dashed with the crowd into the underground and saw the solidarity of the surface disappear as an endless stream of people crushed in after us. We were underground people with the smell of disinfectant in our nostrils and blankets under our arms, standing jammed, shoving and pushing each other. No laughter, no humour. What sort of victory had we achieved? Every family for itself now, and my mother tried to encompass all her family with her bulk, a family that had emigrated into the bowels of the earth. Dignity and joy left the world, my world. Shuffling down I felt as if we were fulfilling some awful prophecy. A prophecy that no one had uttered to me. Something that everyone knew but didn't want to talk about.

The soldiers downstairs forced us to get into trains, to go further up the line. Liverpool Street, being the closest, geographically and umbilically, was the most popular. So we were forced to move on and we tried the next station along the Central Line, and then the next and the next.

I heard sirens. And sirens and sirens. Early in the morning, in the afternoon and in the evening. And we went underground to get away from the sirens and the bombs. Yet they followed me and I heard sirens until the world became a siren. One endless cry of torture. It penetrated right into the core of my being, night and day was one long night, one long nightmare, one long siren, one long wail of despair. Some people feel a certain nostalgia for those days, recall a poetic dream about the blitz. They talk about those days as if they were time of a true communal spirit. Not to me. It was the beginning of an era of utter terror, of fear and horror. I stopped being a child and came face to face with the new reality of the world.

I would scoot out of the train ahead of the family and under the legs of people, unravelling the three or four scarves tied around me. And I bagged any space I could along the platform. The family

followed, and we pitched our 'tent', then we unravelled and un-
wound and relaxed. And out came the sandwiches and the forced
good humour. Here we were back on the trot wandering again,
involved in a new exodus—the Jews of the East End, who had left
their homes, and gone into the exile of the underground. Our
spirits would rise for a while, we were alive for another night, we
would see another dawn.

Now I see that the miracle of Moses wasn't getting the message
from God but in getting all the Jews to go in the same direction, to
make them into one big family. For despite the obvious relief and
friendliness and the sharing of the sandwiches, families were going
in all directions, each trying to feather its own three feet of concrete. And something had been lost without trace. This is what
Hitler brought to the world with his commandments. The Jewish
people of London with their terrific communal feeling were being
torn apart, irrevocably, for all time. But then, so was the whole
world.

'This is what they brought to the world,' my mother said. And
an old man with a sharp beard sitting down next to me, shook
his head knowingly. 'When they start on the Jews a terrible retri-
bution comes to the world. Look at Haman! Look at Pharaoh!'

But I wasn't only miserable, for seizing advantage of my mother's
preoccupations, I managed to get some money out of her. And I got
bars and bars of chocolate out of the chocolate machines and
weighed myself incessantly. Here was a new life, a whole net-
work, a whole city under the world. We rode up and down the
escalators. The children of London were adapting themselves to
the times, inventing new games, playing hopscotch while their
mothers shyly suckled young babies on the concrete. And I used to
ride backwards and forwards in the trains to see the other stations
of underground people.

One night, though, we were very lucky. We were pitched down
at Liverpool Street and Phyllis and I (for now Phoebe had decided
that her name was old-fashioned) decided to venture as far as
Marble Arch. As the train moved out of the Bank Station and
entered the tunnel, it stopped and all the lights went out. There
was a great thud and we held our ears. When we returned we
realized a bomb had fallen down the lift shaft of that station and,

apart from those who were killed from blast, there were also those who had been thrown on the line and electrocuted just as our train pulled out.

I was relieved when a few weeks later my mother said she couldn't take it any longer. She decided to leave London with the family. Up until now she was reluctant for my father and Dave couldn't go because of essential war work. Yes, even my father, almost as blind as a bat, was of some use. And he was glad. Jack was in the Army, so it was just the girls, me and my Mother who were leaving.

'Yes, I'll get Rose from Denham, and we'll go up North,' she said. I slept more peacefully on the stone that night.

Two days later we left London.

5

Blood is thicker than Water

Half the Kops family entered York. My mother, three sisters and myself.

'Here the Jews were massacred,' I said.

'When? When?'

My mother jumped out of her seat. I had to explain it was in history, centuries ago. She visibly relaxed. She wasn't feeling very secure away from her stamping ground, for now we were in England and no longer in the East End.

I was unimpressed with the magnificent York Minster but, then again, buildings never meant very much to me. I was far more impressed with the chocolate factory.

We were driven straight to the local institution where we were to stay for a few days. 'Institution,' had sounded a rather grand place; full of big furniture and smashing food. Little did I realize what was in store. We sat on a wooden bench eating off a wooden table, and the food wasn't bad. It was the people who unnerved me. Old men and women who were slightly cuckoo and some of them not so slightly. One old man was busy making an invisible cat's cradle with invisible thread, a laughing woman beside him carefully took it from him and started weaving the air herself with her dirty fingers. I stared stark-eyed and shuddered.

In the evening there was a film show, 'Alf's Button Afloat'. Talk about eerie, for although it was a comedy the inmates laughed in all the wrong places. When we laughed everyone else was stony silent.

We slept in dormitories that night, I alone with the old men, the women on some other floor. Oh, the smells of old men together in a ward at night. I felt so lonely and far away. One minute I had been a child and now—what?

I lay awake with the sound of the man in the next bed mumbling and snorting and another having an argument in his sleep, and I thought of the bombs falling on London.

Next morning my mother sat quiet at breakfast as if she had the stuffing knocked out of her. Noise left the family for the first time.

'I wonder how Jack is, and Dad and Dave?' she kept on asking my sister, but very quietly.

'It took the war to get us on our feet,' I said, for now money was coming in regularly.

'Such getting on our feet we can do without,' she replied.

Yes, we weren't short of a few bob now. We were making a living, as it were. No longer living from hand to mouth. Those days were gone forever, but so much more was gone forever. Peace and Stepney Green and no-one joked any more. My mother no longer broke into song when she was happy or sad. So there we were, eating porridge in York, that beautiful city. At least people never stopped telling me it was beautiful. But Commercial Road was my idea of beauty, and Wentworth Street and Victoria Park. I had a great empty feeling inside.

I could read my mother like an open book and knew what was going on in her mind. She could only see the war in terms of what it had done to her own family. That was what the war had done, split up the family. There I realized how much Jews needed the family. It was our security. We were obsessed with it, we indulged in it and we enjoyed our indulgence and obsession. For here was our strength, our only safety, our place of worship, the only world we knew. We were conditioned by thousands of years of wandering. Yet it was not only negative reasons that made us cling together. The family was the essence of our faith, and even though some of us had lost our religion on the way we were still held together by the bondage of our bond. And possibly our religion springs from this. The family, the natural order in the midst of chaos, the tent in the desert, affirmed that life was beautiful because it was. And this was and is our undying faith.

'Blood is thicker than water,' my mother replied when my sister asked her to stop crying.

They wanted to get away from York but didn't know where

they wanted to go. And I argued with them when they spoke about
moving. After all, York was a city and I had had enough of nature.
I thought we ought to look for digs there. What is one boy's voice
against four women? So, naturally, we moved.

Into the wilds of Yorkshire.

'Isn't the air lovely and fresh,' my mother said, trying to convince herself.

It was bloody draughty. We were all freezing and depressed.

We were standing in the only street of a little village called
Hamsthwaite, miles away from anywhere. You know the sort of
place, twelve houses, one shop selling everything, a church and a
bus once a day.

'God help us,' my mother said.

But God didn't hear the prayers of Jewish women that autumn.
He was a very old God and a little deaf.

Again we went through the rigmarole of trying to find a place
together. Again I could see the desperate insecurity of my mother.
She was pathetic as she pleaded with the billeting officer. But I was
beginning not to mind the adventure; in fact I was almost enjoying
it.

Of course it was impossible. We simply couldn't be billeted together. Each house took one of us but no-one wanted my mother.
At least one house wouldn't have minded my mother instead of
me, but my mother wouldn't hear of it.

'What's going to happen to her?' I asked the WVS woman. She
told us not to worry, my mother would be billeted in a beautiful
village called Nunmonkton, a few miles away.

We all protested that we couldn't be parted but naturally, or
unnaturally, we were. My mother went, smiling bravely, and making sure that we knew she was suffering beneath it all. I smiled as
I remembered all her admonishments when I was a child. 'When
I'm dead then you'll appreciate me—There's no one in the world
like your mother—I'm a wonderful woman—There's not another
woman in the whole world who has to put up with the things I
do—No tongue can tell what a mother goes through, and
for what?'

Are the nights in Yorkshire longer than anywhere else in the
world?

Yes!

The next morning Phyllis and I set off to visit my mother at Nunmonkton.

I can tell you Hamsthwaite was a thriving city compared with Nunmonkton. Just lonely moorland and a dirty sky. My mother burst into tears when she saw us. We had come in on a bus and we were four and a half miles from the main road. There were no buses back that day.

Phyllis tried to persuade my mother to return to Hamsthwaite with us. She didn't need much persuading, she smiled, gathered up her things, and we all set off across the fields. Me with tonsilitis and carrying two cases, or should I say struggling: one on my shoulder and the other knocking against my knees. Yet, we weren't unhappy because we were so depressed that the only thing we could do was to laugh. And when it poured with rain we killed ourselves, my mother every so often stopping and saying with incredible incredulity, 'Nunmonkton! Nunmonkton! Nunmonkton!' She just repeated it. Her intonation spoke volumes. I don't wish to disparage a tiny Yorkshire village, and no doubt it is the prettiest place in the world, but it is forever stencilled in my mind as the place where I reached the lowest low.

'What am I doing in Yorkshire?' 'Ask me.' I kept on asking and answering myself. So I stumbled on, with sore throat, wet face, bruised knees and gusts of over-emphatic laughter.

A miracle occurred! We came to a sort of road and after sixty minutes, after being absolutely soaked to the skin, another miracle, a lorry gave us a lift. Otherwise there might be three unknown Jewish mounds on the moors.

So we got back to Hamsthwaite. And I could have kissed every brick of those houses and even the church. Well, perhaps not. But my mother's relief at returning was short-lived, by now she was thoroughly disillusioned with the provinces.

'So what's so wonderful about fresh air?' she said. I agreed with her.

They all settled down in the village hall and refused to be separated. I, meanwhile, was at my favourite occupation, wandering, and coming across an empty house, rushed back to tell the others. That was it. No sooner said than done. Up jumped my mother

with her bundle, and my sisters, and off we trotted, I bringing up
the rear, groaning under the suitcases. As I say, Jewish people don't
believe in miracles, they expect them. The door was unlocked.

'So what's wrong with this?' my mother said. 'Loose floorboards,
hanging ceiling, falling wallpaper, a bit of fungus, but who's complaining?'

The way my mother sat down I knew nothing would get her
out of that place. Plague, fire, God, not even the billeting officer,
who came an hour later, red in the face.

'Blood is thicker than water,' was all that my mother would
answer to all his admonishments. Blood, in Yorkshire, wasn't
apparently thicker than water. But my mother had set up embassy
there and the soil and the house already belonged to the House
of Israel.

The billeting officer pleaded with us to be reasonable. Reasonable was not a word in my mother's vocabulary. She could be so at
times, but not when the family was threatened. Then she became
totally unreasonable.

The billeting officer must have seen that I was slightly more
'anglicised' so he appealed to me, explained that the house was
already earmarked for another evacuated family, who were at
present staying with a wealthy woman.

'So why must they move?' I asked. He replied that the wealthy
lady didn't want that London family. And added, more to himself, that she was a very influential old buzzard.

'All right then, they'll move here and we'll move in with the
wealthy lady.' I think he trembled, but it might have been the
draught coming up through the floorboards.

'No, you don't understand, she doesn't want anyone staying
with her.'

My mother overheard, told him what he could do with his
wealthy lady and himself. 'You can axe my arse,' she said. Only
rarely did she use this expression, and only under extremely
dangerous circumstances. The billeting officer stopped being an
Englishman for a fraction of a second. I thought he would swear.

'It's against the law. I could have you forcibly removed. I'm
just giving you a little advice.'

My mother told him what to do with his advice. So he left. Noth-

ing happened and we were congratulating ourselves on victory in
that completely empty house, in that draughty village, when we
realized we had no beds and no blankets.

I searched for that same billeting officer and approached him
feeling terribly nervous, but remembered the old proverb of several
of the Zetters, 'Without chutzpah where are you?'

To my astonishment and joy he gave me blankets and pillows
and helped me bring the camp beds. He was a really kind man. I
felt guilty, tried to apologize for my mother. But he just walked
beside me, silently.

He looked very worried, as if he were saying to himself, 'I'm
going to get hell for this.'

Two camp beds and five people. Two sisters and my mother in
one and me and a sister in the other one sleeping end to end. I did
volunteer to sleep on the floor but this was always frowned upon
in the family, my mother always saying, 'When I'm dead, then you
can get close to the floor.' She wouldn't hear of it.

Believe me, the three in the other bed were better off, what with
the cold that night sweeping through that enormous room. On
second thoughts it didn't sweep through, it just piled up in that
room and stayed there.

I lay awake, worrying, thinking. Maybe we'll survive this war,
and what will I do in the world? But eventually sleep intervened
on my behalf, and I didn't dream.

Next day in the only street of the village someone pointed out
the wealthy old woman who looked daggers. Mind you my daggers
were far sharper and faster and more plentiful than hers. We stared
each other out but I looked away first.

But who was this coming towards me? A priest with a beard?
Surely not. His hand outstretched, and he smiled and shook my
hand. If this wasn't a Jewish face then I'm a Jewish Dutchman
(which I am). 'Shalom,' he said and introduced himself. I didn't
catch his name. It never occurred to me that he had come to see
me or us. Could he have been a relative? I dismissed that thought.
Our family had never run to Rabbis. Yet his face was so familiar.
Maybe it was in the bleak surroundings of Yorkshire that made it
so. Two Jews in the wildnerness.

'I would like to see your mother.' Bad news I thought. Some

bad news from London perhaps. I didn't say another word, took him to the house.

'What's wrong? Is it about Johnny?' She also feared the worst.

'No, No, Mrs Kops. Don't worry.' He was a Yiddisher man with a Yorkshire accent. At first I thought he was kidding, or was a confidence man. And he knew our name. That meant something.

He flourished his hand towards the window, indicating the village.

'How can you stay here?'

My mother agreed with him but told him that there was a war on in the south of England.

'Blood is thicker than water,' he said. 'You should be amongst your own.'

This expression, 'blood is thicker than water,' is the primaeval rallying call for Jews in exile, for families who are in danger of drifting apart, for children who question the necessity of staying within the fold. It's probably as old as the ram's horn, possibly older.

'So what have you got for us?' my sister chimed in, sarcastically.

'I'm glad you asked me that question,' he said. But left us all hanging in the air, exacting every ounce of drama from his performance. This was obviously a transaction. Just beneath the surface of this holy man and his kind voice was the familiar and hallowed ritual of buying and selling. Only God knows what we had to offer. Still he pointed derisively at the impoverished village, before stirring the tea my mother gave him.

'Tell me Mrs Kops. Can your daughter dance here? Can she go to dances here?'

My sister shook her head, smiled and frowned.

'And tell me. Can your boy work here?'

I didn't like the sound of that. I wasn't thinking about working anywhere.

My mother agreed that you couldn't dance or work in Hamsthwaite, and her face got brighter. But I hoped she was more interested in my sister dancing than in me working.

We were all sitting forward, eager and yearning for his next words.

'Come to Leeds. Be amongst your own kind. Blood is thicker than water.'

'Are there Yiddisher people in Leeds?'

'Are you kidding? There are thousands. I should have a penny for every Yiddisher person in Leeds.' He tried to sell us Leeds, as if it was his to sell. He threw in the lot, factories, dance halls, hairdressers. I was suspicious.

'Schmaltz herrings you can get. Shules, matzos, frying oil, the Jewish Board of Guardians. We've got everything there.'

As he eulogized, in the pulpit of his expressions, I couldn't help wondering what a Jewish Reverend was doing in that tiny village rescuing half a Jewish family from a non-Jewish world. But I was still benevolent in those days and dismissed my suspicions. Perhaps that was his sacred mission—the ingathering of the London diaspora to the holy land of Leeds.

He stood up.

'Right. It's all arranged. You'll come.'

'But, but—' my mother said.

'Oo mum,' my sisters squeaked, sort of dancing around her with their hands clasped around her neck all excited.

'Good. Don't worry, I've got everything arranged. A house, jobs, everything.'

And with that he was gone.

In the night my suspicions returned.

An ambulance called the next day to drive us to the fabled city. And the billeting officer, looking very happy, came to bid us goodbye.

I took him aside for one moment, told him that he could tell me the truth because I knew there was something up. He told me it was quite simple.

The wealthy woman had a lot of influence indeed and his head would have rolled if we had stayed in that house. He had thought about it and discussed it with the vicar who discussed it with the wealthy lady. The vicar came up with an inspiration. 'Now they're Jewish people. Where are there more Jewish people?' 'Leeds'. So he had got on the phone to the Jewish community, spoke to a Rabbi and explained the situation. Blood was apparently thicker than water in the religious fraternity. They got on like a house on

fire. After all, business is business. That was that. The Reverend
came.

The billeting officer could see that I was feeling a little appre-
hensive so he reassured me as I got into the ambulance.

'Don't worry, he's promised that everything's been taken care
of. Besides, you'll be much happier amongst your own sort.'

I was pleased to see that he was so relieved, he was such a gentle
man and I wouldn't wish the Kops family on any Yorkshire man,
without some warning.

This all happened within three days and through the frosted
glass of the ambulance window I could see the glazed Yorkshire
countryside flash past.

'Good riddance,' my mother yelled. And she started singing
again with all her heart, the latest popular song, 'Yours till the stars
lose their glory—yours till the birds fail to sing.' She loved popular
songs, belted them out with that rich and peculiar, raucous
Cockney, Jewish accent. She was moving towards territory that
wasn't quite home, but almost. The customs and religion would be
the same, the only difference being a Yorkshire accent.

'Still, beggars can't be choosers, besides a Yiddisher heart is a
Yiddisher heart.' And what could I add to that? She had made
a definitive statement, no more words needed to be said in that
ambulance, but we were all very excited and continued singing
until we reached the Promised Land.

A conglomeration of dirty grey buildings bunched together was
a sight for sore eyes. So this was Leeds, full of smoke and people.
It suited me down to the ground. The ambulance dropped us at
Chapeltown. It sounded very much like Whitechapel and in fact
was a Whitechapel in miniature. Men with beards and women
indulging kids in prams, delicatessen shops and Buba Yachnas.

My mother, who a few weeks ago would have no sooner thought
of going to Leeds than flying to the moon, became a serene and
happy matriarch again.

We were taken to the Jewish Board of Guardians, Northern
Branch, where we expected the fulfilment of the Reverend's
promises. Not a sausage. Not even a Vienna sausage. They weren't
expecting us, and neither were they too delighted to see us. There
were absolutely no arrangements made. The Reverend's name was

invoked and cursed by my mother, silently at first until her voice
rose to a crescendo. They phoned him, but he wasn't to be found.
I thought she would tear the place apart, for she just couldn't believe that a Jewish man would behave so badly. 'A Reverend!
What do you think of it.' She went on and on.

I could feel my temples throbbing and I got so flaming angry
that I told everyone I was going to find that Reverend and to give
him a piece of my mind. I wanted to show that I had become a
man and someone to be reckoned with. So I rushed out leaving
the others there. I wandered the dull streets and fortunately when
I returned, no-one asked me how I got on. They must have guessed
and I felt a sense of personal failure. The people at the Board
of Guardians were more than kind and they fixed us up with
food.

No-one seemed to know the Reverend in question. Someone
suggested that he was a lesser dignitary from some other Jewish
community, others doubted his existence completely, thought we
had invented him. But whoever he was, we never saw him again.

We sat looking out of the windows into the grey city, eating thick
barley soup. People came and went, looked at us, pointed at us.
Telephone conversations. Mild hysterics, heated arguments, until
finally we were taken to a room in the main Chapeltown Road. It
was a freezing November. The first thing that Phyllis and I did
was to scrub the place out. They brought bunks and blankets and
smashing clothing for us, three sizes too big, but who were we to
complain? Trams clanging along outside took me back to the years
before the war, to my safaris into South London. I ventured out,
and just along the road was a delicatessen shop. I rushed home
excited.

'You can get beigels, pickled herrings, matzos and everything.'
So we did. And had such a beano, as my mother would call it. A
rather English expression for the daughter of a Dutch-Yiddish
cigar roller.

That evening I wandered around Leeds and approved.

Briggate was full of life and many characters were hanging
about. A memorable evening because it was the first time I noticed
whores. There was quite a brisk business going on. I didn't fancy
any of those painted birds myself, besides I was stoney broke. On

the way home I noticed the people coming from the pubs, tottering and singing. And I wondered why Jewish people never spent their time or money drinking. I remember thinking out for myself what I thought was the answer.

Most of our money was spent in the home and on the home. A Jewish home was a self-perpetuating community, a reflection of the entire community. The thing that kept the Jewish people together. But that wasn't the only reason why Jewish men hardly drank. It was important never to let our guard down. Being always a minority, the home was the only safe place for us. We always had to be alert, doubly alert. To survive in foreign cities we had to be that much more sober. Anyway, that was my theory.

We moved a few days later to a more congenial but less salubrious flat, in a street notorious for its brothels where some of the girls, much to my fascination, still plied their trade. The house we lived in had, just a few weeks before, been groaning under the weight of groaning men and creaking springs but the landlord got tired of the girls doing moonlight flits and thought he d try evacuees for a change. But ceremony dies hard and men were forever standing outside, gazing at the windows, like mournful dogs watching and waiting for the bitch of the house to appear. And they were forever knocking on that door, my mother having hysterics at every rat-a-tat-tat. 'Don't go Phyllis. None of the girls must go. Only Bernie.' She worried that my sisters might suddenly become corrupted, gave lectures on the virtues of being a nice, respectable Yiddisher girl. She needn't have worried. My sisters were nice, respectable Yiddisher girls. What they had they were hanging on to, and they hung on neurotically. Sometimes just by a hair's breadth.

So there I was answering the door to men who, to put it kindly, looked none too dignified. Still, it gave me a new slant on life, showed me that my mother's saying, 'As long as you've got your health and strength,' didn't quite hold water. She should have added 'and sex'.

'This never could have happened in the East End,' she would say. 'If people wanted that they went Up West.' 'Up West,' was that convenient place where depravity, excess and luxury were available, but far beyond the reach of people like us.

I was fifteen years old now and wore my first long trousers. True, at last my knees were warm, but there was a price to pay. My childhood. I was expected suddenly to be all grown up.

And although I was spoiled immensely, being the only boy in the house, this didn't stop my mother telling me that I had to go to work. She saw that I didn't exactly rejoice at the news. 'Well, not yet—in a few days time.' It wasn't actually the thought of work itself that worried me, but getting up early in the morning. For I used to love to hear my sisters going to work, to pretend I was still asleep. To be all warm and secure. My bed was against the window and I loved to look out at the snow or the sleet falling and see people hurrying through the streets. Then I would cover myself completely with bedclothes, pretending that I was in a tent in the middle of the burning Sahara.

I wanted to do something in life, longed to work at something that I loved to do, had to do.

I began to take the rise out of my sisters and wander through Leeds realizing, after all, how little there was to do there. In the afternoons sometimes I went to the news cinemas or spent a few coppers in the pin-table saloons, trying to pick up a packet of fags, or a bottle of scent, with the small crane. Impossible. It was a mug's game. I knew it, yet always continued.

A tart with a Yorkshire accent spoke to me one day. 'Hello young man, want a good time with a naughty girl?' I looked round behind me to see if she meant me. After all I was only four and a half feet high. No, she was looking right down on me. I blushed and ran away but I was very very proud. I ran all the way home and up the stairs two and three at a time.

'Why can't you walk like other people?' my sister said, for this scooting upstairs was a habit. I did try walking slowly, but somehow stairs were a challenge to me.

And other obsessions started in Leeds. I always had to be the last one starting across a road and the first one over. And walking along a street I simply had to overtake everyone. When walking with my sisters I would say to myself, 'Now I'm going to get them to all cross the road, when I choose, at this telephone box. They would follow.

It was too easy. So I carried out a further experiment. 'In two minutes flat I'm going to get them all talking about Tibet or Christopher Columbus.' I would neatly try to steer the conversation round to that, and sometimes frantic, after the appropriate hundred and twenty seconds, I would shout out 'Christopher Columbus'. So we'd start talking about him.

We would all sit playing cards, a simple game of Sevens, and I might suddenly stop and say, 'We're lost, lost in endless space.' My mother would feel my forehead.

'Have a wash, it'll freshen you up.' There was I, in Leeds, feeling sick with my first bout of angst and she was telling me to wash.

'You don't understand. I've got angst! Angst!' I had heard it somewhere. 'Angst in the pangst,' she laughed. 'Every other boy has growing pains, he has to have Angst-Smangst.'

My sister said maybe it was growing pains.

'Come down to earth. Come down to earth,' my mother said. 'You look like a schloch. Do up your neck and have a wash.' But all my dreams and restlessness couldn't stand up against my mothers endeavours to find me work. She sat late at night with a newspaper going through the situations vacant column, calling out, offering me jobs, 'Here you are—Boy to learn printing trade; apprentice baker; assistant in pickle factory.' There I was, pondering on the nature of things, and there she was juggling with my future.

'It's my life,' I kept on saying.

'As long as you make a living you can hold your head up. Believe me when you've got a few bob in your pocket the world is singing. The world comes knocking at your door.'

It all sounded so horrible, but I eventually decided to accept the lesser of fifty evils. A lather boy in a barber shop.

'Believe me it's a good trade. Who doesn't need a shave?' That was perfectly true. I could even think of a few of my aunts who might benefit from a razor. So that was that.

The barber's shop was in the open Chapeltown Road. The barber was a Yiddisher man who mostly had a Yiddisher clientele.

'The better class clients come here. You'll get good tips.'

He wouldn't let me handle the razor immediately but made me

practise the strokes on a green wine bottle. All I had to do was to rub lather into faces with a brush and my hands. I started seeing humanity upside down, softening up their faces for the barber. I hated it. Sometimes the lather would turn quite grey but who was I to complain? And every so often I went around with a broom sweeping all the hair together. There it all was in one heap, the discarded hair of the men of Leeds.

'It would make nice mattresses,' the barber said as I used to shove it into sacks. He was quite kind.

'Brush their coats as they leave, and they'll tip you.' I became aware of the vanity of bulging, balding men.

No, I was definitely not cut out for this profession. But found it very difficult to tell anyone I wanted to leave. I either hated or loved the customers. I was never indifferent. I could see that Jewish people couldn't afford the luxury of being merely mediocre. They were like other people, only more so. They were either angels or bastards or sometimes angelic bastards.

When I got my wages or tips it gave me no satisfaction. Money suddenly started meaning nothing to me. But when I went home with wages I did feel a certain joy at pleasing my mother.

'Isn't it wonderful to have money in your pocket,' she said. I shrugged but decided to agree.

And my father would send his endless, continuous letters from London. 'I hope Bernie is working. Thank God he's making a living. I hope he continues. Tell him when you can stand on your own two feet there's nothing better. After all he's no longer a child.' I'm sure he must have seen the danger signals in me. I became hypnotized into the job now, for a while.

'How are you going?' someone would ask.

'Thank God, mustn't grumble. Making a living.'

I groaned inside, realizing there was no escape. I was caught up in the wheels of the family and I was being ground up and falling into the same mould.

Bombs were falling on London. Thousands of people were being killed every night. All over the world the same story. And there I was, beginning my war with the family. I felt very guilty. My mother could see my sadness.

I didn't feel like playing cards any more and after work I'd either go to the pictures or go to a library and read the magazines. And when I returned home I would often listen at the door to hear what they were saying about me behind my back. One night I heard my mother say, 'He's the one to take me out of the slums. You'll see. He's the one to buy me the house.'

Her faith in me made me angry. I felt more and more caught in a trap.

Every morning I had to be dragged out of bed.

'Don't you see. How can I get you out of the slums if I'm a lousy barber. I don't want to be a bloody barber.'

The sirens that night saved me. This time it was the most beautiful sound in the world. No work tomorrow I thought. We sheltered beneath the synagogue, my mother repeating every few minutes. 'What am I doing in Leeds if there's an air-raid? This is no good to me at all.'

I agreed with her. 'They say there are terrible raids on Hull and now the Germans are going to concentrate on the North of England.'

Well, they did drop a few bombs on Leeds. This was enough for me to work on so I built them up into an Armageddon.

I told her that someone said they heard the Germans were going to concentrate on Leeds.

'Why should I get bombed in Leeds when I can get bombed in London?' She couldn't bear to be parted from the rest of the family any longer. That was obvious. Just before Christmas she decided we were going back.

'Bombs or no bombs, we're going back to London.'

So I said goodbye to the upside down faces and the barber and to the benign bloody Reverend. God bless him, I don't think. Goodbye to the birds of Briggate with their homely come-hither look, and to the delicatessen shops of Chapeltown Road.

We were returning to the thick of it, to the blitz of London and I was convinced that we would all be killed. Anyway, I thought, that would solve my problems.

So ended the Yorkshire episode of half the Kops family, for blood is thicker than water, and in my mother's words, 'What's the good of a family if it's separated?'

There was little welcome when we got back. Everybody was white in the face and silent.

Except my Dad. 'So what did you come home for?' he said. 'We're being bombed to smithereens.' Then he chastised me for giving up a good job.

London was completely transformed. There were great gaps of jagged space where houses once stood. And we returned to Stepney Green for a while. Now I was no longer worried about my future but more about day-to-day survival. No longer did I collect shrapnel but leapt for shelter as soon as the sirens went. A taste of salt came to my mouth and fear made my eyes twitch. All feeling of community had completely faded. We were all withdrawn into ourselves. Little furtive groups of families groping between shelter and home. There was still a superficial sort of friendliness on the surface, but the roots had been cut. The Jewish community, the family, the spirit, had died. And it was never reborn, not exactly the way it was. An essential ingredient was lost for ever. The inner sense of belonging, together.

'It's all gone. All gone. Everything we ever had is finished. What's happened to us? Oh, by my mother in the grave, what is going to become of us?' That was the way my mother cried. And I no longer tried to overtake people in the streets. On the contrary I stood nervously at junctions wondering, 'If I go down that way, I might get killed by a bomb. On the other hand, if I walk along Stepney Green, on the other side of the road, I might get hit by a bit of shrapnel. Which way do I go?' Every step was a decision and every decision may have been the wrong one.

My sister Essie lived in Gold Street, just along Stepney Green, and the night after our return we sheltered in her Anderson in the garden. It was terrible in there. I shivered one moment and sweltered the next. Later that night we had enough so we went indoors. This time there was no comic relief from my uncles, just a night of sheer terror. The wail and the howl and the scream and the crash. The body of the world was being cremated, pounded, crushed and scattered in space. I looked out at the sky from an empty bedroom. A firework display of death-planes were caught in the fingers of searchlights that poked the sky. In the other room my sisters cried and my mother was shaking her white face at the looking glass, 'Why? Why? What have we done?' I put my hand against one of the walls. It was almost red hot. I rushed outside and found the house immediately next door burning down. And the whole street alight. All around was flame and we just couldn't do a thing but stand and watch the street burn down. But my sister's house wasn't touched. It stood alone in a blackened blazing wilderness that yesterday was called Gold Street.

Fortunately all the people of the street were down the underground. The night was hell, where we rushed around each other, hands over ears, clenching eyes, asking, imploring each other, 'How long will it last?' 'Are we going to die?' 'Tell me it's gonna be all right.' The night-bombers hurried away when the first strands of dawn appeared.

What struck me in the morning was the complete absence of people. I managed to find a Yiddisher bakery open nearby and bought some hot platzels and took them home.

We never got caught by the sirens again, at least not in the evening. We moved away forever from Stepney Green and we never returned.

We moved to Bethnal Green where we spent our hours of day, and in the late afternoon we would make for the underground, with our bundles of blankets. For every day we had to claim our few feet of concrete. The constant worry was whether we would find a space for that night. We lived only for four o'clock when they let us down, when we would hurtle into the underworld, into the trains of the Central Line. Often we would find each station already full up. People ahead of us, who were all fixed up, looked so smug as we panicked around for a vacant slab of stone. You couldn't blame them. We were the same anyway, once we got settled under the burning streets of London. Each night we lived under a different district: Marble Arch, Holborn, Oxford Circus, St Paul's. We never bothered to venture away from the Central Line even though I believe the Northern Line was deeper.

Our one night at St Paul's was terribly memorable. Smoke poured down and a boy dared me to go upstairs with him. I was dead scared but felt compelled to do so. At the top of the escalator the warden warned us not to venture out but we slipped past for a few moments and I stood in the entrance for no more than a few seconds. The whole of the City of London was alight. We rushed down again. I didn't tell my mother what I had seen, and I lay down in silence and didn't sleep the whole night long.

But sometimes we couldn't make the underground for the air-raids started in the morning and went on all day.

We now lived in my sister's house in Brick Lane which had a surface brick shelter at the back of the yard.

When we couldn't get underground a feeling of dread overcame me, for apart from everything else my mother was cracking up. One day in particular I slipped out of the shelter during a quiet patch to get a bit of food. When I returned the bombers were over-head again. My brother-in-law Mick was an air-raid warden and he was standing there among a crowd of people from my sister's buildings. Shells were bursting in the sky.

'What are you doing?' Mick demanded. 'Get into the shelter. You'll all be killed.'

'We prefer to take our chances outside with the bombs,' an old man said. 'We can't stand Mrs Kops and her daughter having hysterics inside.' I could hear my mother and sister screaming their heads off. Mick went into the shelter, shouting at them. They stopped, but oh I remember my mother's look of terror as she cud-dled my sister. That night! I and my brother were larking about in a passage of the building, when we were thrown off our feet by a rushing wind. I never heard a sound but my ears went funny, yet apparently the crash was heard for miles around.

A landmine had dropped on Columbia Market shelter two hun-dred yards away. It fell straight through the lift shaft and exploded down there. I saw a policeman come out weeping and carrying a dead child. It was the first time I had seen anybody dead.

'Cry,' my mother said, 'It will make you feel better.' But I couldn't. Blood was thicker than water all right and all the blood within me was crying out. For opposite, the houses were no more and people I knew were no more.

The King of England came the following morning, drawn and grey he walked slowly over the wreckage. No one cheered because they didn't feel like cheering. But when Churchill came a few hours later, with a cigar sticking out of his fat pink face, a few people did cheer and even I felt like cheering. But I didn't. Despite

Noel Coward's song, 'Every Blitz your resistance stubborning!'
My mother's strength was failing fast and she just couldn't take
much more and we finally persuaded her to leave London again.

'You won't keep me away!' she kept on saying, even at the
station. Again and again she implored me to go away with her. I
told her I couldn't.

I wanted to be on my own, away from the East End. I wanted
to think things out for myself. I had to go in another direction, away
from the family. I had managed to get a job in one of the big hotels
in the West End, as an apprentice cook.

I was going to have my tall white hat after all. The other attractive thing about working in a hotel was that the West End didn't
seem to be getting bashed so badly. As we stood waiting for the
train to leave I told her about my new job, thought she'd be
delighted. My father was.

'You don't need to work!' My mother implored me until the
last moment. The train drew out and we hardly waved. Blood was
thicker than water, for despite being fifteen and cynical, I cried.

Off they went in the direction of Ipswich and I wandered
through the East End alone, getting rid of my father at Aldgate
East.

'Take care of yourself, boy!'

'Yes Dad.' That's all you needed to say. 'Yes Dad. No Dad.' I felt
somehow close to him as I walked away, very close and very guilty.
We shook hands. It was an act of strangers.

I walked to Stepney Green and climbed the seven flights of the
Buildings and stood on the landing, outside the deserted house.
I looked over the East End, the deserted quiet streets. All the children were evacuated. The railings of the park had been torn out
to be made into shells and guns and bombs. The world as I knew
it had passed away. It had died. Gone mad and died. Mr Lindsberg's sweet shop was no longer there. Esther the sweet woman
was no longer there, Gold Street where my sister had lived had
gone up in smoke. Redman's Road and Stepney Green had become
a wasteland of rubble and mounds of earth, of broken springs and
furniture and broken homes. Faces I once knew came flooding
back to my swimming eyes. Faces of people now dead.

I could hear the tap dripping into the sink of the scullery of my deserted house, so I rushed down the stairs and ran towards the main road, towards the West End, towards my new life and my tall white hat.

But I stopped on the way and stood on the bombed site of the family I knew who had been wiped out a year before. The fireplace still stood like a tombstone surrounded by the cemetery of Stepney.

Weeds grew where children once played. Nature returns so soon to reclaim the earth abused by people. But blood is thicker than water. I was alive and wanted to live, so I shrugged and walked away.

6

Smoked Salmon and Songs

I never had a chip on my shoulder about being Jewish when I entered my new world. The only chip I had was in being small. I accepted my background and was neither proud or unproud of my Jewishness but felt fully equipped to deal with my new life. Coming from a large family, my mother had no time to spoil us, we were never indulged, and were always brought back to earth by the others if any one of us acted all high and mighty. I didn't have to fight against my background. I didn't have to travel back to sort myself out before I could go forward. I didn't need to forget my past or ignore it. There was only one way to go—forward, away from poverty. The silver spoon of poverty was my propulsion.

Besides my whole world had been Jewish, there was almost no other world when I was a child, in those most important years. There were no foreigners in my world. Just strangers, people I either wanted to know or didn't want to know. The world was divided between the sad, the mad, the glad and the bad. The same is true today.

I was fifteen and a half, free and alone, stretching my short limbs, and I was growing up fast, not maybe in height but certainly in the gift of the gab that I was rapidly acquiring, probably to compensate for my lack of length.

To be quick on the uptake was necessary to survive in a large family, especially when you were the youngest son.

So I entered the hotel in perhaps the way Don Juan entered hell, taking in my new surroundings with a mixture of awe and acceptance, and I got my white hat.

But it wasn't as high as I had imagined, for in a hotel kitchen the higher up you climbed or crawled, the higher your hat became. Nevertheless I was very proud of my hat and my collection of small knives which I took everywhere with me, even when I was off duty.

91

The head chef was God to me. The distant presence, in his little glass office, where he watched over us, looking out over the whole kitchen, admonishing us when we made mistakes and nodding grudgingly when things were going all right. The hotel stood above a railway terminus and my first impression was the amount of food in the cold storage. Cheese, bacon and butter, things which had become so scarce. Piles and piles of it stared me in the face.

They put me to work making hors d'oeuvres. On the first day I made myself sick on sardines and pimentos. Then I was taught how to make mayonnaise and Russian salad and potato salad. My chef was none too friendly, always chastising me about the lack of strength in my wrists. His breath smelt. I used to wonder why he was so sad.

All my thoughts about being secure from the bombs soon faded when they gave me a bedroom on the eighth floor. It was already occupied by two young waiters, I took the empty bed by the window. For the first couple of days I went about the kitchen stuffing myself with practically everything I could find. They all took the mickey out of me.

'Know why you're so small? You pull your pudding too much.' They all pointed at me and doubled up laughing. They were bloody childish but I blushed. 'You pull your pudding, you pull your pudding.' Though I hadn't heard the expression before I knew they were referring to masturbation, which, of course, I had recently discovered. There were performances of mutual masturbation between the young waiters but I refused to participate. I waited until it was dark, until I could concentrate.

Irish chambermaids came into the room sometimes and one lay on my bed with me but I didn't do anything. I didn't feel the urge to. She touched my ear, blew on me, giggled and waited and ran to the other bed.

'What's the matter with him?' she asked the waiter.

'Oh, he hasn't started yet,' he replied.

One of the boys gave me books on politics and the other one books on sex. So I read while they larked about with the giggling girls, sometimes looking out the corner of my eye to see their progress. I was very interested in the books on sex. I did, however, glance through *Ten Days that Shook the World*.

The world was shaking all right outside, for we were close to the park, where the guns were firing away. Germany was being bombed incessantly now and Berlin was suffering the same as London. To be truthful I must admit my heart sang every time I heard that bombs were being dropped there. I would now like to believe I felt sorry for Berliners, like to believe that I even felt a little ashamed then of feeling so pleased, but I wasn't ashamed. Instead I repeated, 'This is what they brought to the world, may they reap the harvest.'

In the hotel there was a hierarchy and we the cooks were the gods and high priests. The kitchen was a place without daylight, epitomizing the caste system and the class system. The kitchen porters were tolerated, for they were the untouchables, we could be magnanimous towards them. They came round with their plates and we doled out bits and pieces. But it was the waiters who were the very bottom. There was an eternal battle going on to keep them in their place. They were forever scrounging.

'Scum of the earth,' my chef said. 'Never believe a word they say. They'd even pinch the snot from your nose.'

The young waiters who shared my room, turned out to be anti-Semitic, the intelligent one believed in The Protocols of the Elders of Zion. The fact of the matter was they often had to wait on Jewish people, who are by no means unparticular and often liked to have what is known as 'the best' and would think nothing of sending food back three and four times. We argued incessantly, I always lost my temper. 'Why are there no poor Jews?' I told him about the hundreds of thousands of people like myself in the East End. They didn't believe me although they admitted that I was poor. I asked them if they thought I was a liar. They said I wasn't. So I became more furious than ever when they persisted with their stupidity.

'There were no Jews in the Army besides,' one said. I told him my brother was.

'I don't mean you—you're different.'

They hated their jobs and I felt it my duty to smuggle them food from the kitchen. In return I continued reading the manifestos of Karl Marx and Henry Miller. At night I lay in my bed reading, on that tenuous eighth floor while their bed clothes were going up and down with excitable movements, plus the passionate groans from the Irish lassies as they protested. 'Don't, don't.

It was a terrifying crazy world, where I saw for the first time a condition that I later discovered to be called neurosis. Chefs would scream and get into a frenzy as they worked at a fantastic pace.

Once, the roast cook dropped a joint of beef on the sawdust floor. I thought he'd do the most sensible thing, wash it. Not on your life, he hurled it across the kitchen and kicked it angrily round the floor, like a football.

They were a pale lot of men, always drinking beer, pouring abuse on the customers who held them to their servitude. The long day from ten in the morning until ten at night, was a relentless hell of preparation for the two great climaxes of the day. Lunch and Dinner. There was a break in the afternoon but it was impossible to do anything really constructive in those few hours, except sit in the staff room, talk about sport or racing or play cards, or exchange dirty jokes. It was an endless ritual of ants rushing around. We'd make the food, get rid of it, make some more, and more. Day in, day out. The voice of the chef monotonously blaring from the intercom, calling out the orders, slow at first, then faster and faster, until we were automata at some mad ritualistic dance.

I asked one of the cooks if he was Jewish because he had a large nose. I had never been aware that Jews had large noses. But I had fallen for the propaganda of the kitchen, and besides, he did look like a Yiddisher boy. He screamed at me, 'I hate the Yids, they should all be burned.' I told him that was probably happening. I wondered why he got so angry, why he was violent in his language. Hate poured from him like sweat.

A kind kitchen porter enlightened me. 'You see, he said, 'He hates the Jews because he looks like one, because when he was a kid people probably called him one.' I understood in a way. After all, it's no fun being called Jewish if you're not. It was difficult enough being Jewish when you were, what with the persecution and the conflict. That chef turned out to be Italian and started to be really nice to me. Of all the cooks in that kitchen, he turned out the kindest. When I went to him with my empty plate he wouldn't just palm me off with a vienna cutlet but give me a leg of duck, the same as the customers. That chef now has one of the highest positions in the business, has become the head chef in one of the most famous hotels in the world.

I burned myself. To cure it, the chef held it over the flames of the stove. I screamed for mercy, but it did the trick. They began to accept me, and the more friendly they became the more depressed I was. It's more difficult to leave a band of brothers than a group of enemies, for already I could see that this wasn't the life for me.

My father found a flat in a dank, damp, decaying block in Bethnal Green, a tenement that was condemned before the Great War. The walls and the stairs sweated. I went home a few times in the week to give him some food that I had pinched out of the kitchen. A little tea and some cheese.

'Don't tell your mother,' he said. She hated us taking anything that wasn't rightly ours, despite the social rationalizations of my father, but I had no qualms, thinking that my dad was right, that the West End was hardly getting bombed and that people there with money were able to get exactly what they wanted.

'I tell you they've got a secret agreement with the Germans.' He was always on about secret agreements between Hitler and our government. I tried telling him that as Jews we owed our lives to the people of England and to the government who were fighting the tyranny of Germany. He was totally unreasonable. He would have had a fit if I told him that I wanted to leave. For despite there being one war for the poor and another for the rich, despite the fact he hated the West End and the rich, he wanted me to work there amongst the rich. A totally confused man of tremendous energy, completely illogical except in his own mind, where all things were cosily equated, and temper took over if doubt ever arose.

A new kitchen porter started; on his first day I joked with him and he smiled but his frozen eyes stared at me. Then he went absolutely crazy, lifted me up and carried me struggling across the kitchen and held me over a vat of boiling water.

'Let this be a lesson to you.' I really did think he was going to drop me in.

They were mad. All of them stark, staring, raving mad.

In the afternoons I wandered alone through the park killing the few hours, sometimes I ventured into amusement arcades. One day a man followed me so I hurried back to the hotel.

'What can he want with me?' I thought. How strange that a man could lurk around and follow boys. I figured he must have been lonely.

I saw my father again, told him that I was wanting to leave my job. He, red in the face, said I needed my head examined. Maybe he was right. Anyway years later I did have my head examined.

But on this occasion one thing led to another and he worked himself up into a frenzy. He started to bite his tongue and kick the air with his legs. Something snapped inside me. I hit him. For a moment there was absolute silence. Then he lay on the floor, punching the walls with aggravation. I lifted him up bodily and held him up in front of me, surprised at his lightness, thinking, 'I am your father now.' From that moment onwards he became my son.

'I'm ambitious,' I said, when I put him down.

'A poor boy can't afford to be ambitious.' He seemed beaten as he spoke. I didn't half feel sorry for him so I bought him some tobacco.

'But you wanted to be a chef. What do you want?'

As if I knew.

So I went back to the West End, where life in all its facets certainly buttonholed me.

I stood dreaming outside a tobacconist's window.

'Do you smoke sonny?' I turned and a man whose face I remember to this day was offering me one.

'Course I smoke. I'm fifteen and a half.'

'Let's go and have some fun,' he said.

Visions of circuses and seasides and helter skelters that couldn't possibly have existed in wartime London immediately existed in my mind. So I walked along with him, along Victoria Street.

'Let's go down here.' He pointed to a large empty house, the cellar was being used as an air raid shelter. I got a bit scared, but I didn't like to hurt his feelings so I followed him down.

Only when he unzipped his flies did I realize that his idea of fun didn't run to circuses. When his John Thomas popped out I scooted up the stairs and rushed along the street. Over my shoulder I saw him running in the other direction. I felt really sorry for him though I still wasn't quite sure what it was all about. When I got back to the hotel I told my two waiter friends.

'The dirty bastard.' They rushed out of the hotel, looking for him. But I was pleased when they returned without him. Whereupon, over tea, they immediately told me the inverted facts of life. I couldn't believe them, but did.

'Life's so complicated,' I said.

The action of the day had soured me completely, and that night a bomb fell on the hotel. It did no damage but fell on the arch that linked the annexe to the main building. No one was hurt, but this gave me the opportunity I had been seeking.

Next day I decided to consult the oracle—my mother. She was always the one to get me out of a fix, so after saying my so-longs and pinching some food from the larder, I made my way to Ipswich.

My mother was staying six miles from there, at a place called Crowfield. It was called Crowfield because that's all there were— fields and crows.

'Can't stand those birds,' my mother said. But I told her that the black birds over London were far worse to put up with. It was flat, empty, yet beautifully desolate landscape, with a lone windmill near the main road. One house and a field. My mother was billeted with some kind farm people, and I recounted my stories of the blitz to them, like a soldier returning from the battlefield.

'London? I've been there once,' the farmer said.

I gave my mother the food I had stolen. She told me off but ate it, and then I told her about the bombing of the hotel. Told her that the bomb had crashed through and the floors had collapsed and I had fallen three storeys. She didn't quite believe me. But I still had one more trump to play.

'There was this man, see. He was queer.'

'Yiddisher feller? Queer? What was wrong with him dear?' It was no use, I hardly believed it myself. My mother lived and died without the knowledge of these things.

But she must have seen that I needed to get away from my job, and she told me to tell my father that I was not to go back to the hotel. 'If you're not happy there, ain't that good enough reason?'

Who was arguing?

So I returned to Bethnal Green triumphant. My mother had spoken, so what could my father do?

4

So I left and lived in that miserable Queen's Buildings. By the look of it named after Queen Elizabeth the First, or maybe Boadicea. On the walls there were stains and on the mantelpiece plaster dogs without their heads. The furniture was all falling to pieces but I didn't mind that. It was my father I minded.

All the time he went on.

'After all, you're no longer a child. When are you going to start making a living?' Or, 'Without a few quid in your pocket, where are you?'

It became impossible.

It wasn't only his nagging, but the bombs that made me decide to go back to the catering industry. A feeling of death clung to me in the East End, a constant dread of the end of the world. In the West End there was a façade, things were going on. In the hotels people dressed up as though nothing was happening. In Brick Lane stark reality stared you out.

This time I got a job in a very smart hotel in Mayfair. I worked in the cold larder where at first I did almost nothing but cut smoked salmon. Smoked salmon, the great luxury of my childhood. Something I heard about but never saw. And now after stuffing myself with it I got sick and tired of it. There was obviously more in life than smoked salmon.

Many famous people stayed at that hotel. One day a waiter said, 'I'm serving a bleeding king, come and have a look.' I looked and the king looked like everybody else.

I started plucking chickens, and partridges, and pheasants, sometimes running alive with maggots.

'Just burn them,' the larder chef said. 'Get your burner inside and kill them.' I would put my burner in the tail end and out would swarm the maggots through the neck—a whole army of them. It was like the people fighting to get underground. I learned to clean and truss poultry. I turned off food.

Sometimes the young chickens weren't quite dead. One, I remember, ran along the wooden bench without its head. Someone said it was only its nerves twitching.

A month later I was promoted to the oyster room where I did nothing else all day except open oysters, and serve up caviare.

There in the middle of the war I ate whole dessert spoons of it. 'So what's wonderful about caviare?' 'Rich man's anchovy.' But I continued eating it. When no one was looking. It gave me a kick to consume such valuable food.

There were two reasons why I hated opening oysters. One because I killed them when I did. The other because the shell cut right into my hand. The thing that kept me going was the thought that I might eventually find a pearl.

One of the worst moments of my life came when I was promoted out of the larder into the kitchen proper. A whole box of live lobsters were given to me. 'Well throw them into the boiling water then,' the Chef ordered. I wondered why they had to be thrown in live. He must have seen what I was thinking, told me that they wouldn't be at their peak of edibility unless they were boiled alive.

So I hid my eyes with one hand and chucked them in with the other, praying to the lobster God for forgiveness. I am sure I heard them scream. The chef laughed and told me it was only the air in the shells.

Again in this hotel I found the neurosis, the petty jealousies and the incessant rowing between the various sections of the staff. The head chef was about eight feet tall and very distant and very French. And the sous chef was German. Every time he shouted in his native language I cringed. German still affects me this way, unless it's the poetry of Rilke or the Ninth Symphony or the poems of Brecht. I will never ever eat in a West End hotel after having seen some of the things that cooks and waiters do when they prepare and serve food. Some feel it their duty not to wash their hands after going to the lavatory. I have seen Commis waiters picking their noses in the passages between kitchen and restaurant. I saw one bright lad spit in the soup.

One day I was putting six chickens in the oven, covered with lard, I slipped and the chickens landed in the sawdust. The head chef always materialized at an accident, he stood above me screaming his head off as if I'd done a murder. I went to wash the chickens. 'No time, no time.' He picked up the chickens, sawdust sticking to the lard, rubbed in some bread-crumbs, told me no one would know the difference. Another time I was passing about twenty pounds of cooked potatoes through the electric sieve to make

pomme purée, dreaming, as usual, I forgot to put a bowl underneath. The potatoes all plopped on to the floor, into the sawdust.
Again, screaming, he scooped the whole lot up and started throwing in milk and butter, whisking it together like mad.

'What the eye does not see . . .' or the French equivalent.

There are rats in hotels, the four-legged variety as well as the
other kind. And rat-catchers come at night, shine their torches
along the overhead beams and shoot them dead.

One day a baby rat, two inches long, scuttled past my feet during the lunch service. All the chefs shouted, 'Kill it! kill it! Stamp
on it!' I couldn't, my foot wouldn't come down. And when it did
I purposely missed. It escaped. I felt more close to that little rat
than to anyone else in that kitchen. 'Stamp on it. Kill it.' It was all
too easy.

I loved almost everything that moved, except waiters, cooks and
cockroaches. I smiled, could hear my mother saying, *'They're also
human.'*

I went to see our favourite doctor. A marvellous man. He would
do anything for anyone. Get you out of the Army, get you into the
Army. All you had to say was, 'Doctor I need a certificate,' and he
was already signing it. He was already signing it before you even
asked for it. He must have got through more certificate pads than
any other doctor in the world. He knew all our names, our age
differences, how many moles we had on our bums, the kind of
sweets we liked.

I told him I wanted to leave the hotel, that it wasn't good for me.
'So leave,' he said and went on about a doctor called Freud and
how my wanting to leave the hotel was perfectly understandable.

'You'll go a long way if you stick it out.' I didn't quite understand what he was talking about. 'Now take a few weeks holiday,'
he said. I told him I couldn't afford one. He was always telling
people to take a few weeks holiday. 'If only I could send people to
the South of France on the panel.' He patted my hand, gave me
a letter for my father. He died soon after.

I remember my father reading the letter and shrugging, as if to
say, 'If that's what the doctor says, what can I do?'

A few days later my mother came bursting into the room,
returning from Crowfield, saying, 'What do they want of my life?

What do they want of me?' Apparently a German bomb had fallen into that field of crows just in front of the farmhouse. 'Why do they sort me out? Why do they follow me?' She spoke as if the whole Third Reich was all lined up in the world just to make life hell for my mother. Which of course it was. She took her coat off and she was home. Who could dispute it?

No sooner was she home when she sounded the Yiddisher tribal drums and the splintered family returned to the fold, nursing their diaspora wounds, telling stories about the world of England. Not Phyllis though, she became a landgirl.

'Who ever heard of it? A Yiddisher landgirl?'

And I, jobless, and racked with guilt, was being nagged by my father incessantly.

I lay in the bed that I shared with Dave and I could hear them arguing in the other room. How thin those walls were. It made me realize that this thing called security was wafer-thin and how tenuous our civilization was. What was a house but some bricks that separated people from the universe; some bricks and some wallpaper. I sat in my bedroom trying to count the layers of wallpaper, thinking about the families who had lived in these rooms before us. People who had lived and died there. No one had thought of stripping the walls, they just added another layer and furnished the space with some familiar objects and called it home.

I started to search around for work, applied to be a clerk for the railways, sat for an examination at Euston Station.

It was not to be. I failed myself. In the middle of the examination I looked around me at the other boys. I looked at their faces, got a hollow feeling inside, decided that I couldn't go through with it. I put my hand up and asked to leave the room, and I walked straight out and never returned.

I got a job in a metal factory; I stayed two days. Then I got a job in a spectacle factory. It sounded good. Spectacle factory. I stayed five days.

Now I started going to the Labour Exchange and applied for several jobs through them. Office boys, assistant ply-wood learners, smart lad wanted, you know the sort of thing. They took one look at me and I at them and by mutual, though silent, consent we terminated the audition. One day at the Labour Exchange the clerk said, 'What are we going to do with you, Mr Kops?'

I shrugged. There I was getting on for sixteen, with no way ahead, and my family starting to give me up for lost. At sixteen a Yiddisher boy was expected to know what he was going to do in life.

Mrs Plotz lived next door and we shared the same street door. The postman, when he came, always called, 'Mr Plotz and Mr Kops.' My mother didn't like receiving letters. For her, news could never be good. No one ever wrote to tell her something nice.

Mrs Plotz had a dog called Prince. She screamed at it in Yiddish. 'Go out for half an hour.' It understood perfectly and stayed away for half an hour, though once or twice it stayed away for forty-five minutes, but then this could be called a Yiddisher half hour. If she could have gone on the music-halls she would have made a fortune, with that dog, cursing it and loving it in Yiddish.

She and my mother argued continuously and this was a wonderful double act, both competing for the distinction of being the most badly off, and the honour of having the best children in the world. Mrs Plotz had a beautiful daughter, Debbie, all eyes and a great mass of curly black hair. One day she was a child swinging round a lamp-post; the next, she and my brother were making eyes at each other, but it didn't get serious until a long time after.

The raids were not too bad now and we could start to live a slightly more normal life, although we continued going to the shelter.

By now the underground was all organized and we went down Bethnal Green tube station, into the unused extension of the Central Line. We had bunks, and even a canteen, but during the day I played around Bethnal Green, a totally different area from Stepney. Bethnal Green was largely composed of Christian people and before the war it had been a notorious blackshirt area.

Dave and I played on the stairs and carved hearts, arrows and our names on the crumbling walls. We used to share the friendship of a girl called Angela, both kissing her in turn, fighting for her mouth, each holding a different breast. She didn't seem to mind and we weren't complaining.

My mother, now, looked terribly ill, and could not walk more than a few yards without gasping for breath. I began to feel very guilty, especilly when she said, 'You'll take me out of the slums.'

But all my father said was, 'Settle down and earn some money for a change.' He was pestering me to go into his trade; he even offered me his cutting knives. I tried to explain to him how badly he had been treated but again and again he would say, 'A poor boy can't afford ambition, especially if he doesn't know what his ambitions are.'

Dave and I started to draw apart. He rather resenting me not working, and my mother now had to defend me all the time against all the family.

Every day she would slip me sixpence for cigarettes. I, in turn, used to run the errands. When I was sixteen she told me I could have a party and several Jewish kids in the area were invited. I was approached by a young non-Jewish girl.

'Can I come to your party?'

I told her she could.

'Look, I can't afford a present so you can have me instead.'

'In that case give me a sample,' I replied.

I put my hands inside her dress. For a non-Jewish girl she was quite well-made. Lovely, as a matter of fact. We sat on the stone steps where I meant to get a further and fuller sample, but I was frustrated by the air-raid sirens. 'Bloody Germans.'

She came to my party and even though I tried to collect on several occasions I never managed it. I always felt cheated, always wanted to go up to her and say, 'Here, what about that present you promised me?' But I was too proud.

'One day you'll settle down and marry a nice respectable Jewish girl,' my mother said. 'One day I'll see you under the chupah.' I was a real clever bastard in those days. I replied, 'You want me to marry a Jewish girl? Now listen carefully. Would you prefer me to marry a coloured Yiddisher girl or a white shiksa?' My poor mother. 'Don't give me no problems,' she answered and went on frying fish. Jewish girls were marvellous and passionate but you could never deflower one outside marriage. They used to say things like—'If I let you, would you respect me?' And then they'd answer for you, 'Don't be silly, of course you wouldn't.' Then more passionate embraces up to the crucial point. Not that I tried to that great extent to press right home. I'd never had it yet and didn't seem to need it.

A boy lived on the next landing. His name: Leon. An ordinary Yiddisher boy with a nice job, I was always told to 'copy' him. My mother should have known that he had exactly the same filthy mind as myself. We became friends and used to wander the streets together looking for girls, both of us playing pocket billiards.

Mind you he was the intellectual type, and had a fantastic effect on my life. He was a signpost for me without realizing it.

It happened when we were talking about poetry and he gave me a book to read; it was the poems of Rupert Brook and I was very much taken with 'Grantchester'.

But instead of following the author and his works, and others who might have written like him, I looked at the book, at the publisher's name. It was Faber & Faber. So I went to the library and got another book out by Faber & Faber.

Haphazardly I chose the poems by T. S. Eliot. This book changed my life. It struck me straight in the eyes like a bolt of lightning. I had no preconceived ideas about poetry and read, 'The Wasteland' and 'Prufrock' as if they were the most acceptable and common forms in existence.

The poems spoke to me directly, for they were bound up with the wasteland of the East End, and the desolation and loneliness of people and landscape. Accidentally I had entered the mainstream of literature. So I lost myself and found myself, in books.

I devoured books the way locusts would an orchard.

Not that I tried to write poetry. I just read and read and read.

'What's he reading?'

'Books.'

'Books? What for?'

'Ask me.'

My father told me that books would get me nowhere fast. He was wise enough to see the danger signals. Books took me away from the family as I sat amongst them. Farther and farther away. I would sit on the settee as they played cards and I'd look up and see them, wonder where I fitted in. I had fantasies.

One day I was sure that I would come home as usual and they'd all be playing cards and I would watch them for a moment, and then my brother might look up and say something like, 'Who are you? What are you doing in this house?' Then they would all look up and look at me and wonder where I had wandered from. And I would probably protest, 'But I am your brother.' And I would plead to my mother, 'I'm your son.' Then she would shake her head and say kindly, 'Sorry son but I don't know you.' I would refuse to leave. So they would call the police and drag me screaming from the room.

Well it never went that far. But it was pretty obvious that I was more and more lost to them.

'A dead loss.' I heard an uncle call me.

But it was no use. I couldn't hold off the day. I got a job: in a furniture factory near Shoreditch Church. I made the tea and carried plywood about nearly all day.

Phyllis came home from the land.

'What did I tell you? A Yiddisher girl isn't cut out for the land,' my father said.

She got a job in a dress factory. The same one where Rose was working. One day they brought a girl back. She worked with them. I looked at her, she looked at me and I made a date to take her to the pictures.

'At last he's going with a Yiddisher girl.'

Shirley was five feet tall and bursting at the seams. A luscious, overblown Jewish girl, over-emotional, who would swoon if you as much as touched her hand.

'No good will come of this, no good at all,' she would moan, as I pressed her against brick walls, in the moonlight.

I think she could see the muse calling me away, because I used to quote poetry at her instead of the prices of engagement rings. But she was so warm and cosy through the winter months. All the time my family were trying to push us closer, would yawn and go to bed early to encourage us to make good use of the living room. But still she held on to her purity like grim death.

Sometimes we would go to her mother's house and sit there going much too far. And all under the eyes of her mother, but her mother was blind, although with her open eyes I sometimes thought she was merely pretending.

'What are you doing, Shirley?' Her voice would break the heavy breathing and the electric silence.

'Ludo.'

Well, no good came of it at all. But no bad came of it. She made someone a plump happy wife a few years later. When we ever came face to face she would just nod and smile and pass without a word, pushing the pram and her two other children running alongside, into the distance.

Two boys lived round the corner—Alf and Joe Lubin. Mad, passionate, good-looking narcissistic and forever combing their blue black hair. They looked at themselves in the mirror every few minutes. I got to like Joe and I went to his house quite often where he'd be sitting on the lavatory with the door wide open, reading a newspaper and talking to me at the same time. He would sometimes embrace me in the street, cuddle me out of sheer exuberance. Lift me up and kiss me, or burst into song.

The brothers liked Phyllis and often took us to the Odeon in Hackney Road where they shared the same pair of glasses to see the screen; then they argued and shared the same choc ice. It can be assumed they really loved each other. Joe always said, 'Bernie, you've got to get on in the world. Don't accept this crap about learning a trade. Be ambitious.'

Joe worked up West as a songwriter and songs at once caught my imagination, sparked off the poetic side of me; besides Vera Lynn was singing, 'When the Lights go on again all over the World'. It moved me as much as T. S. Eliot, especially when a choir of soldiers chimed in.

Joe thought my work was lousy but encouraged me, and I in return hero-worshipped him. I wrote a song, called 'Quietly flows the Don' and sent it off, for I read in a newspaper advert that I too could be rich and famous within a few weeks.

By return of post a letter came telling me how talented I was and if I would send fifteen guineas they might find time to set it to music. My family were most impressed, but who had fifteen guineas? I remembered my rich uncle so I quickly got his address and rushed off.

I sat opposite him in his office; in his chair he didn't look so small. He puffed on his cigar and studied the letter and said, 'You're wasting your time.' He went on about flights of fancy, that I ought to worry about my mother and settle down and be a good boy. He threw the letter down and told me the man was a crook and he wasn't going to give me fifteen guineas. I could have killed him. He was right, of course. But I never forgave him for it. He became a symbol for everything I despised.

It looked as if the war would soon be over and we wouldn't die after all, and the lights would go on again all over the world. And I wrote song after song. All of them lousy, and I knew it, sang them to my sisters who pulled ugly faces.

The Germans were defeated at Stalingrad and I went on a voyage of discovery into the endless beautiful continent of Russian literature, where I remained happily lost and am still wandering.

Most of us were hardly sheltering now, though my mother and Rose stuck religiously to the descent every evening. Me and my father would go down only if the sirens went.

On March the Fifth 1943, the sirens wailed and we made our way leisurely along Bethnal Green Road. But we jumped in a doorway when we heard the most incredible explosions. But a policeman told us that these were the new anti-aircraft rockets stationed in Victoria Park.

When we got to Bethnal Green Tube Station there were crowds of people near the entrance; police, wardens and rescue workers and ambulances. There was a strange silence. Somebody told us that a couple of hundred people had been crushed to death in the entrance. I was sure my mother and sister were in that crush and we rushed forward, tried to get information. The rumours were flying thick and fast. The only thing we did know was that no bomb had dropped closer than two miles away.

We waited for hours while they brought the bodies out. The longest hours of my life. No-one seemed to know what had happened. A policeman was telling another that the bodies were piled on top of each other and that some people on top of the pile had suffocated while others at the bottom were trapped but still alive.

Almost the last person removed was a seven years old. The child stood up and walked to the first-aid post unaided.

When we finally managed to get inside, I could see lumps of hair in the entrance. We passed the bunks of white-faced silent people, and I was afraid to look as we neared our bunks in case my mother and sister were not there. But I heard her crying, and she cuddled us when we arrived. She thought my father and I were in it; told how the police had rushed along the tunnel from Liverpool Street Station to tackle the wedge of people from the other side.

In the morning we learned the facts. There had been no panic, but the new type shells bursting in the sky had made people rush into the entrance. A middle-aged woman with a bundle and a baby tripped over at the foot of the stairs. A man fell on top of her and people just went over like ninepins while masses more crowded into the entrance. It was all over so quickly. One hundred and seventy-three people were crushed to death, the majority being women and children.

I still remember them shouting out when I got there, 'Open the door. Open the door down there.' And I knew there was no door down there. But the worst thing of all was that it was blamed on to the Jews. Rumours persisted that the Jews panicked, and although this was later denied in parliament, the lie continued even though it was established there were few Jews among the victims. There were quite a few notorious pick-pockets dead amongst the victims.

My mother and sister continued sheltering there, and so did I when the sirens blew, but we drew apart from the rest of the people and whispered.

The heart had been knocked out of my mother. 'Won't they ever leave us alone?'

And we continued living in our home in Bethnal Green; strangers in a strange land. And I continued, staring out of the window, reading books and writing songs, becoming more and more a stranger within my own family.

7

Pimples and Dreams

So suddenly everybody started shaking their heads at me. Before I thought I might be a problem; now I knew it. So what did I do? Lay down and die? Give in? Not on your life. I declared war. Not dramatically but more in my cynicism and silence.

'Just when it looks like the war will soon be over, he has to go and start a private war,' my mother said to me in private. In public, in front of my father, she defended me, asked them what they wanted of my life; after all I was still a baby. I hated that.

My brothers and sisters, my aunts and uncles and cousins and neighbours all shook their heads and put their spoke in.

'He's mad, I swear it.'

'So what's wrong with cooking'

They named half a dozen sickeningly familiar occupations, 'There's a million things you could do.'

There were a million things I didn't want to do, except try to retain a dignified silence.

'Maybe he needs a tonic.' An aunt suggested.

'He needs a good hiding,' my father chimed in, though he wasn't prepared to give me one after his previous experience. He told me if I wasn't prepared to work I ought to leave there and then. My mother had hysterics; asked him where he thought I could go.

'To sea maybe.'

'To sea? To sea? Whoever heard of a Yiddisher boy at sea?'

Although my mother hadn't heard of what the sea meant in Freudian terms, she must have understood. One mother was good enough for me.

So she tried calming the family, telling them I would try to find my feet eventually. But all I found was a headache.

And my father would go on, night and day; talk, talk, talk.

'Wasn't I a good son to my own father?' 'Haven't I been a good
father?' 'What did I do to deserve it?'

My silence was objectionable. No one is silent in a Jewish family.
You can be anything but silent. I wasn't completing the cycle
expected of me; to marry a nice, respectable Yiddisher girl, have
a good trade, save a few bob, and plan for a family and home of
my own.

After all, what more was there?

What more was there? I wish I knew. But my mother thought
that it would all right itself and kept on slipping me a few shillings
every now and again.

During the day I would go onto the roof of Queen's Buildings
and look out over Bethnal Green, at the grey, ugly concrete trap,
and stay there for hours playing my mouth-organ.

And in the house I was becoming objectionable, questioning
every statement that anyone made.

Phyllis started going with a nice American boy named Norman,
who sometimes took me to the West End for a meal, talked to me
about America, about the wide expanse of country, quoted Walt
Whitman and Emily Dickinson. I thought she was one of the best
poets I had come across. Her words made me shiver—

> *'Because I could not stop for Death,*
> *He kindly stopped for me—'*

I worshipped Norman, thought perhaps he might show me a way
out of my confusion. He bought me doughnuts and coffee, told me
how much he cared for my sister. But she wasn't too happy and
often she cried. It was obviously a difficult relationship.

Mrs Plotz from next door would add fuel to the flames.

'So what is your son going to do Mrs Kops?'

'Don't worry about my son—He's going to be a poet.'

'Poet? Shmoet. Can he earn a living as a poet?'

'Sure he can.' My mother boasted, and then went on to explain
that clever boys were always difficult.

Sometimes, during the day, she would cry to me and appeal to
me. And often she tore chunks of her hair out with aggravation
and held it up in her hands to show me. 'Look what you're making
me do. You're making me go bald.'

I hated her. Hated because I loved her. The others didn't matter to me; there was no problem with them. If she had not been there I would have been away in a flash. My love for her held me in captivity, so I hated her. But when things got too tough I threatened to leave home.

'Who'd look after you? Stop it, you're killing me.'

I knew that I was. And it all could have been solved so easily; all I had to do was give in. Yet was it giving in? After all my brothers and sisters were happy enough.

'After all, what more is there in life for a poor Yiddisher boy?'

I continued writing my songs and little poems, but wouldn't show them to a soul.

'What's he doing by the window?' Essie said.

'He's writing; writing about all of us.'

Essie, as nice as she was, pulled a face, but my mother told her that I would be famous.

'Infamous more like it. He'll end up no good.'

It spread around the whole family. I was a no-good. They consoled themselves with this thought.

'It happens sometimes,' they'd tell my father. Meanwhile I prayed at night. 'Oh God give me the strength to live and find myself.' There are two kinds of lost. Those who don't know they are and those who do know. I belonged to the latter variety.

Whenever there was a row I would walk out and go to the reading room of Whitechapel Lending Library where I read the plays of Lorca and O'Casey and William Shakespeare. I was lost in Granada, Dublin and Arden, only to return home to the stinking, festering buildings, to the white face of my mother that gasped for breath. For now her health was failing fast and the more she coughed the more I hated her. I couldn't stand her coughing. Each cough was a nail in her coffin, and in mine.

The coal man wandered around the streets with his monotonous cry and I would lie on the bed in the daytime and fall asleep.

One of those days Dave returned home, must have known that I was asleep, pulled the bedclothes off me shouting, 'Get up you lazy bastard.'

I, dopey from sleep, not knowing where I was in that awful stupor of awakening, flailed my arms about. He, I suppose, thought I was attacking him and he hit me hard on the face.

Blood poured from my nose and my mouth. I screamed and held up the wine-stained sheets and sobbed my heart out. 'I'll never forgive you for this.' And I meant it at the time, for his punching had hit something deep within me. For a year we shared the same bed and we never spoke. We would often pass in the street and never look at each other. One day, however, we burst out laughing, and everything was all right.

But that action made a very strong impression upon me, though of course, it didn't give me the incentive to find work.

My mother cried, warned me that she couldn't give me any more money, 'For your own sake.' Day and night she was bearing the onslaught of my father. He had a one-track mind all right. Like a Zionist, and he couldn't be deflected from his path. I reckoned she was an angel to put up with him, but she loved him without question.

I made a few bob every Sunday in the street market of Brick Lane. For hundreds of years people just came and sold anything. An old woman might stand with just a pair of shoes. There would be the usual mixture of vases, books, old clothes and false teeth. And the market started to spread all over the bomb-sites. At odd intervals the police tried to stamp them out and erect wooden fences, but the street market was too firmly rooted in the people of Bethnal Green. The fences were trodden down or a new market would shoot up in another alley.

I sometimes bought a book for a few coppers, and a little way along the street try to sell if for sixpence. Then I would buy something for sixpence and try selling it for a shilling. Often I lost the lot and would be left with one useless flat-iron, or an ugly plaster dog or a few volumes of the Waverley Novels.

Lew, the old shoe-maker opposite, taught me an invaluable lesson. The secret of selling was buying. If you bought right you could always flog it.

And I searched around for old rags, drove my mother mad. 'What do you want? The skirt off me for lousy fags?'

But she'd always find me something from the cupboard. And

though I was determined not to give in I knew that I was getting nowhere fast.

All night I would pray my usual prayer to my usual non-existent god. 'Please give me the ability to write, to get away from this trap, from this world imposed on me.'

In the day I sat talking to Lew the shoe-maker, asking him how to get rich, for though I didn't particularly want money I thought the same laws would apply to ambitions like writing.

'Dedication. Yes, all your energies concentrated on money. Sell your soul. Lose all your friends. There's no magic. Suddenly you're rich.' He said with a mouthful of nails.

I asked him if he was so sure why wasn't he rich. He told me he liked his friends. And he went on tapping.

Yes. Dedication. All my energies. But who could fight against the love of my mother and who was as trapped as I? Were there others in the world like me? I decided there must be. But I had enough with my own worries.

1944 came and Dave and Debbie were going quite strong now. He still hadn't given her an engagement ring though. In Jewish families you get engaged before your engagement. Then after getting your engagement ring you have a long engagement. Then when you get married you're thoroughly engaged. With kids; and hire purchase; and family. It's amazing how Jewish girls feel left on the shelf if they're twenty-one and nothing has been arranged yet. At sixteen they start looking. At eighteen they start worrying. And at nineteen they should be marrying, according to the aunts and the neighbours. And they hypnotize the poor girls into the whole process. Neighbours chastise neighbours. 'So what's wrong with your daughter? Why hasn't she got a boy?'

A Jewish mother wants nothing more than to see her children married.

It's always: 'Please God by you,' or 'Please God by your children', Or 'May we only meet on simchas.'

I was a shloch. My trousers always baggy. My tie always eggy. My socks full of holes and my shoes hadn't seen polish for at least two and a half years. And since my experiences at the barber shop at Leeds I wouldn't get my hair cut. But apart from that I was quite presentable.

Cecil Gee was revolutionizing men's clothes in the West End. Every Jewish boy had a good suit. And when two Jewish boys met they always felt each other's lapels. 'Good cloth; not bad. Where did you get it?' They would walk around each other looking at 'the cut'. No-one felt my cloth or walked around me.

My sister's American used to help me out with cigarettes, would take me to the PX near Marble Arch and give me whole packets of Lucky Strike. Then I usually wandered into Hyde Park and lay on the grass.

Everybody was saying that the war was over bar the shouting, yet I realized that the thing that had created the war hadn't been removed. The roots of it hadn't been pulled out.

I wrote my first real poem on the grass, about the beautiful clouds in the sky and the way we had poisoned the earth. Then I listened to the speakers. It was the anarchists for me. For I was on my own and had no flag to wave, and no banner to hide behind; but these were strange anarchists, they had both a flag and a banner. But it was more than poetry that made me suffer on the grass. The scent of beautiful girls reached my nostrils and I loved the way they laughed as they passed. I wanted to roll in the grass with one of them. Any one of them; all of them, girls were so beautiful.

And I wrote my second poem called, 'To my Anarchist Lover'. I was longing for a girl. For sex. There I was, full of pimples and dreams.

My spotty face didn't stop me getting on to a public platform, and I plucked up my courage to stand before the jeering crowds at Speakers' Corner. I was on a soap box called 'Poets' Corner'.

'I'm going to read you one poem by Oscar Wilde and two by myself.'

The poem by him was 'The Ballad of Reading Gaol' which I had memorized by heart, although I could not manage more than twenty stanzas before the crowd got too restless.

The characters in the park intrigued me, especially the Jewish man who could talk about anything under the sun for as long as you liked. When I told him how much I admired him he asked me for half-a-crown. When I told him I was broke he bought me a cup of tea.

I loathed the smugness of the Salvation Army. A pretty girl with a white face told us all how Christ had entered her. Later she implored me to accept Christ. 'How? Don't you see if only I could— if only I could believe.'

Suddenly, out of the blue, I was offered a job by Joe Lubin, in music publishing. I had sudden visions of my songs being sung all over the world and having my name in the papers. But when I went for the interview I found out it was only to do the packing in the trade department.

'Never mind,' my mother said. 'You can work your way up.'

So I started work for Noel Gay in the first job I had ever remotely liked. Sometimes I would even meet Mr Gay. He was a real hero to me, the man who wrote 'Run Rabbit Run', 'Lambeth Walk' and 'Me and my Girl'. True, he could hardly live up to the image I had created, but he was the first famous man I had ever met and he was terribly kind. Every time I would put a cup of tea in front of him he would say 'Thank you'. He was very deaf. One almost had to kiss his ear to tell him the time. So I settled down there and all the family relaxed. Peace had returned to my world.

But just at that moment the real war hotted up again.

'There's always something,' my mother said. And not without reason. For all the young men of the family who were in the Army were called away for what we guessed was going to be the invasion of the Continent. Some of my cousins were in the Dutch Army and we dreamed of the day when Holland would be liberated. My mother prayed that the family would be safe.

Dave, because of his eyesight, wasn't taken for the Army, but my mother's single prayer was that the war should be over before it was my time to go. Understandable enough. Despite all the trouble I was causing she still wanted me home.

'Mind you, I want the war over for other reasons,' she said.

About this time the flying bombs started. I was petrified. I was more afraid of these than anything. Maybe it was because the end of the war was in sight, and it would be ironic to die so close to peace. I couldn't stand the way the engine cut out. That awful silence waiting for the explosion.

One day, during the lunch hour, walking along Tottenham

Court Road, one fell on a church just along the road. I swallowed some blast, was thrown against a shattering window of a vegetarian restaurant. My ears went funny and I walked around in a daze for days. Whenever the sirens went I would be the first in the shelter, but after a time people started taking the flying bombs for granted, and even though I stopped sheltering during the day I never became fatalistic like some, who said, 'If it's got my name on it, that's all there is to it.' As far as I was concerned every one had my name on it and I didn't want to take any chances.

I loved working at Noel Gay, where I scribbled songs every day in the hope that they would be passed upstairs and be shown to the *éminence grise*. But, though he was helpful, they never got further than Joe Lublin's eyes. He, like me, was burning with ambition and filled with songs. But I knew my songs were no good. I felt that it was leading nowhere.

My mother couldn't take the flying bombs, she found it difficult to run for shelter. The years of war hadn't made her less nervous. The family were trying to persuade her to go away again. And so was I, for I wanted to go with her; wanted so much to live through the war. But I was pleasantly diverted for a little while, because across the road I met a pretty little ATS girl.

Before long I was walking down the street with her. Before much longer I was holding her hand. I felt very awkward. Me in civilian clothes and she in uniform. We stood on the Embankment, and she fancied that she had a good voice. Doreen sang my songs over the water and let me put my hand down her blouse. One day we went to Parliament Hill and saw a flying bomb drop on the city. London looked like a city built for ants. A little puff of smoke rose and I knew people had been killed.

On Parliament Hill, me scared out of my wits, my eyes on the sky, she let me go a little further and later, in Poland Street, Soho she said, 'Trouble is, once you've had it you want it all the time.' She told me that she feared her husband was probably having women abroad. What a war. I couldn't somehow. There it was, being offered on a plate, but I couldn't. Maybe it was because she wore uniform. I was longing for it, and here was my opportunity.

After all, I wasn't going to get it from a Jewish girl; not without an engagement ring. And even then, I wasn't so sure.

So I pulled my wandering resolutions together. 'I'm bloody lonely,' she cried, and I got her a taxi. She went home to her mother and I went home also, wanting to kick myself on the way. When I got home my mother told me she was leaving London again. It was all right with me.

We arrived in Northampton, out of the blue, as usual, and we wandered along the main street when, of all things, we came face to face with some neighbours.

'Mrs Green! How wonderful to see you.'

My mother embraced the woman, who didn't seem very pleased to see us. They had been there for more than a year and were worried we might move in with them. My mother noticed her coldness. This hurt her so much, brought home to her at last what the war had really done to people. So she said goodbye and we were about to move on when the woman said, 'At least come home and have some tea.' We did, and we sat through tea very quietly. When we left, Mr Green handed us instructions to reach the various offices that dealt with nomadic families like ours.

I tried to defend Mrs Green, but my mother wouldn't talk about her. So I cursed her and my mother told me to shut up. So I shut up and my mother pleaded with me to say something.

We were very lucky. My sisters and my mother were billeted with a wonderful family. Eight boys and one girl and their parents called Aunt Liz and Uncle Charlie. And I was billeted along the road with Aunt Liz's sister.

My mother and Aunt Liz were very similar people, yet both had such entirely different backgrounds, but both lived entirely for their family.

Uncle Charlie sat in the corner, giving endless minute and jovial instructions to the happy brood of brothers. One of the brothers had been courting the girl next door for five years or more, and all the others weren't yet going with girls, even though the eldest was over thirty. They were all very gentle and ragged, and chipped and hopelessly spoiled their young blushing sister. On Saturdays they would spruce themselves up and go dancing. They would pour grease on their hair, slick it down, and try to get me to do the same.

I started to smarten myself up, for there was a plump lass along the road who I was mooning for.

Meanwhile, at my own digs I sat alone and wrote songs, and mooched about the house. Also to pass the time, I mucked around with the boy next door, playing in his house. His father was abroad and we used to go through the drawers when his mother was out and read his letters which were full of the most purple declarations of love, what he wanted to do to her and what he would do. 'I'll sweep you in my arms, carry you upstairs, throw you on the bed and do you.' He was also a bit of a poet. She once read me one of his poems. 'Darling I love you, you mean the world to me. Upon the sands of Africa, I always dream of thee—But when this war is over I will never roam—I'll stay with you and love you in our little home.' Ugh; but slightly beautiful. War helps men to commit murder and write poetry.

The local meeting place for boys and girls was called, 'The Bunny Run' and there, as posh as I could be, I came face to face with my rosy round girl. Her name was Susan and she was sixteen. I walked away with her. She hardly spoke but giggled all the time.

Behind the houses, in the long grass under the dappled sky, I never quite made it. But, Oh! What bliss. One of the few really great moments of my life was almost undressing her on a warm summer's day. Alone in the fields with a stamping horse and me showing off, reciting Shakespeare's sonnets between swoons. She was illiterate, but passion and literacy do not necessarily go together.

So we'd meet every moment we could and I'd just strip off her clothing and kiss her. And she was such a happy girl, always smiling. She told me she had been backward at school; and still couldn't add up. Come to think of it I could have taken her. Come to think of it, why didn't I? We would grapple for each other's bodies at every opportunity; in passages, under the table, and, once, at a funfair we lay consuming each other with the sound of mechanical music through a hedge.

Up till then my mother's cry was, 'You'll marry a nice respectable Yiddisher girl, you'll see.' But she seemed to like my girl and didn't shudder at the little gilt cross I bought for Susan at Woolworths. My mother was becoming a bit more broadminded. Her travels through rural England were teaching her that people were pretty much the same the whole world over.

So I went fishing with the boys, on the River Nene, and mushroom-picking with my sisters, and passion panting with Susan. But there was still the question of work. My father had given me a present before I left. The tools of his trade. Northampton was the centre of the shoe industry, so he took it for granted that I would follow in his clicking footsteps, gave me his hooked knives and his blocks of abrasive to sharpen them on. He thought at last he had me; so did I.

I started work in a shoe factory. At first I carried bales of leather as big as myself into the factory, all day, for weeks on end. The smell of the leather made me retch, but no matter how I tried I couldn't develop a skin allergy. The physical smell of the factory became completely nauseous.

But beautiful Susan, with the happy eyes, with her blouse buttons almost ready to pop, waited for me after work, made it all bearable. And I popped the buttons and kissed her breasts and passed the evenings breathing in the beautiful fragrance of the Northampton fields and the cheap scent from Woolworths. That girl was empty; beautifully empty.

I was promoted into the factory proper, where they gave me a bench and leather and patterns, so I sharpened my father's knives. It was probably more the thought of what happened to him that made me hate the job so much. I couldn't understand how he, hating his working life so much, could now bequeath it to his son.

I became quite obsessed with hatred for my father, and all my confused anger was directed towards him. Until then I could never have dreamed of admitting to myself that I didn't like him, so it became quite a relief to find that I actively disliked him, that I didn't have to kid myself. In our family it was a sin to have favourites, even though, of course, we did. But we would never admit it to ourselves.

One beautiful day I wanted to go to the lavatory, but in the factory you couldn't just go. You had to hold up your hand and catch the overseer's eye. He would nod, and then you were at liberty for a few moments to relieve yourself.

I went into the lavatory where it said, 'No smoking'. I sat behind the locked door and smoked. The foreman came in. 'What do you think you're doing in there?' Smoke was everywhere. I pulled the chain and faced him. Very grandly I said, 'I would like to tender my resignation.' I left him gaping and walked straight through the factory smoking my head off. All the men watched me as I slammed the door on the leather industry, on clicking, the job that had ruined my father's sight.

I got a job in the office of a flour mill. Two girls worked in the office so the days fortunately passed quickly. And in the soft evenings, in pictures, or in fields, I would embrace my yielding girl. But, I'm afraid I had been leading her up the garden path, for I told her I was a brilliant songwriter with a wonderful future, had built up a myth that I was really a song plugger of the Noel Gay Music Company. She was so proud of me and told everyone. They all believed it.

A letter came one morning telling me to present myself for a medical: I stood naked in a line of men and felt indignant at the lack of privacy.

I didn't pass the medical and I was confused about this. I hated the Germans, wanted so much to get a crack at them for all they had inflicted on my family, the Jewish people, the world; yet another part of me wanted no part of the war, wanted to lie in those green fields of Northampton, horizontal with Susan.

My mother was delighted. But I was worried sick, wondering why they had turned me down. The illness of my childhood obviously had lasting effects.

I took Susan to London one day. The last rockets of the war were falling on the capital, but that didn't matter somehow. I lay on my bed in Bethnal Green with her, having planned the big seduction, but it didn't work. She didn't belong to that background. We didn't belong to each other. She seemed so naive and young, everything she wore was wrong. She reeked of her cheap scent. It was all ridiculous. She sat on the bed with lipstick smudged over her face, and I had nothing to say to her, so I took her back to

Northampton and then I got the sudden impulse to return to London immediately and for good.

The day before I left there I played a weird joke on them all. I went up to my bedroom, put two pillows around me, put my mother's coat over that, tied my hair in a scarf, rolled up my trouser legs, put lipstick on my mouth and glasses on. I went downstairs and knocked on the front door, and pretended to be my eldest sister Marie. I sat down and fooled them for half an hour and they made me tea. My mother knew it wasn't her daughter, but she didn't know it was me. 'So why did you come Marie?' she said.

'To tell you that Bernie can go home now because the war's over.'

Then I revealed myself and my mother was very cross. I wanted to cause a row, to give me the excuse to return. I needed some sort of big blow up to be able to face up to Susan with a reasonable explanation.

I told Susan that I was going for a little while back to the music business, that everything was going to be all right and she would either come to London or I would return there. She knew I was lying and I tried not to make love to her as I spoke, but even on that last night I couldn't keep my hands to myself. But she was so beautiful and fresh and young, and I was returning to a city that was so battered, so old and so tired.

So I went home and got my job back at the music publishing company, and waited for peace and for my peace. Phyllis also returned to London, but she was desolate. Her American boy friend, Norman, had just written to her that he wasn't returning. He had found a girl in a concentration camp, a lone survivor of an Austrian family. He wanted to dedicate his life to her, for he himself had been a refugee from Hitler and went to America as a young boy.

Phyllis wept for days, 'It would be easier if I didn't understand, if I could feel bitter, but I do understand,' she cried. I felt very sorry not to be seeing Norman again. But we had other things on our minds for we learned that all our family in Holland had been killed in Auschwitz, all but one cousin.

They even dragged out my old uncle who was too old to walk.

What a victory! Was there a single family in the world not touched by the war?

A friend from the West End came to my house in Bethnal Green. He called himself an intellectual. 'Look here old chap, they're not all like that. You can't condemn a whole nation, you must be logical about the Germans.

I wanted to throw him out of the house. 'Don't ever ask me to be logical about the Germans. Allow me this one burning hatred. It is too soon to ask me to forgive. If I lived for a thousand years it would still be too soon.'

I just didn't want to know about the Germans. Story after story came. Stories that tore me apart. My pimples had gone and my dreams had turned into nightmares, nightmares that would stay with me until I die. 'Six million! Six million!' my sister cried, but I couldn't see things in terms of mass, for each separate individual member of my family died gasping for breath at the hands of one monstrous acquiescent nation. All other people were innocent until proven guilty. But from then on it was the other way around with Germans.

In Bethnal Green we never had toilet paper, and if I wanted to be alone I had to go to the lavatory. It was the one place of privacy and there I read the squares of newspaper. I figured out that the most terrifying thing of all was that ordinary acts of human decency were now being called heroism. When one man gave another a morsel of bread he *was* a hero, a real hero, yet what a comment on our society when such a normal act between man and man becomes heroic.

I hung around in those last days of the war, unable to feel any excitement. My mother returned from Northampton and the family gathered together again, played cards, ate fruit and nuts and sang songs. But the world had changed.

I sat in Shoreditch Churchyard near where Shakespeare's original actors were buried, wondering how I could continue living and making my living in such a world. A songwriter! Who wanted to be a songwriter?

Suddenly the bells were ringing and everybody was cheering and dancing and kissing and I went down to the Embankment with the crowd, but amongst them I thought of those other crowds; those of my family and people like them who had perished, who had suffocated, gone up in smoke; I thought of all the young men like me who no longer had dreams, who lay rotting under the earth.

And I walked away from the mad dancing crowds as all the ships' hooters started their shrill chorus and everyone began to sing. I was trying somehow to gather the threads of my life together and dream a new dream, to look forward out of the chaos and through the horror of our time.

8

So suddenly he's an Actor

Denmark Street was like any other street of business. Songs were
the commodity and the characters standing around might have
stepped straight out of Wentworth Street. They were the purveyors
of nostalgia for the masses. During the lunch-hour I spent all my
pocket money in the pin-table saloons of Charing Cross Road.
Consequently I was always stony broke.

I was making no headway and might just as well have been
packing margarine as song copies. But I did meet people, different
people, singers and entertainers, people on the stage. Fabulous
colourful types. Their stories whetted my appetite, even though
they were always telling me how terrible show business was.

An accordionist took me to the Welsh dairy one lunchtime,
bought me a cup of tea and a cheese roll and told me a different
kind of story, his story.

He had been in a concentration camp with his wife and his son.
Being a young able-bodied man he was given a job to do. This
way he saved himself. Quite casually, he talked. 'I had to feed
bodies into the crematorium. One day the bodies of my wife and
my own son came along. I fed them into the flames.' He must have
registered my look of dread. 'No, that wasn't the terrible thing. The
terrible thing was when I did it I felt absolutely nothing.' There
was no emotion in his voice.

He asked me about myself. I told him I was ambitious. He said
that he wasn't, that he continued living but he was finished. A
dead man playing an accordion. I asked him why he didn't kill
himself. He shrugged, paid for the tea and we left.

Then I knew that I wanted something beyond Denmark Street,
something 'beyond a paper moon and a cardboard sea.

The family gathered on Friday evenings but the roots were
somehow severed. The spirit was maintained on the surface, but it

wasn't the same. There were always plates of sweets and nuts on the table and the boys and girls would speak in gibberish and sing scattily, as they played rummy. Phyllis and I didn't play. My mother did and she used to look across at me as if she understood what was going on in my mind.

I had finally come face to face with myself and knew I had to get away from the family as soon as possible.

My mother looked so old now, once she sat down she would stay in that same place all day, except to go to the gas stove. She never lit the sabbath candles any more. Even the candlesticks were broken.

Now I didn't want to be a songwriter but I still defended that curious calling against my Dad. He kept telling me to learn a decent trade.

'Irving Berlin hasn't done so badly,' I said.

My father should have bothered his head about Irving Berlin. He had never even heard of him.

'He's a Yiddisher boy, an ordinary boy who made a fortune out of songs.'

'A Yiddisher boy named Berlin?'

One day passing the Troxy I noticed there was an amateur talent competition, so I entered. They asked me what I did. I said 'sing'. I couldn't even sing in my bath, but they tried me out and said I was good enough to enter. I wondered what their rejects must have been like.

So one night there I was on the stage singing, 'I'll be with you in appleblossom time.' The family came and they were all very excited. The lights dazzled me but I could see all their grinning faces in the front row. My horrible voice grated out and much to my surprise I didn't come anywhere.

Back in Denmark Street I wanted to be out of it. For suddenly it was the theatre for me, not show business but the theatre of Lorca and Shakespeare. I told my parents. My mother remained silent.

'So suddenly he's an actor.' My father ridiculed and asked me what was wrong with songwriting. I told him.

'So Irving Berlin didn't do so bad.'

'So what about Eddie Cantor and Charlie Chaplin?'

I shot names of Yiddisher people who had made it.

'And what about Sarah Bernhardt?' I added.

'You're no Sarah Bernhardt. You'll never get nowhere. You've got to have influence, rich parents, drive, initiative, talent and ambition.'

'But I've got ambition.'

'A poor boy can't afford to have ambition.'

What did I have to do? Swallow myself to prove I was ambitious?

My mother encouraged me. I think she realized that if I was out of the way peace would return to the house.

At Noel Gay's I asked a few performers how you actually got on to the stage and I was told to look down the columns of *The Stage* and write hundreds of letters.

I wrote one letter and got one reply. A few days later I deschloched myself because I was invited to meet a gentleman at the Eccleston Hotel, Victoria. He had a camel-hair coat on and I didn't like the look of him.

God knows why he chose me. I was to work as assistant stage manager and be a student of acting at the same time and receive a salary of £2.10.0. He gave me a contract. I held it up like one of the dead sea scrolls and showed it to my family. They looked at me with a mixture of surprise, anger, and wonder. My mother kept repeating, 'What did I tell you?'.

Off I went to Lincolnshire, where I learned that being an assistant stage manager meant having one long headache.

It was a completely new world for me. I knocked on the door of a dressing-room to announce, 'Half-hour to curtain up', then I just barged in. There was a most beautiful girl, stark naked.

'Well don't stand there gaping. Help do up my bra.'

I did. She was having an affair with the boy who was having an affair with another boy who was having an affair . . . and so on. We all shared the same digs. There was no chance for me.

My first stage appearance was in *Blithe Spirit*. Talk about baptism by fire. We were a girl short, so instead of the little maid who is visited by poltergeists, I played the part being a rather quaint young man servant. Her lines made me sound rather odd. Noel Coward should have known. I was even scared to think he might come to Gainsborough. They told me not to worry, he wasn't expected in Lincolnshire. It snowed but the theatre was packed. The week after it was quite fine but no-one came.

The next play was *A Bill of Divorcement*. There was I, dreaming of Lorca and they thrust Clemence Dane on me. As assistant stage manager I had to find props and make the wine from burnt sugar and water, carry furniture and the can back for anything that went wrong. In that particular play I had to ring the telephone at what was supposed to be a most important moment. The bloody bell wouldn't work. So I rushed to the entrance, knocked, shoved my hand around the canvas door, 'Telegram Madam'. I was congratulated. But business was none too good and our notice was pinned to the board. I wrote almost fifty letters to various companies offering my wealth of experience and I was lucky.

A few weeks later I travelled to Crewe to join another company. In my digs was the entire cast of a female impersonation show. They used to run about at night having rows and crying, 'take back your ring. I'm not married to you no more'.

Crewe was the other end of the world. People came to the theatre but we were doing plays like *While Parents Sleep* instead of *Juno and the Paycock*. I asked the producer why. He pointed at the full auditorium. 'That's what they want.'

I started turning my thoughts towards the West End. The West End, of course, wasn't interested. Neither was the East End, or any other end.

One night I was awakened in my sleep by the producer who was trying to get into bed with me. 'What is this?' I shouted. 'Don't be so bloody daft.' His eyes were glaring mad, so I locked myself in the lavatory and stayed in a sitting position until the morning.

When it came, so did my notice. I had just about enough money to return to London. There I invented some story of illness in the company, for the family, but my father kept on saying, 'I told you so.'

I wrote again to adverts in *The Stage*. Meanwhile I worked for my brother-in-law, sandpapering and staining chair legs.

A telegram came. It said, 'Travel immediately to Thornhill, Cumberland.' At last it seemed I was to get real drama. The Repertory Group was the name of the company, and it sounded marvellous. All the family clubbed together to give me my fare.

I travelled north to Egremont, under the great hills of the Lake District, and when I reached the small village of Thornhill I thought there must have been some mistake.

There was just a tiny church hall and a few houses and a great sweep of moor and emptiness behind. It was all very beautiful but hardly the place for the great classical tragedies. I was drawn to the church hall by the sound of a hammer. Inside there was no-one about. Just a lot of junk, and several hampers.

'Anyone here?' I called out. A little man tottered backwards, gingerly, down a ladder and said in the most beautifully modu-lated voice, 'I'm John Denver, the producer of the company.' He had a hammer and nails in his hands. He was about sixty years old. His hair was dyed, rather inexpertly, and had gone wrong in patches.

'I'm just fixing up the stage,' he said. Then he asked me if I'd ever acted in *East Lynn*. I'd never even heard of it. 'Never mind, we'll get you through.' He handed me a script, a cue script, show-ing just the last line of the previous person's dialogue and my lines. I was to be Richard Hare and was expected to learn the part for the evening.

'Oh don't worry, go back and study it. We'll have a run-through this afternoon.' Then he gave me five more scripts. 'These are your parts this week.' Harry Hardcastle in *Love on the Dole*, I was also the secret in *Lady Audley's Secret*. The juvenile lead in *Hindle Wakes* and small parts in *The Bells*, and *Ten Nights in a Bar-room*.

They had found me digs so I went back there and cried. Then I remembered his advice, 'Have a little doze, with the part under the pillow. That way,' he assured me, 'the words will percolate into your brain.' They didn't, but I couldn't sleep. I tried to find out about the company from a girl who, like myself, had just joined. She was in the room next door.

It was called a fit-up company. They travelled from village to village with a repertory of about forty plays. A different play was performed every night. 'Once you learn all the parts it's plain sailing,' she said.

The company was run on a commonwealth basis; we all took an

equal share of the takings, but the boss and his wife took an extra share. I met the company in the afternoon. I was bereft and speechless. They had a run-through for my benefit. It lasted ten minutes. They had been doing those same plays for more than forty years, and their parents and grandparents had been at it before them, right back to the rogue and vagabond days. These players bore little relationship to the theatre as we know it, and acted in a melodramatic style that hadn't really changed since the strolling players of Elizabethan days. I learned there were many companies like this in England, each with its own territory, and none of them had their eyes on the West End, none thought of advancement. They were content to travel and perform and make a living. Anyway, at that rehearsal I admitted that I hadn't even learned two lines. John Denver said, 'Oh, you'll say so-and-so and so-and-so, and I'll say so-and-so, and you'll reply so-and-so and so-and-so, and so-and-so.' But I still must have looked terribly worried, 'We'll stick your lines around the stage. That speech outside the window, these lines on the table—don't worry.'

I worried. At tea-time I realized why I had got the job. There was still a shortage of young male actors in England. A lot of the women were dressed in male attire. My young brother in the first play, Charles Cobber, showed signs of senile decay. But I was tremendously excited, and I suddenly felt alive. My heart beat fast, the moors of Cumberland were to be my provincial battlefields. Here I could make all my mistakes away from home. The company seemed to be made up of all the descendants from the oldest theatrical families of England. They undid their hampers and made up, and then we prepared the stage. It was no more than seven feet in depth and about eighteen in width.

Half an hour before curtain up the people of the village arrived bringing their own chairs. John Denver in his make-up sold tickets and I in my East Lynn costume sold programmes in the aisle.

Five minutes before curtain up, the hall was crammed. The boss came up to me. 'Incidentally, what else do you do?' I didn't understand. So he told me that each member of the company was expected to do a little turn in the interval. Charles juggled, Marigold sang. I told him I could try standing on my head, but I'd probably fall over. He thought rather not.

5

They managed to get me through that evening, I uttering not a word except, 'Here I am in sight of my father's house and I dare not even enter—' Then I simply gasped but no more words came. George took over my part as well as his own. 'I know what you're going to say. You're going to say I'm a rat. Well I'm not. And it's no good you telling me that I'm a lousy swine. . . .' He winked when it was all over.

I slept that night with the words for tomorrow night under my head. But it didn't work. I simply had to do it the hard way, by learning it line by line. Memorizing the part by the shape of the words on the page and the way they were situated. Gradually I learned the whole repertoire as we travelled around Westmorland and Cumberland, under the shadow of Scafell and Snaefell. Through Keswick, Ambleside, Appleby and Cockermouth, sometimes playing above footlights that were illuminated by gas. And it became a sort of holiday, along the grey blue coasts of Cumberland, where Wordsworth lived and dreamed. Lugging the scenery was the hardest work of all, for I had the hardest job, being the youngest male. All the other men were either cracked or cracking up. All except John Denver with his eternal damp dog-end in his mouth and his cheeky mad twinkle in his eyes.

There amongst the most beautiful hills I heard the news that the A-bomb had been dropped on Hiroshima and the war was over.

A letter came from my mother, 'War is over for ever and ever—' Now, in London, they were dancing in the streets, now in Japan they were dying in the streets. I walked into the countryside alone and climbed a small hill and just sat there, feeling completely drained of all emotion. We were on our own now. Mankind. Terribly alone, growing beyond evolution.

I loved and died and cried and died, went mad and died and loved and went mad. Sometimes I made love to my leading lady who was well over sixty years to my eighteen. On the stage, of course.

Often I died in such an uncomfortable position that I would stand up and die all over again. Once upon a death a splinter from the floor stuck up and tickled my nostrils. I sneezed.

'Rigor mortis,' the heavy man said.

We had a pianist who played appropriate music during the performance. One day our aged leading lady entered but the pianist's mind was elsewhere. She walked straight down to the front of the stage and shouted at him. 'My fairy music please.'

On Saturdays we played a matinée for the children. And made up the words as we went along although we had a rough outline. Kids are a tough audience. But I learned more from those Saturday matinées about comedy and tragedy than at any other time in my life.

Our first venture into modern drama was the play *Night Must Fall* by Emlyn Williams. But there was no Mrs Bramson, we were one lady short. So I played the part as Mr Bramson, and got suffocated by the young maniac. Some of the dialogue between us sounded somewhat dubious.

So we moved around the lake district, shifting our own scenery, through the idyllic, desolate landscape, sometimes cut off with a whole village because of a snowstorm.

We painted our own posters and stuck them up for miles around. In blinding rain I once cycled towards Penrith, tacking my posters to tree trunks, watched only by some rather shaggy, indifferent sheep. I watched the rain washing away my newly painted words and then the wind ripped the posters from the trees. I was so wet and miserable I just sat down and cried.

But I drew my regular share of money, learned the art of improvization, and naturally fell in love with the young girl in the company. She ignored me, dramatically, so that everyone knew she too had fallen.

It was a local girl, who kept me warm after the curtain came down. But she asked me to take her to London so I took her friend out instead. She wasn't so pretty. But at least she didn't nag me for the metropolis. I took her to pictures in Whitehaven and wandered through the countryside reciting *Blood Wedding* and *Juno and the Paycock* to her. She hardly understood a word, but it didn't matter.

I wrote a poem about Cumberland for I fell in love with its loneliness. I never wrote about the sea. I respected the sea but it made me feel insignificant. What could you ever say about the sea? The sea could speak up for itself, I felt. But the lonely mountains were not so frightening. They inspired me. The poem was the first poem

I ever submitted and it was published in the *West Cumberland Times*. This was not surprising since it extolled the beauties of the county.

I started to feel restless and because I now had quite a bit of experience I decided to have a change. So I applied for and got a job with a similar company at Shrewsbury. Mind you, they claimed it was slightly better class. The plays in our repertoire included *While Parents Sleep* and the Aldwych farces. Then we moved to Wales, to a mining village. The best audiences I'd ever acted before.

By now I knew all the melodramas off by heart and I loved them, played them in the style of the company, quite straight. And I loved the Welsh family with whom I stayed. The old man, a miner, played the violin, his two sons, David and Ianto, played the viola and cello. I told them I was Jewish. They gasped, 'We thought Jews had horns.' But they carried on playing and liking me.

I travelled for nearly a year and a half this way, falling in love with local girls and trying to love the hateful girls of the company. Still I hadn't made it with a woman. It was worrying.

My family always wrote asking when they could expect to see me in the West End. Had I been a fishmonger I would have stood a better chance of becoming a star with my name in lights. I became more and more restless, but I stayed with the company.

In Bacup, Lancashire, I was to play a negro in *White Cargo*, so I started putting the appropriate black greasepaint all over me, the producer thought I was crazy. 'Just put it on your face—they all know you're not a negro.' He was absolutely right.

We got very used to each other and I became proficient, even though I realize I was a lousy actor. The girls of the company were cows. Sometimes when I embraced them on the stage they would look down at my flies with a terrible grimace in order to make me dry up. I did. I got so used to the plays that my mind would wander while I was saying the lines. 'I hope the landlady hasn't got fish and chips for us again tonight.' At the same time I was pointing to the heavy lead, 'What have you done, you've killed your daughter, you've killed your daughter.' This was the curtain line, and I waited for the curtain. It wasn't forthcoming. There was no-one there to bring it down so I added, 'I will now go and bring the constabulary,' and I brought down my own curtain.

We were respected in the town, but it was difficult to keep up appearances on our meagre earnings. Cardboard went into my shoes to keep out the rain. I turned my own collars over and over again. After a time I chucked it in and travelled to Penrith where I joined a young group of melodramatic players. We did exactly the same plays but with experimental lighting. It was there I met her, my first *femme fatale*.

She had the most dazzling mass of red hair I'd ever seen. 'Frightfully, Frightfully Lorna,' I called her. She was upper crust, but I wanted to bring her down a peg or two. She drove me mad in the digs at night, with both desire and irritation. All of the young company lay on the floor smooching and I begged her for herself. After all she'd given it away so many times. I said, 'Once more won't hurt.' I was then just five feet three inches tall but lying on the floor it didn't seem to matter. She promised to think the matter over. I pleaded with her but she said she was determined to turn over a new leaf and be a good girl.

'Turn over a new leaf tomorrow, start being good after me,' I implored her, but she stayed chaste for a week and thereafter started ignoring me, so I left the company.

I joined another fit-up near Norwich. But I didn't like the face of the producer, nor his voice. And I was getting a bit fed up with squalor. It was just hard grind for no dough. The romance of being an actor was wearing threadbare.

I stayed in digs that I shared with a Scots girl, rehearsing for two days while it poured with rain. On the third day the weather cleared and I'd almost learned my part. We were all set to open that evening; over tea I persuaded her to leave. We gathered up our luggage and walked along the dark lanes towards Norwich, at the time when the curtain should have been going up. She and I were playing the leading parts. I hated myself for my action, but had to do it, somehow.

When we got to Norwich we sat on some steps until the morning. I stared up at the sky telling her about my universe phobia. 'I'm lost, I'm lost, I'm lost,' I said.

'Shut up then,' she replied.

In the morning I sold my overcoat in a junk shop and she hocked her bracelet and we returned to London by coach.

This was the pattern for quite a time. One company after the other. Dreams and squalor. How often I fell to sleep hungry. Sometimes we would be locked out of the church hall because we couldn't pay the rent. Then I would hitch-hike back to London to be fed an enormous meal by my mother and a lecture by my father.

Then I'd shoot off again, getting money somehow, borrowing a few shillings from faces I knew and once a few quid from the Actors Benevolent Society. So it went on. Up and down, delirious or sad. Exhibitionistic and intense. I'd leave London full of hope with borrowed money and return after a few weeks full of despair. Everyone told me I was wasting my time, but I thrived on their discouragement, it fed me. I was gathering sustenance within. I hoped their discouragement would reveal my road ahead.

I started to want something more. These fit-up companies were all very well but I realized that this way I would be going round and round for the rest of my life. I wanted to get somewhere and I wasn't looking for security or contentment. I didn't get it. I returned to London and started doing the round of agents. They took one look at me and shook their over-fed faces. But in a café in Gerrard Street I met a man with a pseudo-American accent. Just like that, he offered me a part in a new play he was touring. I didn't believe him because at that time London was full of phoney Yanks. However, this offer turned out quite genuine. The American had written the play. He was producing and also starring in it.

A few weeks later we started the tour. I was playing an Italian gangster. It was a terrible play and a terrible part, but the money was the first real money I had earned. When we arrived at Bolton I saw we were billed as an 'All-American cast', so I had to speak with an American accent in my digs and in the streets. I also invented an American identity.

One day we were invited to look over a cotton factory so I asked the mill girls questions in an American accent. Later we had lunch with the directors. I felt awful. There wasn't one American in that cast of fifteen, though one of the girls had been to Canada.

We played at Collins Music Hall in Islington three weeks later. The people there, used to music hall, just wandered in and out during the performance. In the front row I saw a woman suckling her child. They treated the whole thing as a comedy; almost every tragic line brought hysterical laughter on the first night. And the reason for their laughter? I, the Italian gangster, made my first entrance pretending to have rushed across the roof-tops of New York, escaping from the police with a gun in one hand and a knife in the other. On that night I caught my trousers on a hook outside the window. When I entered, it pulled my flies open. No-one noticed at first, but then I had to rush forward and stand centre stage and thrust the knife at the producer's throat.

'His flies' undone,' someone screamed in the audience. They just wouldn't stop laughing and jeering, and we had to bring the curtain down and start all over again. We played it for comedy after that.

The play folded and I returned home, but things were so difficult in the family that I used simply to creep in at night and go straight to bed. One night my mother was waiting up for me.

'Where have you been? It's twelve o'clcok.'

I told her it was about time she faced the reality that I was almost a man, that I was shaving and that I was having women. Of course I wasn't. She cried, 'Why do you tell me these things.'

I told her that she should rejoice that I wasn't having men. She looked at me as if I was mad. I hated myself.

I used to wander sometimes through the East End with friends from the West End.

'Isn't this beautiful, this desolation?' one said.

'No, it's horrible. It stinks, and there are bugs in the walls. I see no beauty in it.'

Most of the Jewish people were now escaping along the north-west passage to Golders Green via Stamford Hill, but not my family. They stayed in Bethnal Green, I could hardly bear to visit Stepney Green any more. The air was thick with ghosts.

I started writing furiously, purely for myself. Things I saw around me, things I felt inside me. Though all my clothes were falling to pieces, I tried to keep a semblance of smartness for the round of agents, but gradually I realized I was fighting a losing battle against myself.

For a while I became a film extra. It was degrading work. Some film extras fought to get in front of the camera, some fought to be at the back. I was of the latter sort. Once I was on an all night call in a fairground scene, going round on a merry-go-round endlessly. It was freezing and I was put on the big wheels. Sometimes I was caught up in the sky between takes. Then we'd be assembled on the frosty fields and told what to do, as if we were idiot children. Often I was kept awake by the dear old ladies who were being madly gay. Patched-up old girls forever jabbering about their fabulous pasts. Were there ever that many stars in the world? 'And I said to Larry—and Viv said to Ivor—and I said to Edith—'

We were all misfits under the moon. Pinched and white and smiling mechanically, like figures out of Hogarth. Moving like somnambulists behind the stars, cheering and waving and murmuring and chilled to the marrow.

In the morning it was pathetic returning on the tube. Everyone washed out. Old ladies doddering back to their lonely furnished rooms. Nodding to sleep on the Central Line and powdering their faces and mascaraing their eyes at Shepherds Bush. And the aged queens camping around and giggling, with sadness and longing pouring out of their eyes. Actors who don't make it are the loneliest people in the world.

But I earned quite good money and was able to bring a smile to my father's face.

'My son's in films,' he said. And all the family went collectively to the cinema to see me appear once amongst a crowd of hundreds. In one film I saw myself chasing myself. The casting people had made a mistake, I was both the pursued and the pursuer.

Often I would lose all my earnings at a game of cards.

The man who organized the extras in those days was called Archie Woolf. He was a lovely man; well, not lovely physically. He'd smack you on the bum and say, 'Go down to Pinewood for two days.' In that crowded office you'd hear extras talking to extras, 'Do they want tall men or small men, blond men or dark men, fat men or thin men?' 'How many days is it for?'

Being a film extra depressed me enormously, for it showed me how I would most likely end up if I didn't make it as an actor. And the thought of being an actor appealed to me less and less.

I started spending my days in the National Gallery for it was warm in there. The paintings of Goya, Velasquez and Rembrandt excited me but no more than the girls who passed. I ventured into the National Portrait Gallery but got scared of the loneliness and the terror on the faces.

I started going regularly to the café in Gerrard Street where the actors met. They dressed well, boasted continuously and were always on the bum. All except one man who wasn't an actor. He impressed me very much. His name was Paul Potts, and he told me he was going to Israel for the *Manchester Guardian*. He was a poet and a radical and very excitable. I said to myself, 'This is a real man, one of the few I've met.' Despite the fact that he was bloody rude to me.

About that time I read the poetry of Mayakovsky. His suicide note played on my mind. I found it beautiful and terrifying. I loved Russia and the beautiful dream behind Socialism, but was becoming confused. One minute I wanted to change the world, the next moment I loathed it, wanted only to change myself, to harden myself against the coming night of the long knives. For I was sure of an imminent showdown. In the family and in the world. To survive, one first has to acknowledge that war has been declared. The city was a battlefield. I became exhibitionistic for I needed the antagonism of people. Discouragement nurtured me. I took to quoting poems aloud in the streets, people looked at me.

'Your son is going mad,' neighbours said to my mother.

In those days of 1948 people were not so discreet. I stood on the roof of Queen's Buildings declaiming, and I wandered the West End spending my days at the Westminster Reference Library and at the Express Dairy Restaurant near Leicester Square.

I became very friendly with a young man called William Pettit. I spoke incessantly. He listened, got some vicarious pleasure from my iconoclasm. A few weeks later I opened the newspaper to find that he had killed a married woman and the police were searching for him. The newspapers were full of it. A few days later there was an evil smell on a bomb site near the Bank. They found his decomposing body there. He loved the woman he killed and he wasn't able to cope. After killing her he killed himself.

I used to wander the streets of London. 'Christ I want to love someone, want someone to love me.' I was twenty-two years old and already felt I was a failure. I started menial work. The lower the position the more I liked it. My mind was free to enslave itself, to create its own captivity. Now I re-entered the hotels but this time as kitchen porter. My mother was patient and I hated her patience. If only she would do something to make me leave home. If only she was a cow.

My father was ashamed of me, went red in the face when he spoke to me. 'You're a writer, so become a reporter,' he said. But I didn't want to. I could never confuse that work with creation. Not that I was ambitious to be a writer, it was just that writing meant freedom. A means of striking, of asserting my independence.

I returned to the theatre. A group of young actors decided that the masses needed art. That this would start a social revolution. So we tried Dickens and Lorca in the Isle of Wight, in hospitals, in schools, and in Halls. J. B. Priestley came one night. There were about six people in the place. He sat in the two bobs smoking his pipe and left without saying a word. The masses of the Isle of Wight didn't appreciate us. We moved to Southampton. There a local woman joined the company, we rehearsed a new play in her house. During the rehearsals I noticed the woman's daughter.

I went into the bathroom and suddenly the girl was kissing me. There was something odd about her, something both odd and old.

'I could lay right down here for you,' she said.

'Why don't you?'

Rehearsals finished. The girl told me she would be travelling with us when we started our tour of Hampshire. She told me to contain myself. That I could have her within a few days. Suddenly I loved life. The universe was a beautiful garden. The world a smashing place. I could have kissed the coalman, embraced the fishmonger.

A week later we opened in Basingstoke and the girl arranged that we shared the same digs. When the curtain came down I dragged her home, begged her to hurry to bed. At first she wouldn't hear of it. She started talking, the way women do sometimes. 'I hate men,' she said, over and over again. She was bonkers, but oh what a beautiful shape beneath her dress.

'All right, you can have me,' she finally said.

She ordered me about, told me to get into her bed, then went into the bathroom. I lay there with my heart practically leaping out of my body. This was to be my baptism of fire. Basingstoke of all places would be burnt into my memory.

'I'm naked,' she called from the bathroom. So I looked, but the light was switched off and it seemed like an hour until she slid into the bed beside me. I didn't know what to do so she did it for me. Just my luck! To get a nymphomaniac for my first time. I had broken the spell. I was away. I had had my first woman. I was worshipping at her shrine. Afterwards I put on the light and just looked at her body and smoked.

'I hate men, I hate men,' she kept on saying.

She moved out of the digs the next morning and ignored me for days.

The company moved back to Portsmouth a few days later. The girl refused to speak to me but her mother took me to one side, told me she knew what had happened, that I was to beware, that her daughter was a bad girl. The mother was a spiritualist and told me I would succeed if I stayed away from her daughter.

That night I waited outside the house for my woman, my first woman. She came out, passed me by and walked along the beach, took off her shoes, stared at the water. I rushed up to her and begged her to speak. She remained silent, looked at me as if I were a stranger. I knew then that my life ahead was filled with complications. I watched her for an hour as she stared at the sea. Then I walked away.

What a beginning. I was utterly fed up with the theatre, with girls, myself, so I hitched back to London. But the rows became unbearable, so I spent most of my time wandering around the West End.

I met a most beautiful girl in the street. The sun shone right through her summer dress. She was very proud of her natural attributes. She was Jewish so I took her home. Glad at last to present a Yiddisher girl to my mother who gave her a soft-boiled egg.

When we left the house she told me she had a baby so I took

her rowing on the Serpentine. In the boat she told me she had two babies, and both by different men. She herself had been an orphan. We were lying on the bottom of the boat, in the middle of the lake, cuddling and looking at the sky.

I arranged to meet her that evening but she didn't turn up, so I rushed around the streets. I finally came face to face with her in Leicester Square, outside a milk bar. But she looked different; her face was plastered with make-up, her eyes with mascara. I asked her how she could sell herself to anyone, she swiped me round the face, then burst out crying.

I led her to a No. 6 bus, my arm round her. When we got home my mother said of course she could stay the night. After all, she was a nice Yiddisher girl wasn't she?

About two in the morning I slipped out of Dave's bed and crept into the living room on the settee beside her.

She wasn't such a nice Yiddisher girl in their sense, but she was a wonderful Yiddisher girl in my sense. The next morning I thought I'd be courageous and tell my mother at least half the story—that she had one child. It worked.

'The poor, poor Jewish girl. It just shows it can happen to the best of us.' I told my mother I liked her and she said she could stay for the time being until she found her feet.

The family tolerated her—at first. But she wouldn't look for a job. 'She's an orphan,' I explained.

'What's that got to do with it?' my mother replied.

Every night now we slept together, though I'd creep back into my own bed before dawn. My brother would moan and turn over in his sleep. We were not on good terms now.

My girl started showing too much of her body around the house, sometimes lying virtually naked on the sofa. I didn't mind. But my mother screamed one day, 'Maybe dad will see her, or Dave. Then what?' She had a beautiful body, but how can you tell a Yiddisher mum that nakedness is next to holiness?

But then somehow my mother found out that she had two children. 'Two,' she yelled. 'Two!' 'You can make a mistake once but not twice.' I asked why not twice. 'Are you so sure she's a Yiddisher girl?' she said. Anyway she had to go, so I found her a room in Whitechapel Road, where I visited her for a while. Sometimes she wouldn't be there when I arrived and I would wait in the darkness for hours. When she came we would make love. One night embracing her I found some marks on her neck, marks that I hadn't made. We argued and she told me to get out. As I left I noticed my photograph on the mantelpiece was hidden behind the looking glass. I waited outside the house to well after midnight when she suddenly left. I climbed up a drainpipe, broke into the room and took my photograph, tore it into small pieces, scattered it on the bed, and I left again. On my way home I met her along the road, pleaded with her.

'You're a hopeless, romantic child,' she said, and slapped me round the face again. Then she quietened down and we had a cup of tea in an all night café, where she tried to explain who and what she really was.

She wasn't a full-time whore, but went on the streets to get enough money to support her children. They were being looked after in a very expensive nursery. 'I want only the best for them,' she said and showed me a photo of them. They were beautifully dressed. She told me that she got great joy in giving herself to men. She didn't actually enjoy it physically, but it gave her pleasure to give her body to sad men who couldn't make it with their wives. It was all she had to offer the world. She couldn't settle and needed to be free. Sometimes she kidded herself that she could turn back the clock and start a new life. But it was impossible. 'And you must decide also. Living between two worlds is the worst thing.'

I couldn't keep back the tears and offered her some money. Then I remembered I was absolutely skint. She paid for my tea and I left her there.

I returned home bereft, and trying to look happy. The tears wouldn't stop. I started crying like a baby.

Nobody said a word except my father. 'Trust you to find the one bad Yiddisher girl.' I got very angry and smashed some of the already breaking furniture. My mother had hysterics, my sister had hysterics, my father had hysterics. So did I.

'Leave me alone, please. Leave me alone.' I pleaded.

'No, you can't make the same mistake twice.' They went on and on.

The trouble is we make the same mistake over and over again

but I couldn't explain it to them, besides I was as disgusted with myself as I was with them.

'So you're an actor. Then why don't you leave. Go and act, we're fed up with you acting round here.' My father again.

'Still, a poor Jewish girl,' my mother said. 'She was an orphan.'

'So why don't you act. Leave home and act.'

But suddenly I didn't want to be an actor any more.

I lay curled up on the bed, covered with blankets. The days of innocence were behind me, I was face to face with the stark reality of the present and the horrible fear of tomorrow that was only too inevitable. I had run out of excuses. There was no way out, no-one to turn to. And an obvious silence reigned and shattered the household.

9

'I'm a Yiddisher Boy – Gimme a Chance'

One Dutch cousin, a sole survivor, returned from Belsen and I heard her story; as she spoke I could see the various members of my family being dragged away into Germany, and in the middle of the night often I would see them choking to death. My hatred of the Germans burned into my being. It consumed me and I cannot say I was ashamed of my hatred.

In the family everybody was now getting settled, except me. Even shy Rose found a nice boy, and Phyllis stopped crying over Norman, fell in love with Alf Gold, a seaman since returned from the wars. And Debbie sat cuddling my brother Dave, 'Tchutch,' 'Tchutchie, I could bite lumps out of him.' She pinched and twisted his cheeks. He loved it.

But the more happy they became the more menaced I felt. Sure, I loved their happiness, yet I was being suffocated and drowned by the family. And my father soon resurrected his faith in the conventions of the world, pleaded with me endlessly to settle down to a normal life.

'I should throw him out. That'll make him come to his senses,' I often heard him nag my mother through the wall.

'Over my dead body,' she would reply.

Yet I wanted him to win the battle, wanted the matter solved once and for all, for me.

One evening I drifted into a café off Charing Cross Road. My confusion suddenly seemed quite commonplace. Everyone looked mad there.

The Swiss Café gave me a real sense of security for the first time in years. The characters accepted me just as I was.

Art students, artists, models and layabouts, all misfits like myself. I was a member of a new minority where my Jewish neurosis

suddenly became an attribute. So I became a permanent fixture
and at first it was a giggle, meeting people as mad as Duncan, the
ex-doctor who handed the girl beside me a bunch of withered
flowers and kissed her gallantly on the forehead. She told me the
story of those flowers. A few days before he brought her the flowers
that he had found in a dustbin. She accepted them with a sort of
nervous thank you, but they were tattered and she wanted to
dump them, but knew that he searched the dustbins of the area.
That night she dumped them in Maida Vale. And here he was
again, presenting her with that same bunch of flowers, this time
a little more tattered.

Most of them nagged me to leave home, so now I got it two ways.
They told me to write, to paint, to sculpt. In that café everyone
was, or pretended to be, an artist. Everyone doodled or threw ash
on paper, poured tea and ink on to it and rubbed it all together and
held the scrawl up to the light and looked at it like it was
a Michelangelo.

Each night I returned to Bethnal Green, crept into my bed and
crept out in the morning and tramped to the West End again.

There's a time when a human being craves love and comfort
and is not too particular where it comes from. Homosexuals were
kind to me. They were always kind to the lonely or the ugly. One
boy, Tommy, begged me to go back with him. Christ I wanted
love so badly, and he told me I was a good-looking boy. So I went
to his room, but wouldn't allow any funny business.

'Look, we're all queer and if you're not why are you afraid to
let me?'

'Look honest, if ever I go queer, you'll be the first,' I said.

I was the sort of Yiddisher boy who had his head screwed on
in the wrong direction.

I got to like him and his friend, Ray, very much. They used to
dress up like women, as Victorian ladies, and go off to Victorian
drag parties. They would pass the café waving grandly or benignly
at us. They were both night telephonists and their rooms were quite
out of this world. One day it was Second Empire, the next it was
Greek classical, and the next Japanese.

Tommy finally fell on his feet. Announced one day that he had

fallen in love with a Catholic priest and was going off to live with
him in America.

'But where will you live?' Someone asked.

'With him of course.'

'But what does God think of all this?'

Tommy took one quick look at the sky, 'She thinks it's rather
wizard.'

They were always referring to Jesus Christ as 'That old Queen
in drag', 'Get her, on that camp old cross.' They were terribly sad
deep down, but covered it with a perpetual happy effervescence.

That café reversed all my standards and my ideas crystallized.
I carried on writing, mostly poems of hate against the Germans.
I was very pleased with one particular poem called 'Advice'.

> *'Listen to the priests my son, and always heed*
> *their sermons,*
> *They'll help you love the human race, and that*
> *includes the Germans.'*

I just couldn't cope with the human race, and so I was happy
to have fallen amongst low-lives.

There was David Levine, a fabulous pianist, who gave piano
lessons to keep himself going. We sort of teamed up. People said
we looked alike. He was the most intelligent, the most complicated
and intriguing person I had ever met in my whole life.

He called himself the bad half of me, and used to rave on for
days and days. He was way beyond me.

Then he told me he was a drug addict, rolled up his sleeves,
half proud and half sad, to show me the scars. He took me around
the West End revealing his hiding places for the drugs. In a café he
would put his hand behind the lavatory cistern, bring out a little
brown packet. In another lavatory he unscrewed the handle of the
chain; there in the hollow was the packet. 'Thousands of people pull
this chain every day.' He clutched the packet like the holy grail.

That was his great kick, hiding drugs in public places.

'Our theme song should be "I'm a Yiddisher boy—gimme a
chance",' he said, and offered me some drugs.

'Don't need it,' I replied.

'You will.'

The fatality of his words chilled me. I refused the drug, but our theme song stuck 'I'm a Yiddisher boy, gimme a chance'.

When David was particularly stoned he wandered the streets with glazed eyes. 'Rachmuniss' he cried out. 'Rachmuniss.' Compassion.

Everybody stared.

He loved to take chances. Often walked up to a policeman with a stick of marijuana. 'Can you give me a light?' He would tell them it was asthma cure.

We'd wander along Shaftesbury Avenue and suddenly he'd dive into a dive, play a piano fantastically for a few moments and rush out again, me following him. 'Must get my nose altered, must get my nose altered.' He was always holding his nose, always going on about the hole he had in his head.

I tried working for him, knocked on doors asking ladies if they wanted piano lessons. Most of them looked at me suspiciously. It came to nothing.

We had the most incredible rows at street junctions, just like lovers; but when we had some money we went to a Yiddisher restaurant near Piccadilly Circus, had a salt beef sandwich, him crying out 'Rachmuniss—I'm a Yiddisher boy, gimme a chance'. One day he begged me, implored me to smoke some marijuana, so I did. Nothing happened. No magic curtain went up, I just felt a little sick.

David was happily married, believe it or not, to a nice respectable Yiddisher girl. He took me home and joggled his daughter on his knee just like any other Jewish father. 'What do you think of my Francesca? Isn't she the most beautiful child in the world?' He and his wife had a wonderful pastime on Sundays. They'd dress up in dinner jacket and evening dress and gatecrash Jewish weddings at the Wembley Town Hall, and eat until midnight.

'What side of the family are you on?' someone would ask.

'The other side,' they'd always reply.

She was a devoted wife. If ever he slept in the West End, or was away for four or five days she'd search for him and take him clean socks and shirts, and some food.

So I started smoking greengage, or charge, or tea, or stuff, or pot, or marijuana. We always called the same thing by so many names.

It was also called Shit. 'Shit' because the boys who went onto the white stuff, the cocaine and heroin addicts, the main-liners, no longer got a kick from a reefer, consequently it was 'Shit'.

These boys were always sure that I had to follow their path. Like religious maniacs they were. 'First it's benzedrine, then shit and then you'll pop. You'll see.' They made my flesh creep.

And I got involved in the kick of hiding it around the town. But I got scared one day, wanted to run far away, my heart started to beat like mad, my life suddenly started to frighten the living daylights out of me. So I shot off to Paris with five quid and a dream, but I had the dream flung in my face. I hated Paris from the first moment. It was hate at first sight.

Whenever someone smiled I could see the open hand. The way to see a city is to be broke. Then it reveals itself to you. Paris had no heart—it was an old queen with a fabulous plastic surgeon in attendance. Perfume under the decaying armpits.

So it was marvellous to return to London where, for a few pennies, you could have a cup of tea with nobody worrying you. Or you could sit in a museum for nothing. I killed a lot of time with a threepenny ticket on the Underground, where all day I went around and around on the Inner Circle, in the warm, sleeping off my benzedrine nights.

But London soon seemed inhospitable again, seemed bent on self-destruction and so did the world. This time it was the Russians. Suddenly the Russians were our enemies, and the Germans were our friends. Not mine.

The Berlin air lift was upon us and I laughed, 'They'll have us yet, those Germans. They'll destroy the world.' But it was no laughing matter. 'Can we not learn? Every fifteen years or so the cancer breaks out, The German cancer,' I said. My friends told me I was stupid. It was the Russians not the Germans. But I was totally unreasonable. 'There should be two thousand little Germanys. It should be cut up into thousands of little pieces,' I said then, now and always.

London scared me. It seemed vulnerable to destruction.

At the Soho café I met an intense smiling boy who had just come out of the paratroopers. He had large ears and a large heart, and wanted to paint. We decided to hitch-hike away from London.

'The world can go bugger itself.'

We stood on the Great North Road with no future but the road ahead. When the car stopped, the driver asked us where we were going. We told him anywhere. 'I'm going as far as Manchester,' he said. 'That suits us,' we replied.

I got a job in Manchester in an hotel, as a kitchen porter. But Manchester was more depressing than London. I kept myself warm with a local girl who was twice my size, but suddenly I departed as quickly as I came, returned to London.

My family were beyond imploring me. When I walked into the room silence reigned. You could cut it with a bread-knife. I started to carve wood. I always carried a penknife now and a piece of wood. I wasn't sure if the wood was to justify having a knife or the other way round.

A week later I went off to Paris again. It was still there, still the same. I wrote poems, picked up dog-ends in the ashtrays of the cafés. And returned once again to the café in Soho.

I slept with a girl from Ealing who came for local colour. She was talented but without life in her eyes. 'Are you just off to Paris?' someone said. 'No, I've just come from there.' It was always like that. People coming and going. Sometimes I wasn't sure if I was coming or going.

Several members of the family took me to one side, told me that my mother hadn't very long to live. 'You ought to try to please her.'

But she never appealed to me; she'd just look sad and she'd smile and slip me half a crown when she could. I would rush straight to the West End and buy a stick of marijuana. I was so sure that it wasn't habit-forming. 'I can give up this stuff any time —that's why I don't mind smoking it,' I told everyone.

Some nights I never went home, just sat in Lyons Corner House talking about art and dreams and destruction. Then I'd wander the Embankment early in the morning. I tried to get a job washing up at the same restaurant where I had talked the night away.

I stood in a stinking queue with other misfits, tramps and drifters. I was taken on.

I got a job on the conveyor belt putting one cup on each tray as it came along. Terrible soulless work, but it left my mind free for confusion. When the manageress wasn't there a few of us would hurl plates and cups, hundreds of them, at the wall and smash them. Just to relieve the monotony.

I became ultra exhibitionistic, quoting poetry about the forth-coming cataclysm, which none of the kitchen staff understood or seemed to mind. I had become a court jester. My mind floated, my automatic hand continued putting everlasting cups on ever-coming saucers.

I met a Jewish girl in Soho, a sad beautiful intelligent evocative bird, all buggered up with socialism, Zionism and family.

She told me she thought she was pregnant. But not by me. I thought I was doing something symbolically necessary by saying I'd look after her. So I smuggled her home onto the settee where she had me.

'Who have you got in there?' My mother called.

'It's all right Mum, she's a Yiddisher girl.'

I supposed that she would suppose that one must be thankful for small mercies. She wasn't.

The girl had the grace to take herself and her problems to Israel, which had problems enough of its own. She told me she needed a cause, so she went out of my life.

We had no cause. We were caused. And we had no effect.

Soho started to fill with nice girls who wanted to give themselves but were always torn in the battle between their emotions and their intellect, torn between socialist youth camps, family con-ferences, whilst they read their books on Buddha and Henry Miller.

'I'm a Yiddisher boy, gimme a chance.' This was my theme song, not only with girls. But I could feel myself slipping out of my depth. I was on the unsteady slide to oblivion.

One day my sister gave me a pair of shoes to take to repair. I took them straight to the West End and sold them for five shil-lings. I bought two sticks of charge and I soared out of the terrible depressing world, got lost in a telephone box and became deliri-ously happy reading the names of people in the telephone book.

Now I really loved the drug. I thought it was forbidden because the governments of the world wanted to suppress people, didn't want them to be happy, to know too much. I picked a thousand sounds out of the air and earth. I heard them altogether, separately and in union. A symphony composed with birds and people and machines and wind and water. All night I lay in a state of composed paradise, looking at the textures of my clothing with wonder. The next morning I felt empty, useless and ashamed of what I had done with my sister's shoes.

But she forgave me. A week later she was most reluctant to lend me half-a-crown, but she did. I went straight out of the house, bought her a bunch of flowers. I never returned the half-a-crown.

I saw a lifeline in an advertisement in *The Stage*. 'Young actors wanted for sharing company travelling to Africa.'

I enquired and was told they'd be delighted for me to join them if I could find fifty pounds. They were making for Tanganyika, to perform dramas to the people who were involved in the groundnut scheme. It sounded crazy and just right.

But who in the world had fifty pounds? I asked my mother and my father, sisters and brothers, knowing full well the answer. But you never know. Miracles do occur. I thought they might club together to get me out of the way. But fifty was way beyond them.

But I had to leave the country by hook or by crook and I thought of 'by crook', but I wasn't cut out for that sort of life. The only thing I could pick was my nose. I couldn't even pick a winner. There was no Zetter in me at that time. If there were just two horses running in a race and I backed each one each way, they'd both be disqualified.

Then I remembered the organization who had helped me out in times of stress. The Jewish Board of Guardians! With a double dose of chutzpah and a stick of hashish working through my nervous system, I plucked up my dutch courage and approached them.

To my amazement they listened to my story and to my astonishment they decided to help me. But not quite in the way I wanted.

'Yes we've decided to help you so we're giving you some new clothes.'

'Can't you make it a little cash?' I pleaded. We are a practical race; the answer was no. They gave me a note which I took to a store at Aldgate.

And so I got some beautiful new clothing to the value of thirty-five pounds, clothing that I was never to wear. I took it immediately to the West End where I flogged it for twenty pounds.

I felt awful about doing it but I had to get away. All the faces of the people I knew seemed twisted. David Levine frightened me, his eyes stared at me with a burning depravity. He was now hooting like a bird and moaning like an animal. In Charing Cross Road he bent down and made me examine the top of his head.

'Look into the hole and see all the stinking rot of the world.' Even the faces of my family were no longer familiar. If I stared at them they would become strangers, their flesh would start to coagulate.

I kidded myself, with the others, that there was no addiction to marijuana. This was the worst kind of addiction. The psychological craving had taken root. There was no easy way out. Words had started to bubble out of me. Words with no apparent meaning. If words were pennies I would have owned the world. And a particular fear had obsessed me. I thought I might rush up to a policeman and spit in his face and curse him.

It was a tremendous relief to be leaving.

And all the family contributed a little amount towards my departure. I kissed my crying mother goodbye and left the house and the street without looking back.

Two days later, I arrived in the lemon sunlight of Marseilles and joined the company. Although I hadn't brought the full amount, they were very pleased to see me because they were desperately short of money. The producer immediately took everything I had. I didn't like the look of him. It was mutual.

They had converted a massive RAF lorry into a caravan and this was to be our travelling home. Meanwhile we stayed on the blistering Mediterranean coastline, ten of us and a dog, all cramped within.

It was a crazy scheme but the world was a nuthouse, so who was I to kick? The idea was to cross to Algiers, then across North Africa, and then down, but suddenly we were thrust into the middle of one of those eternal French strikes. No boats were leaving for anywhere and so we were stuck for nearly a month.

The mistral howled at night and we got to know each other. In the day we tried to rehearse. Imagine us on the beach reading from the scripts of 'George and Margaret' under the indelible sky, watched by beautiful dark smiling children as they dived into the dazzling water.

But the cash was dwindling fast and Marseilles is no joke without money. There were twins in the group, giggling virgins. 'We'll soon put a stop to that,' I said to Derek, the only person I liked in the whole company. But we didn't get anywhere with them. What they had they held. I found a pretty little French girl along the beach who, in return for English lessons, rewarded me with all the treasures she could afford. Quite a booty but not the entire catch.

The strike was long and food got short. But the producer didn't seem to be doing so badly. He still smoked his Hi-Life cigarettes. And a few members of the company were having it off with one another. But my Catholic girl stopped coming and winter was approaching. Derek and I were stony broke. We lived off a diet of cabbages and onions stewed together with Oxo cubes. There was a tremendous store of food in the caravan, but it was stored away for a rainy day. Derek and I tried to break into it, for although the sun was shining, it was very cold winter in my heart.

I told Derek he could pass for a Jewish boy, which gave me an idea as we tramped the streets of Marseilles, one of the most relentless, violent cities in the world.

'We'll find a synagogue and say we're Yiddisher boys, give us a chance.'

So we wandered down Rue du Synagogue and came face to face with the rabbi. I expected him to say 'Well boys, what can I do for you?' Instead he mumbled away in French. Whoever heard of a Yiddisher man with a beard speaking French?

'We're Yiddisher boys, give us a chance,'—'Nous sommes garçons Yiddishe, donnez une chance.'

He understood not, or pretended not to, but smiled fiercely like our Jewish God and gave us a ticket. We went to the address stated, found a camp which welcomed us, and people who immediately gave us a big meal. Then it dawned on us that the object was to ship us to Israel. We scoffed the meal and dashed out of the place. Zion was not calling us; well, if it was, we were not listening. 'If we fought for Israel, only the Arabs would benefit', I rationalized, as we beat it from the area.

A crisis meeting was called in the company, and there were heated discussions about calling it a day and going home. 'On, on, let us go on,' I demanded. Fortunately most of the others wanted to. That day we were visited by the French police who told us that we were not the sort of tourists they liked, and would we leave France immediately. That settled it.

We decided to journey through Spain, across to Tangier and then across Morocco, the Atlas Mountains and so on. After all, it's only a few inches on the map. At the Spanish border we were rooked by Customs officials, were told we needed a carnet to get the caravan over. Only a solid citizen of Spain could sign us in and they would do it for a small fee. They were full of cold smiles, it was no good arguing.

It was like a dream; that first sight of the Pyrenees. We came into a village in the semi-darkness. There was an officer on a white prancing horse and a straggle of soldiers slogging behind picking up dog-ends. And long queues outside bread shops. When we tried to get bread we had to pay three times the price, not having ration cards, which the custom officials should have given us.

We were twenty miles inside Spain and almost broke. The façade of friendship started to crack.

Derek and I cliqued together, for now, instead of one company, there were groups and splinter groups. The producer went to open the emergency store. It had been rifled by someone. Just a few tins were left and a few packets of tea. No-one knew who. Unfortunately, it wasn't me, because by now I hated almost all of them.

The first week or so we stayed in country places, in beautiful lonely landscapes, where the songs of gypsies were sometimes blown by the wind. Our money ran out, but the producer still managed to chain smoke. I had one stick of hashish left, smoking but a puff every day. When this went I tried smoking ordinary tea. And I went dizzy, wanted to be sick, but there was hardly anything in my stomach.

We met an Australian boy in Barcelona who was travelling south. He was quite well off and gave us money for petrol. So we continued southwards looking at our maps, eyeing each other suspiciously, and we prayed, for the steering was going a bit wonky.

The people were beautiful and in one city some were living in caves, children with flies buzzing in their eyes and their bellies swollen from starvation. I think that was the worst sight I ever saw. I threw out an old pair of plimsols. A dozen kids rushed forward. Some of the actors laughed. So did some of the kids.

We scrounged and scraped some vegetables and cooked them at night in the open. By now we were barely talking to each other, except Derek and I. But the two virgins tittered through their privations and retained their maidenheads, with much difficulty, from the members of the company. Near the Sierra Nevada we climbed, I remember, for days and days, slowly winding upwards towards the sky. Surely we must soon descend? I thought. And then at dusk we saw our journey before us, the endless winding road down, but the steering had gone completely berserk so we stayed up there until the morning.

We were visited by the Civil Guard. I asked one of them why they shot Lorca. He didn't understand. I pretended to put a pretend rifle to my eye and made a cracking sound. 'Lorca! Lorca! Garcia Lorca!' The civil guard suddenly became human, they were just boys in uniform. They tried to explain that it was the communists. Lorca's songs were sung all over Spain.

A sad, beautiful country under a frightening régime and a beautiful sky, with a sickle moon clutching the clouds. The earth full of scent and foreboding.

Next morning came the descent. Derek and I sat on the back of the lorry. We didn't speak but we both knew what the other was thinking. Six inches to the left was the ravine and we were determined to jump off and survive if there was an accident.

I looked behind me at the actors inside the lorry and knew that if I saw them hurtling down that ravine it would have left me cold. I could hear myself saying 'Oh well, there go eight actors, no great loss to the English theatre.' If I saw their smashed bodies I wouldn't have turned a hair, but God was on the side of mediocrity that morning. We got down safely.

We stole oranges to survive. From the trees we pulled them murderously. So we had oranges for breakfast, dinner, tea and supper. Oranges, fried, boiled, grilled and baked. One day, however, we came across tangerines. What a relief. But not to the dysentry. I lost a stone or two in weight and Granada, beautiful Granada, left me lifeless and cold. 'Granada, beautiful, far-away and alone.'

We went to the British Legation but they were never there, either at tea or lunch.

We camped outside the city, a cluster of children with sores on their mouths approached us.

'He spicka English, he spicka English.' They pushed forward a little bare-foot boy with henna'd hair. He recited some famous words in a majestic falsetto. 'I name this ship SS Britannia. May God bless her and all who sail in her.' That's all he could say. I gave him a copy of *Three Men in a Boat*.

We moved on and each white village was dominated by the great shadow of the church that seemed to cover the whole place. Spain seemed a lonely place, with the wind blown flamingos and men asleep on donkeys, and the most beautiful turquoise skies and thin beautiful women, soldiers on the bridges in their olive green uniforms and three-cornered hats.

I had no film in my box camera but pretended to snap people. Women would rush into their house and change for the event, to stand before me with their whole family of flashing teeth. Then click went the empty box. People stared at us as we passed. Spain was then still untouched by tourists, still licking its wounds.

Often we got plastered on anis and fell to sleep on the earth, and woke in the morning, each nursing a dreadful hangover, going about our menial chores, grunting like wounded animals, ignoring each other. How we hated each other. My dear theatrical madly gay friends of Marseilles had become my rather deadly enemies. It taught me a valuable lesson. Friendship would be a word rare in my vocabulary from then on.

Malaga! The sea! And nearby Gibraltar.

By now I was so hungry that I wasn't hungry any more.

Malaga passed like a white dazzling dream of Moorish arches and the sea hanging from the line of the horizon like a blue sheet hung up to dry.

We crawled into Gibraltar. The shops amazed us, each window bursting with meats and watches and cakes. The caravan rested. Derek and I were suddenly alone.

Gibraltar is in the sterling area and all the boys and girls had wired their mummies for money.

A few hours later we saw them in the main street looking all clean and happy and well fed. They waved, told us they were staying at decent hotels and were going home. Not one of them even offered us a cup of tea. 'Be seeing you,' smiled and walked away. The eight of them were all friends again and were being madly gay.

'Where are you going boys?' A homosexual voice and a kind face greeted us. He was a colonial gentleman and was a member of a mission to comfort sailors. We weren't sailors but we needed comforting. He got us fixed up for the night and took us out to a meal of steak and chips. When I came to eat it I couldn't face it, didn't feel hungry. I could have kicked myself. But the man didn't try to collect our gratitude. So that cheered us up, resurrected our little bit of faith in human nature.

Gibraltar is a rock; and that's all there was, rock. A claustrophobic depressing place, overhung by a perpetual cloud. The next morning I taught Derek the few Jewish prayers I knew. The prayer for drinking wine and the prayer for food and the first six letters of the alphabet. Then we made our way to the offices of the Jewish community.

'But I'm not circumcised,' he said.

'They're hardly likely to take down your trousers for a few matzos.' This reassured him.

The representative of the Jewish community was not too pleased to see us, so we sang our battle hymn 'We're Yiddisher boys, give us a chance'.

'A chance to do what?' The man spoke with an Oxford accent. He even had an old school tie on. He kept looking at Derek. 'Are you sure you're—Jewish?' he asked.

Derek swallowed and assured him he was.

To change the subject I dropped a hint that we were secretly making our way to Israel, to be of some service to that state.

Possibly he could see no pioneering light in our eyes for he told us to go back to England. We told him we would rather stay in Gibraltar. I think that was a bit too much for him to bear. Two Jews on the bum would be a source of embarrassment to the

Jewish community of Gibraltar. On the wall was a map, and there was Africa. Africa, a whole new continent, just a spit away. I could even see Africa out of the window. It was drawing me. It was a new continent. It was singing to me. He must have heard the swan-song. 'I'll give you your fare money to Tangier.'

So who were we to argue?

We took the cash and travelled to Algeciras in Spain, where we intended to get the ferry across, but the Spanish police took one look at us and we were immediately grabbed and bunged into prison. No explanation, just some excitable lisping, and there we were in a stinking, infested little cell.

That night we heard people singing in the street.

We were very thrilled because we had a feeling they weren't going to shoot us. And they didn't.

Next morning, they opened the door as mysteriously as they had shut it on us. And there we were, on a boat. Before us, on the other side of the sea, the blue, misty coastline of North Africa was beckoning.

Our trousers were tattered, all our belongings gone, our hair long, our faces dirty, our feet smelling and our pockets empty, and the whole of Africa before us. And what had I to offer the new continent?

I knew my acting days were over for good and all. So what had I to offer the world? The future? I had nothing to offer and I had nothing to say. Nothing but my theme song, on that rocking crowded boat.

'I'm a Yiddisher boy, gimme a chance?'

10

Distressed British Subject

The romantic blue coastline soon changed into the most confusing harbour of Tangier. Derek and I stood on the quay surrounded by a swirling, smiling swarm of screaming Arabs

Could they be shouting, 'We're Arab boys, give us a chance?'

We pointed out that the suitcases were practically empty. They got the message and drifted away, so there we were in Morocco, with fifty pesetas between us—and the night coming on and all the smells and sounds of pulsating Africa. We wandered the harbour area, looking around us, with wide eyes and mouths.

'Yoo hoo boys,' a fat female American voice called.

Something always turned up, my mother said. Apparently it had. But my mother would have got a bit of a shock if she could have seen the way fate had dressed one of its emissaries.

She waved a plastic handbag at us and we rushed and embraced her. She was a whore we had met in Marseilles, who was working her passage around the world. 'I'm working in one of the best houses in North Africa,' she said.

She was well over forty, so we didn't have to say a word about our plight. She took an arm of each of us and took us to a respectable house. 'Not where I work, you understand. I like to keep business and pleasure apart.'

We wondered what was business and what was pleasure to her. We stayed at that house for a few nights at her expense, and she seemed thrilled at the thought of helping two emaciated, starving, latter-day actors.

She told us business was booming and that she was very well in with the mistress of the brothel. We were not to worry, she would get us fixed up somehow or other. But I carried on worrying, not having the essential commodity for whoredom.

The house we lived in was run by a Spanish lady.

'Don't tell her what I do boys.' The fat American whore said. As if it wasn't obvious.

The whole of the Tangier football team were billeted in that house. Our house in Stepney Green was like a Trappist monastery in comparison. I retreated to my usual place when I wanted to be alone, the lavatory, which was the only spacious place in the whole house. It was like a throne room with a hole in the middle of the floor. You had to squat on footprints.

Outside the window the sun dropped like a stone into the purple sea. We rushed out into the street into the Soco Chico. Then it hit me. The excitement and fear of being on my own in a far country. No-one would help me get out of a difficult situation.

A shoe-black pestered me 'Clean your shoes mister, clean your shoes mister?' He smiled at me in seven languages. Clean shoes were the last outposts of my empire but I had no money to spare so I refused him. He threw some mud over them saying with that same smile 'Clean your shoes mister, clean your shoes mister?'

A beautiful old man, with a carpet over his shoulders came up to me with a far-away look in his eyes. I guessed what he was selling apart from carpets. Hashish. So I bought at the crazy low price and smoked my head off. The beat of my heart took on the tempo of Tangier, but I kept my fists clenched. The music did something to me and I sat in the Café Centrale, watching money changing hands. It appeared that if you wanted to be a business man in Tangier all you had to do was put a notice in front of you where you sat. 'Kops—Export Import' and you were in business. I had neither the notice board nor the inclination.

People kept buying us drinks. Most of them had ulterior motives, though at the time we naïvely accepted. People told you their life story if you looked at them for no more than a second.

One small stateless Jew, five foot one with a beret and a cigar stub, befriended us. He told us to beware of two thousand things and five thousand people. He sat pointing out the undesirables. He kept on about spies all the time. 'He works for our side, but he works for theirs.' But he never told me which side he was on, whether it was the Zionists, the Communists or the Salvation Armyists. He showed me a photograph of a young man, told me that it was him ten years before. 'I went to Spain for a day trip.

They kept me five years. In that time I aged twenty years. They garotted me almost to the point of death, but wouldn't let me die.' We asked why.

He shrugged like the eternal Jew. 'Ask me?'

I watched the passing parade of girls and boys flirting. It reminded me of Mile End Road on Saturday night before the war.

Then a carriage came through the street, pulled by a horse, in it about eight whores and two queers.

'Just to remind the Tangerines that they're still in business,' our friend said.

I smoked, got high and sat by the sea. Indian Hemp was suited for such a place. The tempo of this world was the same as my mind. In London, smoking charge was confusing, for I crossed a road in my time to find the traffic very much in its own time. Here I was synchronized. It was blissful. One needed peace and quiet to take drugs. I became religious, started reading books by Ouspensky and Gurjieff. I was really gone.

In the waterside cafés I sat with old Arabs, drinking mint tea and eating chunks of thick bread. I went out on a fishing boat, helped in my own crazy way to haul in the nets. I got paid in mackerel, which I then grilled over charcoal on the beach. When the fat stopped dripping and sending up puffs of smoke they were done. It was one of the best meals I ever tasted. But I stuck the job for two days only. My fear of the sea put an end to my new vocation.

Often a policeman would come in and share the hashish pipe. And the eternal music from Egypt wailed through the radio. It all sounded the same to me at first. But I got used to those five day operas, found they were beautifully intricate and sophisticated.

The war between the Arab states and Israel was in full bloody swing. In the crowded café one of the Arabs said in his excellent English, 'By the way you are Jewish aren't you?' It was no good denying.

'Anyway, we are first cousins,' he said, 'what's the difference? Besides, those Arabs in Syria and Egypt, they're not real Arabs.'

He told me I was a better Arab then they were.

One of them, a little man with a guttural voice, reminded me of my brother-in-law Mick. They all reminded me of someone or other, and it made me realize how people all over the world are so much the same. Each community contained the smiling boy, the shy girl, the bombastic little man and the worrying mother. Anyway this Arab bloke asked me if I had yet been round the brothels. 'I make sure you get it official Tangier price.' He dragged me to every brothel in Tangier that night. As the door opened he clenched his raised fist, indicating a prepared phallus, saying 'This boy, friend of mine, official Tangier price.'

At one of the whore-houses stood the American floozy oozing out of her sequin dress. She greeted me as a long-lost friend. Then she had a private animated discussion with the madame while I waited. I had heard that effeminate boys were used as cooks in brothels, and would sometimes be delivered up unto a man if the price was high enough. I hoped she hadn't cast me for such a role.

It was all right. I was offered a part-time job. I was to get a percentage for any tourists that I took to that particular house. 'You'll get in with the class, being English.' Englishmen apparently loved the Arabs, and I was to transmute that love into passion. Birds or boys, or anything else. Madame could supply the kinkiest demands.

'You'll get paid more for exhibitions. If they buy you a drink accept. It will be coloured water. We pay you later.'

It sounded marvellous, though God knows what my mother would have thought. But in Morocco in 1948, when the sun was down, life was desperate and you had to survive somehow.

Business was lousy. I picked up three Americans, a woman with glasses and two tall men. 'Guess who's having who?' she said to me. I couldn't. It worked out that they were all having each other and collectively. They asked me to fix up an exhibition. No sooner said than done. Two girls on a bed. One black, one white, pretending to be Lesbian, the girl underneath moaning in amateur ecstasy. But the Americans loved it, sat wide-eyed through the performance. We all stood around the bed watching the animals. It was all so silly.

Still, they had saved money to come to Morocco and wanted some beautiful moments to remember for their old age.

So I made a few bob and stayed on at the Spanish house for a week or two and took others to similar exhibitions and stood there yawning and drinking coloured water, pretending to get excited with the sweating, panting boys of England and America, not forgetting Scotland.

Often I was offered my percentage in kind and, although I didn't want to be unkind, I refused. Man does not live by bread alone, but at least he must have bread.

Familiarity certainly bred contempt. I was contemptuous, not of the whores but of the customers, so I decided with resolution to hand in my notice.

In the great square I stood watching the Berbers, the storytellers from the hills; the women loaded down with sticks, their men walking ahead. And the donkeys; I dreaded to think what the RSPCA would have thought.

I was living now in the Casbah, amongst the Arabs, therefore I was shunned by the British. I walked into the British Library and they would all stand several feet from me. The people who lived in those beautiful white houses on the hill did not invite me to tea. Instead I drank mint tea and stared at the sea. I had gone native. People stopped staring at me in Tangier, except the British who glanced momentarily and then pretended they hadn't really seen.

But I was still a Yiddisher boy and felt it my duty to graft, to make a few bob. Just to keep my hand in. After all, these were the hard times, the rainy days my parents warned me about. As soon as I started thinking of the family I felt broke and insecure. So I argued with myself. 'Things will get much worse,' I said to myself. 'Nonsense,' I replied. And I was right. Things did get much worse. I started to miss money. I stopped being an Arab at peace with the world and started being an unskilled down-at-heel European nomad. I was thrown out of a sort of hotel in the Casbah. So I took my few belongings to the beach where I slept near my favourite Arab café.

My last money went on an advert in the newspaper. I was willing to teach English, the ad read, but as English was the only language I could speak, it was difficult to see how I was going to bring this about.

The only answer was from a Spanish boy named Eduardo. He was on the run from the Spanish Army. I gave him my first lesson by way of sign language. He was very demonstrative, walked through the streets with me, the way most of the Arabs did, holding my hand. I was most put out but I didn't want to hurt his feelings. Besides, he was a customer.

He was a lovable swine and very shrewd; he became my friend, so soon I was giving him lessons free of charge.

Eduardo was always talking about his patron, who turned out to be a Portuguese queer who was having him in return for a room and food.

I knocked on his door one day to beg some food. Eduardo came and was greatly relieved to see me. He thought I was his patron.

When I got into his room I realized the cause of his fear, for he opened a wardrobe and in it, cowering in a corner, was an Arab girl, stark naked. Fifteen years old. She dressed hurriedly and he dismissed her. Then he fed me.

Eduardo managed to feed me for a week or so and gave me a little money so I moved into a Tangier version of a doss-house, where I suffered the most incredible tortures from the thousands of vermin that invaded my bed in droves. As if I wasn't in enough trouble : what with dysentery and no news from home. And needing a girl so badly.

So I turned to the Jewish community. They gave me some matzos.

Most of the Moroccan Jews were going to Israel, I was asked if I would like to go. I said yes. It was the first word that came into my head. So I was ushered into a room where there were two men with moustaches, who asked me where I came from, why I came from, where I was going and why I was going. They hardly looked at me. I felt insulted. 'This is me! Me! Giving my life to Zionism' I wanted to shout. But their faces seemed to suggest that Weizmann could manage very well without me. Nevertheless they told me to report there the next day. 'We're sending anyone,' they said. 'We'll teach you to fight.'

'I don't want to fight. I want to write.'

That did it. I left and that's the way I never went to Israel.

So I hung about the Moroccan equivalent of the Jewish Board of Guardians where I suddenly saw a line of people who looked like Arabs except for their black skull caps. They were Yiddisher people. But they hardly looked like landsmen, to me with their long nightgowns on.

I wondered where they were going so I enquired and found that it was the anniversary of the death of one of the most famous Rabbis of Tangier. They were all going to the cemetery to celebrate. There would be hard-boiled eggs and drink. That was enough for me. I joined the procession, walked along, moving my head backwards and forwards, mumbling, pretending to pray.

I sat on a tombstone, surrounded by people, noshing away, my mouth crammed with egg and my eyes swimming from anis. All of a sudden, the women made the most incredible whooping sounds. 'What's that?' I asked.

'They're driving away the evil spirits.' So I should care. I whooped also. It did me a little good. An old man of seventy, with about two hundred children, invited me to his house saying 'My house is your house'. I don't know if he meant it but I was satisfied just to have some of his food. I wasn't in the market for property. Even for free.

When we got to his place he clapped his hands and his wife came running. We sat down and had a proper meal, his wife dancing attendance on the table. These were Jews? These dark happy people? These were my brethren? I could just see the ladies of Stamford Hill putting up with that. I dropped a napkin on the floor and was about to pick it up when he shook his finger at me, pointed at his wife as if to say 'Give them an inch and they'll take a yard'. He clapped his hands and she picked it up. Then a very sexy, biblical girl of fourteen came in and sat on his lap. He offered her sweets and fondled her, but not in a fatherly fashion. He introduced her as his second wife. His hospitality was infinite but it didn't extend as far as that dark darling, unfortunately. He was a wealthy merchant and helped many poor Jews of the area, who mostly lived in frightful squalor. According to Jewish law a Jew is allowed as many wives as the country where he was living allowed him. But he said he needed only two—one for work and one for love. They took off for Israel one day. Their eyes were alight with the promise of the Holy Land. How I envied them as we waved goodbye. They were going to a new land, a modern democracy taking the customs and habits of centuries. Some good things and some bad had been acquired during the dispersal. The Jews were normalizing themselves. How would this man and his two wives and his ancient God fare in the process?

I met Charlie the Arab again who had a business proposition. He was ships' chandlering and wanted me to work with him. Boats didn't dock in Tangier but anchored about a half a mile out at sea. The idea was to row out and offer souvenirs and nick-nacks to the passengers and crew.

'You speak English, we make good business. Good kosher business. We make fortune,' he said. Visions of plenty made me walk into the main entrance of a second class hotel. I signed in and had a big meal. On the veranda I saw the boats out at sea. I was going to be a great Tangier business man, so I called for and smoked a cigar.

The next day we set out in a rowing boat, all loaded up with horrible leather bags, cheap cigarette lighters, attaché cases and so on. The ship was further than I had imagined and looking back Tangier seemed so far away. The ship loomed ahead. Called *The Brazen Head*, it came from Glasgow and I clambered aboard, whereupon I stood with a group of appreciative sailors. We haggled away until the captain, more formidable than the ship, stood before us. He had heard me speak English.

'If you're not off my ship in one second I'll have you thrown overboard.' He spoke with a thick Scots accent. I pleaded with him, asked him why he allowed the Arabs to stay. He said he wanted no stowaways and went red in the face, so I didn't argue any more.

I lay in the rowing boat waiting for the others. The sea became very choppy and the sky menacing. Tangier seemed to fade right away and I was tossed into one of the most fearful half-hours of my life. I was helpless on the sea, frozen, unable to move. I thought of the great depth beneath me, fearing that any moment the waves would leap up and claim me, or that I might be overtaken by an irresistible urge to throw myself into the water.

The Arabs returned laughing, minus some wares. They rowed back to the shore with me lying at the bottom of the boat with my eyes closed. My ships' chandlering days were over.

But on landing Charlie told me not to worry. He had a better idea, which he explained over coffee, while I trembled the fear out of me.

We were going to become very rich by buying British Army surplus goods. All Charlie needed to do first was to get some real money together. Then he shot off, promising to turn up in a few days.

So there I was, homeless again, without food, under the cold nights of North Africa. The days were not too bad what with hashish from the communal pipe, but every time the sun fell like a stone into the sea the world became filled with dread.

I lit a fire on the beach and stayed there. After a time I didn't feel the hunger so much, and, with the lack of food, my mind became very clear. There was no excitement in this hand-to-mouth existence. I was terrified of the figures lurking around. Life was very cheap in North Africa. I was unskilled, unwashed, unwanted, just like so many others.

'Won't you come and have some tea?' a charming Scots voice said one morning. It belonged to a dear old lady who took me to her little boat. She had a soft daughter and a smiling husband. On the windows were chintz curtains, and I had some home-made scones and a wonderful pot of tea. Butter wouldn't melt in their mouths. I later found out they were quite notorious smugglers, though what they wanted with me was anyone's guess. It might have been plain straightforward charity.

I sat in a bar doodling on the plastic, noticing the proprietor's daughter, who had olive coloured skin, eyes full of the Jewish sorrows.

'Would you like to marry her?' the old man said. He smiled so I thought he was joking. So I said, 'Of course, tomorrow.'

'No, next week,' he replied.

The girl was wiping dishes impassively and I left the place. Eduardo, who went in there a few nights later, told me that the man was in deadly earnest and that I had committed myself. I wondered why quite a well-off man would throw away his lovely daughter on a worthless lay-about like me.

'Perhaps so she can become British.' Eduardo told me that there was also fifty pounds in it for me. He advised me to accept so that we could all have a party, but if I didn't intend to go through with it, I had better steer clear of the place. So I did. I certainly wanted fifty pounds and I certainly could do with the sad Jewish girl, but marriage? I wouldn't wish myself on anyone. Derek and I drifted together again.

So I mooched around flat broke, but my stomach wasn't empty. It was Passover, and the Jewish Community gave us packets of matzos which I sat munching by the blue sea.

It was such a relief when Charlie approached with smiles, cigarettes and fresh plans.

Derek and I were to go to Gibraltar on the morrow, to approach the British authorities and buy any surplus goods we could, like lorries, tanks, battleships. We asked Charlie for the money. He gave us our fare, told us to telephone him as soon as we settled the price. He had some crazy idea that the British could talk to the British. The next morning we washed our feet, had a shave and set off for Gibraltar, with nothing but a return ticket, and a little money for food.

When we got to Gibraltar everything was closed. It was a Bank Holiday, and the Commander-in-Chief was nowhere to be seen. We didn't even meet an admiral. We just sat around on that dreary rock pulling faces at the Barbary Apes. In the light of Gibraltar it all seemed rather pointless, our journey totally unnecessary, in fact quite mad in the extreme. Besides everywhere we went the people looked at us. In Tangier we could pass in a crowd.

For a moment I toyed with the idea of applying for assistance to return to England but decided not to. I couldn't return defeated. So we left Gibraltar minus our battleship.

On the ferry back we spoke to an English merchant navy officer. He was smaller than me and he couldn't have taken more than a size four in shoes. He asked us all about ourselves and we told him everything. In those days I couldn't keep a thing back, believing in the ultimate goodness of mankind. He listened sympathetically. He then told us he had four weeks leave and was spending them in Morocco. He said if we played our cards right he might be able to get us a job on his ship. We liked that idea.

When we landed he asked us to take him to the best hotel. So we threw off a cluster of Arabs who wanted to carry his bags, and took him to a pretty classy hotel where he signed in. 'Boys, you're staying here with me,' he said. So we signed in too, my dirty hands smearing the registration book.

Later we had a colossal meal amongst the snooty guests who looked at us in disbelief. He said he was loaded, took out a wad to prove it.

Later we took him to the Soco Chico and we sat there for hours. He insisted we have our shoes cleaned. There were no bottoms to them but the uppers didn't arf shine. Then he gave the shoe-black more money than we had seen in weeks. Neither the boy nor we could believe it. Then, the little man started buying useless things in the Indian shops. The Indian shopkeepers looked at him dubiously as he loaded us up with articles but they couldn't resist the temptation of his cheque book.

We lived it up in the hotel; champagne, fois gras, the lot. Then he said he was going out to buy a car. We were very suspicious by now because he seemed to be getting more and more agitated. When he had gone we rifled through his case and found his birth certificate. 'He' was a 'her'. At least that's what it said on the form. Our officer was a woman in disguise. Then we remembered the smooth skin, the high-pitched voice and the tiny feet. When he came back we waited around for him to undress. He wouldn't. 'I've got to get away boys. I've got to get to Casablanca. I've been a naughty boy.' He was puffing at cigarettes furiously.

'You mean a naughty girl' I replied. He rushed out of the hotel and we wondered how we were going to pay the bill. But he had left his luggage so we hoped he would come back. Our nerves were frayed and Derek and I decided to part for good.

I was now really desperate. That night I had a coffee opposite the French Embassy with a Yiddisher boy, from Manchester, when a sweating Portuguese gentleman started to talk to us. He told us how much money he was making and offered to pay for our coffee.

He took a parcel out from his inside pocket, it was as big as a shoebox, and was crammed with thousand peseta notes.

'Put not your trust in banks, especially the banks of Tangier,' he said.

Later the Manchester boy told me a little about him, for he had kept his eye on the old boy for days, watching his movements, following him everywhere.

We decided to get that money and beat it over the border to French Morocco. We shook hands on it.

That night at the hotel we made more detailed plans. One of us was to chloroform and hold him while the other took the money. Then we were to get away in a hired car.

I never questioned the morality of all this. Let's say one is led gradually to the abyss, until the only thing that worries you is the fear of being caught.

It was all fixed for a few evenings later. I was getting deeper and deeper into a mess but I reckoned that only one sin could wipe out another, or justify it.

But in the night I couldn't sleep, tossing and thinking of my family in Bethnal Green. My mother! What would she think of me?

I paced the room, and I paced the beach at the first sign of dawn, then I realized I couldn't go through with it. It was simply against the grain. I had a feeling that this would lead me into paths where there was no way back. Here was the thin end of the wedge. It wasn't merely the act. It was the money. No good would have come from it. I was always superstitious of cash and the way it came.

I had other fish to fry, though I hadn't bought them yet.

I was very worried about telling the other boy that I had funked, and when I did he jeered at me, and told me he was going through with it. But by breakfast time it was obvious that the whole scheme had collapsed.

The lady disguised as a sailor returned with a car and the most contorted look on his face. I was so relieved. He picked up his luggage, paid all the hotel bills and pleaded with me to go to Casablanca with him.

He had a fistful of money. 'Look all this is pinched but we'll have a marvellous run for our money.'

I shook my head. He gave me five pounds worth of pesetas, and that was the last I saw of him.

Now I was all alone in Tangier and the police came to question me. The officer had been bouncing dud cheques from Edinburgh to Tangier, had even bought the uniform with one of those cheques en route.

'No, I don't know where he is,' I said. They threatened that I would hear more about it but Tangier had taken its toll, I worried about nothing. Yet I worried about everything. What with a mother in England doing her nut and me going down the drain. I knew she was worrying about me, I could feel it. And I wanted to prove to the family that I was someone, that I wasn't just another piece of human flotsam. I wanted to prove to myself that I was going somewhere. So I did—to the British Embassy.

I must say they were quite human for officials. I was told that I would have to write a letter stating that I was a distressed British subject. So I tried to look as distressed and as British as I could. It was easy being a subject. I had been a subject for discussion all my life.

They took my passport and told me that a boat to England wasn't expected for a few weeks; meanwhile they would put me up at an hotel. It turned out to be the same hotel I had just left. The management weren't at all pleased to see me. I had been instructed not to order anything 'à la carte', so I did. I knew that I would have to pay for it all one day. If I was going to be rich in the future why shouldn't I share in it then, and if I was going to be broke in the future, you can't take blood out of a stone.

The British Embassy gave me a little pocket money each day and they never made me feel ashamed, but I was angry with myself to have landed in such a defeated position.

I bumped into Eduardo again. He was very pleased that I had food and shelter but he could see that I was unhappy. 'What else do you want?' He must have seen me undressing the overdressed girls with my eyes.

'You call yourself my friend, and you never tell me? You want woman, I find.'

We sat for a while and then his little girl friend came along. The naked one in the cupboard. He could see that she would do at a pinch. As far as I was concerned she could do with more than a pinch. 'You want her?—you shall have.' He was always promising to lay down his life for me. It was good to know that at least he would lay down his girl for me. So he shouted at her in Arabic;

she took one look at me and shouted back. He shouted at her, she shouted at him. It seemed she didn't like the idea. 'Good! She will come to your hotel.' Then he shouted at her again. 'I have told her to take nothing from you.' I explained that I had nothing to give.

That night I bribed the night porter with a packet of 'Casa Sport' the cheapest cigarettes. He let her in. We were suddenly alone. She took off her clothes and got into bed. I pulled her out and gently led her to the bathroom. Then I took her to bed. She couldn't speak one word of anything but Arabic—I couldn't speak one word of Arabic. It didn't matter. I awoke her several times in the night. She was very tired but went through the motions rather beautifully, with closed eyes.

In the morning I tried to teach her a little English. I wanted her to stay in bed all day but she had to hurry away to work. I watched her dress, as I lay in bed smoking, watched her lovely graceful movements. We were linked, the Arab and the Jewish world. There was fighting in Israel. Her people and mine were killing each other. First cousins! We were linked, she was an ordinary girl from the streets of Tangier, moving like a princess of myth. All human life was contained in her form. All beauty came from our having each other.

I jumped out of bed and embraced her but not so that it would lead to lovemaking, but she yawned and smiled and so we made love again. With the morning outside yelling its head off. Before she went she took up one of my most valuable possessions. A gaily coloured scarf. She tied it around her head. I said she could have it but she shook her head, remembering Eduardo's warning. But I pushed her out with the scarf. She came back for several nights when we slept naked together. This was the way to join people together. It was a wonderful Arab-Jewish union.

A few nights later, with her in my arms, I was awakened by the night porter who opened the door. 'Someone to see you.' In barged a tall Englishman with a bowler hat. 'I'm Inspector ... from Scotland Yard.' I thought I'd had it, having always felt guilty for no reason whatsoever. I suppose it was just the Jew in me conditioned by years of bitter experience.

The inspector sat down, took not the blindest piece of notice of the girl who scampered away. To my great relief the inspector didn't want me. He had come for Derek who was wanted as a witness for the prosecution in a rather important case coming up at the Old Bailey.

I told the inspector that I had no idea where he was. He then asked me to go out and have a cup of tea with him. So we wandered along the streets of Tangier in the middle of the night. It was just as crowded as any other time. There he was, standing in full English stockbroker's regalia amongst a crowd of drugged, chattering, squalling, buying and selling Arabs. 'Aren't these 'erbs dressed funny?' He stood there sneering with all the authority of Scotland Yard. We sat down and ordered tea. He was quite a nice bloke really, as policemen go.

Later he found my friend in Casablanca and managed to get him back to England. A few days later I met the other boy from Manchester; he was also returning to England. He had a carrier bag full of dirty old socks, underneath that was a pound in weight of marijuana. He told me to do the same, that if I managed to get it safely through the customs all my troubles would be over.

I never saw the girl again, or Eduardo, for at an hour's notice I was flown to Gibraltar where I was rushed on to a ship making for Liverpool. I had nothing but a jacket, a pair of trousers, a shirt and a pair of shoes. Some people on board gave me a few odds and ends and an immigration official gave me my passport which I had to surrender at the other end.

There was a strange kind of hilarity aboard the ship, a claustrophobic feeling of being cut off from the world. Most of the time I stared at the sea. The passengers got very excited when they spotted shoals of porpoises, but every knot gained was another nail in my coffin.

I thought of throwing myself over the side but it was always either lunchtime or teatime or bingo. And people just wouldn't leave me alone. But really it was the end of my world; I had died. Soon we would return to land. England! Where you were expected to know where you thought you were going. Where we were all yes-men in no-man's land.

Already I could see the coastline of home and I was returning defeated and terribly alone. My family were waiting for me but

I hated them. God gave us our families—thank God we could choose our friends. But who were my friends? I didn't know anybody, nor wanted to.

There was just the grey sea and the sky and the ship tossing on the black waves and the persisting thought that I should kill myself. I was sick of governments and politicians and family and work and I was on the run from myself, trapped between nowhere and nowhere. To my right was the beautiful soft, countryside of England, the country that gave me birth and sheltered me and I loathed it.

We landed at Liverpool. I had no luggage so naturally the Customs were very suspicious and stripped me to see if I had any opium growing under my armpits. I was returning defeated so the indignity of the search was just something I expected.

Another immigration official took away my passport and gave me a rail ticket to London. And so I boarded the train.

I was trapped in this country now and I had a vision of the apocalypse. It would all be destroyed before my eyes. I had always been morbidly bound up with death. 'Shit sticks where it touches—'

'You always find what you're looking for.'

The sayings of my family played through my head to the accompaniment of the sound of the train wheels.

I was returning to a family that I didn't want, who didn't really want me. They wanted something that I couldn't give, wanted me to be someone I never could be.

I was a refugee from a continent not yet born, a disciple of dust, expecting only chaos as my legacy. Everything had turned sour. I was attracted to dross, but I couldn't go to the dogs completely. I wanted desperately to use this opportunity to break with my family forever, but I knew once in London the pull of the home would be too much.

The train hurtled through the dark inhospitable landscape, past the depressing mongoloid slums of provincial towns and I was a person torn by my past, without a passport into any future.

11

On the Floor

A few days after I returned I took to sleeping on the floor. The bed seemed to tilt and the floor seemed none too safe. The whole flat seemed to be moving in on me. Instead of lying beside my brother I got a few blankets and slept in the corner of the living-room.

At first nothing was said and there were few questions. I just wrote furiously during the day. I couldn't control the flood of words, words I understood when I was writing them but which were meaningless a few hours later. It was like verbal diarrhoea. They had apparently decided to tolerate me, so I wandered around the house high as a kite on marijuana.

My young sister Rose got married. That meant all of them settled except me. She sat on a white settee dressed in white and I sat declaiming in the middle of the room, addressing the wedding guests as if I were conducting a political meeting in Hyde Park. They carried on drinking their advocaat and cherry brandy as if I didn't exist.

All the time I sat on the floor. This aroused the anger of all my relatives. They smouldered in silence. All except my mother.

'When I'm dead, then you can sit on the floor,' she said, referring to our traditions of mourning. 'You're killing me! Why are you killing me?' But still she slipped me money.

I had one drawer in the only sideboard. Once it was full of old clothes, now it was full of pieces of paper with my words on. I couldn't stop writing. I watched my hand holding a pen racing across paper.

I was afraid of walking in my sleep in case I walked to the river and threw myself in. Before I closed my eyes at night I tied a tie around my wrist and to the leg of the table. I was also afraid to hold anything in case I crushed it in my hand. A new nephew was born. I held him one day and started to sweat and I got an urge to throw him out of the open window. I quickly thrust him back to my sister.

I took to refusing as much food as possible. I became thin and bedraggled. Then I took my shoes off and wandered the streets barefoot. Wandered around the East End with my manuscripts in a carrier bag. This was the only way I could carry them. I was afraid to hold them in any other way. There was no-one to help me, for my fears transfigured my actions into aggression. People became afraid of me.

'Pull yourself together,' some said. 'You're killing your mother.' Pull myself together? What a useless expression!

What could I reply? I wanted to shock, wanted people to stare at me in the streets. I needed their mockery. The rules no longer applied. I had been bequeathed a madhouse called the world. My head was filled with the moaning cries of my dead relatives. I relived their last gasping moments over and over again. Before me was the wasteland of coming destruction. I could see the coagulating cities. Madmen were in control, old madmen, yet I was expected to know my place, to take my place in the madhouse, to acquiesce, to stand in queues and nurture an apathetic family. To become a fully paid up member of the inhuman race.

I took more drugs for there was no ground under my feet, just the sloping floorboards.

The day went on before my eyes but I couldn't enter. I began screaming at bus queues and would run away up side streets, breathing heavily in doorways. Sometimes I would follow old ladies and when they looked in shop windows, I'd creep up behind them, growl like a wild beast and watch them jump. Then I'd rush away hating myself, laughing and crying my eyes out.

Conflict was an easy word glibly tossed by intellectuals in the West End. All the time they told me to leave my home and my family and become one of them. But I loved my home and my family. I couldn't tear myself away. I had to return again and again. I still hoped for a way out.

'What are you doing with your life?' my sisters would say.

'What are you doing with your death?' I'd reply.

The pencil made a groove in my finger.

One day I was walking and writing in Whitechapel High Street when two coldly smiling men stopped me. When reasonably dressed young men with darting eyes stand before you they are up to little good. So I guessed they were policemen.

'What have you got in the bag?' They pointed to my carrier.

'I'm so relieved, officer,' I said. They got excited, thought I was about to confess a heinous crime.

'This is my masterpiece. I've been writing it for ten years and no-one has seen it. No-one wanted to see it. At last you do. I'll read it all to you.' I took out all the notebooks and they smiled weakly, and backed away from me. I've never seen policemen move so fast. 'Thank you. Thank you very much.'

But I was being torn apart and wanted destruction. I was disgusted with humanity, with myself, wanted to apologize to insects.

I felt so bloody sorry for my family to have to put up with someone like me. I argued with myself all the time and people stared at me, avoided me as I walked the streets. Sometimes I would walk with a limp, pretending to be lame. Sometimes I would blow out my cheeks or screw up my face, pretending to be deformed.

Near my home one night I was attacked. I didn't feel the blows. It was like fists thudding into dead flesh. I saw stars. On the floor I could see it was a policeman hitting me. I didn't hit back and I didn't feel indignant. I was sort of expecting it, wasn't I at war? There was no anger on his face. That was the awful part about it. He just lashed out and then walked away. To this day I can't remember saying anything to him. Yet who knows? I was so far gone that maybe I called him a filthy name. My only thought was to get rid of the drug, get rid of the drug! I never carried it in my pockets but always in my clenched fist, for such an occasion as this, but he was gone before I could get rid of it. So I smoked and everything became beautiful again and I staggered home as happy as Larry. When they saw me and the blood on my face they screamed. That made me burst into tears.

The next day I decided to turn over a new leaf and enter the world of the living dead.

My brother-in-law, Alf, was a door-to-door salesman. One little case filled with gear, and a street. That's all that was needed. He sold toilet goods, braces, brushes, things that never meant anything to me, but things the world couldn't seem to do without. The boys in the trade called it 'on the knocker'. He promised to teach me the ropes.

Everybody was so happy. At last I had come to my senses. Alf lent me a suit and took me to a warehouse in Houndsditch and lent me money for my gear, so off we journeyed to the suburbs. Suddenly there I was in the creeping disease of Croydon, with things that I didn't want to sell, selling to people who didn't really want them.

One foot in the door, a smiling face and a line of endless patter. But two sticks of hashish to keep me going. So I knocked on the doors of the wastelands spieling my words to the Zombies. My heart wasn't in it. One face tried to turn the tables, tried to sell me religion 'Believe on the Lord Jesus Christ and you'll be saved'.

'Saved for what? Don't you see, lady, if only I could believe.'

I was terrible at the job, made a few shillings in the same time my brother-in-law made a few pounds.

I'd sit on a garden wall kicking my legs, shaking my head, saying 'They don't want me at their house'. Alf would laugh for a second then tell me that whether they wanted me or not I had to graft. So I'd knock some more. Sometimes though, the door would open on a very expectant lady, all prepared to spend her husband's hard earned cash on something she could have bought down the road at Woolworths for half the price. 'What have you got?'

'Cataclysms, lady.'

'I don't want none of those.'

To keep myself going I invented a special identity. 'Good morning Madam, I'm travelling for dead poets and armless painters. This is our yearly call.'

'We've got everything, everything,' their usual reply. 'But Madam, you don't know what I've got. Crucifixions! Holocausts! Brochs!'

'Yes, we've got everything. We've got that, we've got that.'

'Crenk you madam, crenk you madam, thank you madam.'

We'd both smile horribly.

When I came to a Jewish house I would know by the muzzuzah on the door. 'Morning Madam. I'm travelling for Jewish dead poets and armless Jewish painters. This is our yearly call for Passover.'

I cried at one door. I had no idea why. The lady asked me inside and made me a meal. She asked me what was wrong. I told her times were bad. Meaning the state of the world, not the state of my finances. She bought £5 worth of gear, so I took the rest of the week off.

One woman said she had everything but could do with a nut-cracker so I offered her one, asking for half-a-crown. She told me it was too cheap, so I picked another one out of the case, exactly the same as the first. 'This should suit you, it's seven-and-six.'

'What's the difference?'

I was holding one in either hand, I even forgot which was which. 'So isn't it obvious? The cheap one is made of pig-iron.'

'Pig iron?' She looked like she would vomit. I told her, however, that the other one was plated and tempered and moulded and hardened and would last as long as there were nuts in the world. Longer. So she bought it.

This taught me a lesson—I sold more when I asked for higher prices. But the lesson didn't cut very deep for I was fighting a losing battle against myself.

Everybody was telling me how well I looked and my brother-in-law was complimenting me on the way I was catching on. But I hated to get proficient at anything so trivial.

The suburbs smelled of death. I could see the imminence of war in the suburbs. The houses reeked of despair and sadness. As the doors opened it would pour out and poison the streets.

Every face had a tragedy, every house had a story both to reveal and to keep secret.

The thing that finished me was when a woman who answered the door was followed by her imbecile daughter, who crawled on all fours. She bought a comb for the child, saying 'I have five children but she's my favourite. When they go wrong you love them all the more somehow'. She asked me in for a cup of tea but I backed away from the house. I still see the poor girl creature trying to comb her hair, using the comb upside down, and the mother turning the comb round and showing her the way, as she must have done thousands of times before.

I'd lasted out for three months and that all but finished me.

I took my shoes off again and the house went silent, while I sat around writing.

When the evening paper came I pretended to look for work and I did look down the Situations Vacant column. I underlined certain jobs and would go out to make a few phone calls. 'Hello, I've just seen your advertisement in the *Evening Standard*. Can I talk to the Personnel Officer?' 'Hello! I've seen your ad for a clerk. I've just phoned to say I don't want the job.' Then 'Click' from my end.

But I did begin to work, though I never stayed at any one job more than a few days. As soon as I had mastered the simple technique I'd walk out. In the few weeks since giving up the knocker I had more than twenty bosses and told them all what to do with their positions. 'I give you my lovely time. All you give me is lousy money.'

The position with my unemployment cards became very complicated. The Labour Exchange sent for me, told me that I really had to settle at something. Then they started to go into my history. 'And what did you do in 1944 and in '43?' I tried recalling the horrible years of my servitude. It went on and on. Then I hit upon a brilliant idea. 'I lost my memory,' I said. Their faces became suddenly kind. They spoke more slowly. 'When did you lose your memory?' 'I forget,' I replied. 'I remember, there was a war but I think it is over. Is it?' They nodded their heads and told me not to worry.

Life became completely impossible at home. I couldn't blame them really, even though I did. I wanted to say something so much to my mother. When the fog came down and she started coughing I wanted to say something kind to her, to tell her that my journey into myself was because I didn't want to see her suffer any more. But no words would come.

So I came into my Kingdom of Soho where I could be as mad as I wanted. I was a jester in a court of jesters, in a café called 'The Alex' where I wrote the day away and wandered the streets ridiculing the wage slaves. The bums of Soho became my family, the café my womb.

There has been an attempt to romanticize the bohemian past of London and though it sheltered me I found it largely terrifying and sordid, but it was my home, a place where I could be myself, where I didn't have to answer questions unless I wanted to, where my bare feet were accepted.

Tearaways, layabouts, lesbians, queers, mysteries, and hangers-on. We just sat in the café, waiting. Waiting for another day to kill itself. Every time the door opened we looked up as if we were expecting someone. We wandered from café to café. 'Have you been to Tony's? Who was there?'

'No-one.'

The regulars included the would-be poets, the sad girls from Scotland, the artists without studio or canvas. The kinky men searching for kinky love. I'd sit until someone came with money to buy me a slice of bread and a cup of tea. I was particularly interested in a man with mauve hair who spoke very beautifully and always wore the same upholstered smile. He was gentle, always said to any stranger, 'Tell me the story of your life,' what's more he listened.

There was also Iron Foot Jack. The King of the Bohemians. 'A bohemian doesn't work to eat, he eats to work,' in his soft Cockney. One of his legs was shorter than the other. He claimed a shark had got him in the Coral Sea. Once he started a new religion in Charlotte Street called 'The Children of the Sun'. Black Larry was one of his acolytes. Old girls from Kensington came to pray naked and of course paid for the privilege. 'When you die your carcase goes to the moon and your soul goes to the sun.' Jack was always surrounded by acolytes and young girls from the provinces, 'mysteries', whom he called 'My little dollies'. He had thousands of friends but when he died just a few people went to the cemetery. That was the way of Soho. Iris Orton, a poet, put a few wild daisies on his grave.

All these things opened a new world for me and I spent all my days writing, notebooks describing the incidents, but minding my own business as much as I could. One day four spivs came in.

'Warn Orlando, warn Orlando,' a lady called The Fox screamed at me. They thought I was implicated, got me against a wall and held a knife to my throat. I thought my time had come but suddenly one heaved a chair through the huge window and they all rushed out.

There was always a tremendous amount of violence, especially on Saturday night when everybody was either high or drunk.

Iris Orton befriended me. A strange girl with a cloak, who was a beautiful poet. She edited a magazine and published my work; she was the first person to take my work seriously, encouraged me to continue, though I would have continued anyway. At that time I thought I was possessed by the ghost of Rimbaud. Occasionally I slept at home but often I stayed in a bombed house near Goodge Street. There in the dark cellar amongst the fungus, I smoked and dossed down—I dragged in dumped furniture and made myself quite comfortable.

I met Mac the Busker and agreed to busk the queues with him. We arranged to meet outside the New Theatre where we would act duologues from *Hamlet*. But I funked it at the last moment, but despite that Mac and I remained friends.

And there was an excommunicated priest called Michael. I stayed in a house at Notting Hill with him, where one night he ran naked over the rooftops with a flaming cross in his hand after having eaten the contents of two benzedrine tubes. In that house, Tony, a painter, with blazing eyes, told me to take up the brush and paint. I did. I painted his nude girl friend, then made love to her. Took her away, wandered the streets, took her to my own cellar until she drifted off into another corner with another boy. The café was full of men looking for men and girls looking for girls. The girls I knew liked me for my bare feet and bracelets. But one day a normal boy came in looking for a normal girl. Everyone was surprised.

In the corner of the café were the four Trotskyists, out to convert the world, but all they could do was argue among themselves. They split up eventually into two rival groups and became deadly enemies.

The beatnik scene started in Soho in 1950. The girls with their white faces and long hair, living entirely for kicks. Allie and Patsy and Booey and Beau and Johnny all left the scene for Canada, and from there went on to California. They were the new pilgrim fathers taking the New Zen to the New World.

I still hid my drugs round the city. It was part of the ritual. I got my drugs from those dirty eccentric creatures who loused around. These characters were the carriers. They were too filthy for the police to search, who are largely suburban and fastidious.

One of the spivs, a perpetually smiling American, got religious one evening and circumcised himself with a rusty razor blade. Blood spurted everywhere, he nearly bled to death in Charlotte Street.

I pounded the pavement, flying in a dying city. Screaming out and gone. They called me a character, so I suppose at last I belonged somewhere.

'Leave home, leave home,' the Soho people kept saying.

'Easier said than done'; I wasn't prepared for the final plunge.

I had girl after girl, was enjoying great success simply because I ignored them. When they spoke I told them to shut up. Part of me was getting its own back for past humiliations. They'd wander into the café, see me engrossed in writing and couldn't bear my indifference. One beautiful girl came to the table, smiled, put her hand on my knee and moved her head in the direction of the door. She was different. I followed her out and in her room near Covent Garden she revealed herself. She had the most beautiful copper-skinned body. We stayed in bed for two days and on the third were joined by another poet. We took it in turn to have her. On the fourth day I sat in the café waiting for her to come in. She did, and went to another table and went off with another boy.

Iron Foot Jack managed to get hold of a cellar in Neal Street, near Seven Dials. Trotsky's printing press was down there. I stayed one night. Hundreds of characters came, including the Countess. The noise was terrific. The police raided the place. A policeman said to the Countess, 'What are you doing here?'

'Oh officer, I'm just passing through.' The Countess was always finding wonderful things in the street. One night she offered two different shoes to a girl at my table—'Nothing wrong with these dear. They're only odd'. That was us. 'Only odd!'

Everyone loved the Countess, despite her having a tongue like a whiplash.

She with her schoolboy's cap perched on her head and her one saucy pregnant ear-ring dangling from that penetrating incredible face.

A good-looking American poet, named Douglas, arrived on the

scene. We became very friendly. He told me he was hoping eventually to become a woman. We remained friends.

Douglas could always put his hands on some money. One day he dragged me, not unwillingly, to the Dorchester Hotel.

At two o'clock in the afternoon we were drinking cocktails. The waiters looked askance at us. As I drank I thought of all the people in factories, my own family slogging away. Douglas spent in an hour the amount my brother would earn slaving for a whole week.

A few days later Douglas committed suicide. He went home drunk and turned on the gas.

Bohemia became depressing but at least nobody got at me all the time. And the desperation of its inmates helped to pass the time.

One night I saw two mates hitting an old man outside the café. Their fists thudded into his wet face and he was smiling at them in a strange kind of way. His glasses were shattered on the ground. I tried to stop them but they looked at me as though I was crazy and beckoned to me to join in. I walked away.

Another suicide, a rather quiet Jewish boy. His suicide note was passed around the café. 'Please! Please! Whatever you do, stay off drugs.' The note seemed to speak personally to me. As I read it I was inhaling the beautiful smoke deep into my lungs. I thought a lot about suicide, had fantasies about its causes. I imagined there was a girl called 'the suicide carrier'. She went around infecting poets and dreamers, although she herself was immune. Had I slept with her? Was I going to get the disease? All day I sat with the fear that I might destroy myself. At other times, in more rational moments, I worked out that these Soho suicides were merely people who couldn't face up to mediocrity.

They lived in a world of make-believe for a time thinking they would make it on a grand scale. Then one day they came face to face with themselves and they just couldn't stand the shock. This was something I would have to face myself, eventually.

I could feel two forces within me fighting for control. One dreaming of creation, the other demanding destruction. At the moment it was touch and go who would get the upper hand. Just like the world.

But there were some who lightened the burden. Jackie, a lovely girl of seventeen, who was on the run from the law. She always got into the most awful scrapes with terrible people, yet always emerged as pure as driven snow. This was my first really platonic relationship—we really were just good friends. I never thought until then that I could go around with a beautiful girl without wanting her.

Besides, Jackie was going through a lesbian phase. She had run away from home and when the police found her they sent her to an approved school, where she was initiated into lesbianism. Fortunately, later she reverted to wanting men again.

There was also Bill, a poet. 'My lords, here is a soul for burning,' he shouted in his Welsh lyrical voice. All my girls fell in love with him. I couldn't hold them once they saw his handsome face. Everyone was spellbound by him.

And there was Chico, the painter, only seventeen. He had been found starving and painting in a bombed house. The newspapers called him a genius; a terrible thing to live down. Nevertheless he could speak fluent Chinese, Spanish, French and Dutch, and he could paint in every known modern style from Van Gogh to Mondrian.

And Ronald who one day asked me in the street if I had any money to spare. I had exactly half-a-crown. He said that would do, so I gave it to him, whereupon he threw it down the drain. 'People are bigger than money,' he said. It taught me a big lesson. Never to listen to him again.

Christ I didn't want to die, I wanted to live forever, but something was pulling me down, amongst the legions of the lost, cut off from the world, in a café of an unbelieving, hard-working, money-making Cypriot.

Sometimes we would decide to colonize a new café so we'd search for a Greek who would tolerate us. Preferably an empty café with a few men playing billiards. And we'd tell the owner that he'd have lots of customers. Not us, but people who would come to see us. The Greek would nod his head and so we would descend like locusts on to the tables, eating our slices of bread and butter, tapping songs with spoons and scribbling on the plastic surface. And talk—talk—talk. Then the week-end Bohemians would come and call it living; we called it dying.

I decided to have another bash at working. So I started pearl diving in the cafés around Wardour Street. I'd slave till Friday, get my measly three or four quid, get high with the crowd, start raving, and return to that same café with a real sexy girl and blow almost all my wages on one meal. The boss wouldn't be too pleased to see me. By way of explanation I would shrug at the waiter, 'You see I'm not really poor; I'm a millionaire who worked here for the hell of it.'

Yet still I couldn't make that final break with home. I returned several times a week to fortify myself with some of my mother's food.

A few of us got a room near Camden Town. An empty room with orange boxes. I cut myself and smeared the blood all over my hand, stood on my friend's shoulder and made a bloody handprint on the ceiling. It stayed there for years.

I hated the lavatory in that house; couldn't wait to pull the chain and dash upstairs. I came upstairs puffing one day and Bill told me he felt exactly the same in that lavatory, he too always ran up the stairs. I made enquiries. Next to the lavatory, in a poky yellow room, two babies had been burned to death a few months before. The parents wanting a drink went to the pub on the corner, left the radio playing full blast. Nobody heard the children screaming. But I did after that. Chico lived in the house with us. He now looked like an El Greco painting. His canvas skin tight over the stretcher of his skeleton. I was now painting more and more but one day I chucked it in. My world was one of words. Talking and writing.

It was no good being good at a few things. I had to put all my energy behind the thing that I did the best—writing. Writing gave me a sense of danger and excitement, so I knew it was the only way I could travel. Friends told me to take it easy. I told them there was always a sacrifice you had to make no matter what it was. My eyes stared out of my head.

We wandered the night for dog-ends, but the practical Jew in me made me search the better-class streets of Mayfair. I figured that people who could afford to walk through Mayfair could afford to get their health checked so there was less chance of getting TB. Besides they smoked a better brand of cigarette. I never asked anyone in the street to help me out. The world wasn't interested in my journey, or in my private suffering. Why should it be? No-one had asked me to enter the arena but now that I was there I was committed to the end.

Our room became quite cosy and we didn't have to pay for our electricity. Outside the window was a cable taking juice for a radio relay system; we tapped it and had points all over the room.

My mother implored me. She could see destruction working within me, so once again I decided to have a last fling at the world to see if I could possibly settle, but more to prove that it was completely hopeless. This was to be my last rendezvous with the conventional world.

I am an extremist. Most people could go right through Soho and come out the other end and settle down respectably, but I was like one of those suicide boys. I had to give myself completely to the thankless muse. If I had gone into business I would have made a fortune. I would merely have sacrificed everything to achieve that end.

But my mother was ill so I had a wash and a shave, cleaned my shoes, and got a job as a commis waiter at the Albany Club in Savile Row. Suddenly I was serving Danny Kaye and Margaret Lockwood and the Yiddisher tailors of Sackville Street.

I got a fabulous wage which I rushed straight to Soho and usually blew on hashish. I also gave a few pounds to my mother. She was pleased. 'At last you're like other Yiddisher boys, with a few pounds in your pocket.' All I had in my pocket were a few sticks of greengage.

The headwaiter offered me a rise. But I was getting too liked at the club for my own comfort. The friendliness of ordinary people was disarming. How could I wage a war against those I liked? So it was time for me to move on.

I went to Scotts of Piccadilly where I worked as commis wine waiter, but I descended the stairs one night with a tray in my hand declaiming Paradise Lost. The place was packed with diners. Milton and Dover sole didn't mix. I lasted but a few days after that.

Then I landed a smashing job at a gentlemen's club. Everybody was very kind. Mind you a few of His Majesty's Servants kept very weird friends. One of my friends came in one night with a member.

He winked at me as I served sherry. He was a male prostitute on the 'dilly'. He told me he was hoping to find a rich sugar daddy. It looked like he had succeeded.

I was in charge of the drinks and one night at the card table I overheard a conversation from some of our politicians. One of them was moving a glass around the table, 'Gentlemen, if I had my way, tonight, one bomb on Moscow, one bomb on Peking, finish.' I wished I had one bomb to throw at him. All I had was my hashish bomb.

I was asked to help out in the restaurant one lunchtime. A renowned liberal publisher sat at one of my tables. I wanted to say to him, 'All my life I've wanted to meet you. I'm writing a book, I want you to see it.' He looked so kind.

'Soup, sir?' He didn't look at me, he just waved me away brusquely with his hand. 'You lousy bastard,' I thought. He called himself a radical English gentleman. Many of those old tories could have taught him a lesson in civility and kindness. I've mistrusted professional do-gooders ever since. They're so busy loving humanity they haven't any love left over for mere individuals.

I've since met many humanitarians who beat their wives, or socialists who are fascists with their children. It's so easy to hide behind a banner. Maybe they need to love the masses because they can't love people.

The world was singing late one afternoon and all the waiters were happy. I served His Lordship a drink. 'He wants a double brandy and I want the evening.'

Outside the park looked so green, daffodils shone in the sun, and people were wandering around hand-in-hand and I had a contortionist to meet. I thought of her. The girl with the agile thighs. She was willing to give herself to me whenever I called.

His Lordship repeated the order. Meanwhile I took a few quick drags from my stick of charge and approached him again. He in his dinner jacket, me in waiter's garb. 'Isn't it strange sir, we both wear this ridiculous garment? The point is, who is the waiter and who is the lord?' He went red in the face and I went straight to the head steward, told him I was packing it in. He implored me to stay.

'I'm leaving,' I said and walked straight out. I couldn't find my contortionist in the café so I rushed back to Bethnal Green.

When I got home I told my mother. She wept bitterly. 'What have you done? Don't tell me, don't tell me. What have you done?'

I left the house all depressed. In Soho they told me there was going to be a bit of a party in the East End so we struggled down to Whitechapel Road. An American deserter, a few mysteries, two painters, a poet, a few hangers on and a book thief.

The usual sort of crowd started drinking and mucking about in a room opposite the London Hospital. It turned into an orgy. I participated. It wasn't too bad at first. People just giggling and having each other. Girls yawning as they were being done. One girl went through every man in the room, including me. After I'd had her she was pulled away to perform with two other men. I looked out of the window. Just along the road I was born. There opposite was the London Hospital, and further along Stepney Green, empty and cold.

When I looked again at the ritual in the room I couldn't re-enter the proceedings. And it was horrible to see—sordid and completely terrifying. All we needed were animal faces to complete the picture. No, animals had dignity.

At four in the morning the girl who had gone through every man rubbed her thighs against me again. But she was crying. I asked her why. She spoke with a typical East End Jewish accent. 'I can't stop—I can't stop.' And still her thighs revolved against mine. She told me her mother lived just up the road near Stepney Green Station. 'Do you think I should go and see her?'

I told her yes.

At six in the morning most of them were gone but the girl remained, her face all smudged with mascara and she sang over and over again 'My Yiddisher Momma' as she cried. Then she prepared to go, told me she had decided to visit her mother. But even as she was opening the door she had one last rub with her thighs against the few remaining male members.

I caught an early morning bus to the West End and went to the house of a musician friend, where a small way-out jazz session was still in progress. I lay there smoking, with my eyes closed.

Suddenly I started to write furiously. The room started to float in space, started to swing in nauseating endlessness. I then saw what I thought were strange doors that started in the room, doors that led nowhere, doors nobody else could see. I took long journeys along corridors that weren't there, writing all the time, writing. 'Someone has got to die. It is either my mother or me. It must be her.' Then I heard strange metallic birds calling me. They sounded like my mother. The way she called me home when fog descended, or when a terrible storm thundered. 'Ber—nie, Ber—nie.'

I got the urge to rush home and I wasn't surprised to find white faces confronting me. 'We've been trying to get in touch with you. Where have you been? Mum is very ill.'

I went to the bedroom and she lay there, pale, and looking at me. I knew.

'I'm sorry,' I said. She smiled.

'You'll be all right.' 'Won't she be all right?' People said as they came into the bedroom.

I knew it was either her or me. Someone had got to die. She smiled. 'What are you doing with your life? Life is sweet. Pull yourself together.'

'I'll try,' I said.

She needed oxygen. All the children took it in turn to hold the mask to her face. When it was my turn I couldn't. I thought the mask might suffocate her.

My brother took over and I left the bedroom. I knew the die was cast. I sat down on the floor of the living-room and wrote down all that was happening, while I waited, waited.

12

Death in the House

Death had entered the house. I could feel it clinging to me and I wanted to rush out into the streets. But I was caught up in family and in ceremony. For the ceremony had begun, there was no escape from it. Death had entered the house. You could see it on the faces of my brothers and sisters. But death lay wholly on my mother where she lay sleeping in the bedroom. I consoled my weeping heart with the fact that it would soon be over.

There was a terrible relief to see my mother like this. For now I could no longer have guilt at the way I was treating her. I would soon be free to go my own way.

I was about to be born and I lay on the floor as these most horrible thoughts came into my mind. I was afraid to go on thinking and I stared wide-eyed, incredulous, looking at myself in the mirror. How could I feel this? Or think this? How could I stop my thoughts? A child needed his parents dead. One generation fed off the other.

So the late morning came and all the children kept on saying to each other things like, 'I think she looks a little better.' 'Doesn't she look a little better? She's not so pale.' 'What do you think Bern?' I agreed she looked better.

There was no getting away from the house, so I smoked to get away from the family. I drew the Indian hemp deep into my lungs mixing it with air and blew it out of the window. Soon I hovered above the room and could see my own body leaning on the table, and I could hear my own voice singing songs I'd never heard before.

She got a little better later and for a while I thought she was going to be all right. Perhaps it was merely the drugs and my vivid imagination after all.

So I returned to her bedside, where she again smiled but I knew that she was really trying to say, 'You're the only one unsettled, please try to settle down.'

And I remember what she had once said about me. 'He'll buy me the house, he'll take me away from the slums.' And there was something I wanted to say to her, 'Forgive me for killing you.' But I didn't say it. I couldn't gather enough sound together.

So I continued writing down what I saw going on around the bed and in the living room. I floated above the family, feeling like some terrible recording angel. Writing was keeping me alive. As long as the hand moved from left to right across the page I would be safe. But writing spelt danger in the long run, took me close to the edge. But I needed the edge, needed the danger. I drew sustenance from chaos.

Then I decided to make a sacrifice. I got the bottom drawer out of the wardrobe, tore up every poem I had ever written, tore them into hundreds of pieces and started to burn them in the fireplace. If I could keep the fire alight I was sure that she would live, and if I could rush to the window and see a bird in flight, then rush back again and keep the fire alight, she would definitely become well.

'What are you doing?' Rose said.

'Preparing a miracle,' I said.

But she was too pre-occupied and said a small 'oh' as if people did that all the time. But the fire went out, for all the poems were burned. Just the ashes remained and I crumbled them between my hands and then I washed the black off.

People came and went, including the doctor, and I raved all the afternoon, more quietly though, because I had been told several times to shut up. So I lay my head on the table and tapped my fingers on the wood, and as I sang I wrote some more down which I did not burn.

'I'm lost. I'm lost, lost, enough for all of us. Naked we come and naked we go. How bloody cold we are. We buy and sell but when all is said and done nothing ultimately belongs to us. Not even our own bones, nothing but our dreams; our dreams belong to us.

I was losing my grip of the world. This, apparently, was all there was to it. I had seen it all. From now on it would all be repetition.

Later they told me I could go out if I wanted to, so I went to the West End.

It was Sunday afternoon. The familiar faces were plodding the streets schnorrering fags and coppers from each other. I sat in an Italian café. This was in the days before expressos. The blind café owner fancied himself as a tenor and so did practically all his customers. They all had a go at singing Italian arias.

My contortionist wasn't around. Shirley, a sad Jewish girl, sat beside me. I had seen her around. She smiled and I held her hand. Then we started kissing. She had very sympathetic eyes and I reckoned we would hit it off for a little while or so.

I phoned my sister's home from the café. She told me not to worry. My mother had been taken to a hospital near Shoreditch Church and she was a little better. So I returned to Shirley, smoked some more hashish, then wandered through Soho with her, happy and high. We went to a cinema, started necking in the dark and felt all frustrated, so I phoned some friends of mine in Camden Town and they said yes we could go over there. So we did. But somehow we couldn't make it.

Meanwhile, in the other room, Bop was playing the guitar and his wife, Pearl, was playing with her child. I liked Shirley, she was really a good kid and she too was utterly lost. I couldn't find her because I was twice as lost.

Besides, death was whistling down my bones. The whole of Camden Town smelled of death. And the sky was wearing black, and the drug inside me changed the chimney stacks into waiting vultures. My friends called us in for tea and as I sat there talking, their faces all fell away.

Bop suddenly became a leopard, Shirley became a hyena, Pearl became a tiger and the child became a monkey. They were real animals waiting to pounce upon me. And the sun in the sky seemed to be exploding. I screamed and screamed.

The whole room seemed to be laughing. The cup and saucer in my hand started to scream. I threw it against the wall and I stood outside my body, which I could now smell putrefying. Then the wild animals in the room started laughing at me. Instead of passing out I rushed down the stairs and flew along the street hoping that my body had followed me.

I stood by the canal looking into the muddy water. Some children played near the bank. One shouted at me. I waved back.

I looked over my shoulder to see if death was stalking me. There was no getting away from it. The fingers of the water were beckoning me. 'Maybe I will jump without being able to stop myself. Maybe my body will dive after my spirit. Maybe I am already dead.'

I started to feel my face to prove I existed and whirled my arms around and around. I wanted people to notice me, wanted proof that I still existed.

I walked towards the junction, went up to a policeman and asked him where I was.

'Camden Town,' he replied suspiciously.

I got a bus back to the West End and I felt better now. The Soho characters waved at me. I belonged. Now everything was all right again. I wandered, writing.

I returned to the café in Charlotte Street. As I entered the door everyone looked up and looked down again. Yes, I existed all right. I was just another no-one. Time slowly slid past.

I felt something tugging me, pulling me towards the door. The effects of the drug had worn off but the tugging was very real. I walked slowly as if in a dream, but precisely, as if I knew where I had to go. I was being pulled, pulled out of the café. It was no good fighting against it. It was one of the strongest forces that I ever felt. I walked automatically to the bus-stop and was sucked on to a bus. I got a ticket to Shoreditch Church.

The grey hospital building looked like a prison. Some of the family had just left but no-one was there now. She was on the danger list, therefore was allowed visitors at any time. The sister said they thought she was a little better.

So I stood at the foot of the bed. Her head tilted towards a bunch of flowers on a locker. She was asleep, breathing quite normally, it seemed, but her face was like marble. It was fixed and peaceful, and dying had given her face a calm distinction, a certain nobility. She had always been imprisoned by the city, had never emerged to claim her true heritage, a peaceful place in the sun. But now she would be leaving the city.

My eyes filled with tears, the whole ward started to drown and I couldn't stop the tears flowing down my face. But I smiled with embarrassment when the nurse came up. Then I saluted the sleeping mother, a salute of benediction and acknowledgement, covering half my face with my curled hand, and I left the place, rushed down the stairs four at a time.

I went to Stoke Newington to Phyllis' house, where the family were assembled. I told them I had seen her and that she looked much better.

Ten minutes later my sister-in-law came screaming up the stairs. 'Mum's dead, Mum's dead.' I thought at first she was laughing but realized she wore an expression of extreme agony. Something out of a tragedy that had lost its producer.

I stood in the middle of the room as if I were planted to the floor. Meanwhile all my sisters danced around me. All the children were going up to each other, the permutations never ceased. 'It's not true,' 'What are we going to do?' 'Oh Rose,' 'Oh Jack,' 'Oh Marie,' 'Tell me it isn't true.'

My father wailed upon the floor and beat his breast. He looked like a wounded animal. My eldest sister was tearing out her hair. Phyllis screamed at me, 'You said she was better, you said she was better.'

My sister-in-law had arrived at the hospital two minutes after I had left. My mother had died in that interval. I was the last one to see her alive. She had definitely been pulling me. 'Blood is thicker than water,' she always said.

I wanted to write the whole thing down and at this moment I knew I was a writer. It didn't give me much pleasure. I would have given anything fully to enter the grief and cry like them. Instead I stood stock still, expressionless, handing out words of comfort to my sisters. Then I went to the lavatory to write it all down. I didn't want the others to see me.

Later in the day I felt wonderful and terrible. I was free at last. The cord had been snapped. I wanted to stand up and sing and laugh my head off but sadness was expected of me and it was easy to be sad. So the tears came. It was easy to cry but the tears didn't come from deep within me. The essential core of me hadn't been really touched. I was high on marijuana and floated above the assembled family whose dance of death had become more stylized. One sister every so often would go to another and both would weep on each other's shoulder. But though I was high and free, I thought of the body of my mother lying in the hospital mortuary, watched over by the professional body watcher hired for the occasion, according to the laws of our race.

'She's younger than all of us. She's unborn.' They shook their heads at my words but Phyllis became very protective. The atmosphere was unbearable. For I kept on swooping down to earth with a vengeance, called back by the concentration of grief. And for a day and a half I wrote every second I breathed, pulling out of myself the entrails of words. Creation was a disease within me. I had to get it out of my system. But it never ceased. The more I pulled out, the more spilled out. Drugs had opened a door inside me and I couldn't close it again.

I didn't feel great, I felt empty and small and utterly hollow.

It's hard to assess the meaning and power of a Jewish mother. She is practically always a matriarch, holding the family together, bending it to her will, making a living bit of sense out of the senselessness of the universe. When she dies the family is splintered, destroyed. The children become separate planets shooting their own directions into space.

We buried her a few days later, I in a borrowed dark suit, unshaven. My tie was cut by a man from the synagogue. I repeated Hebrew words after him. And I prayed in the language that I didn't know. Phonetically I read out the Kaddish, the prayer for the dead, as I stood pale and calm amongst the weeping relatives. Drugs were getting me through the ceremony smoothly. And as I prayed I found myself dovening, moving backwards and forwards in the nature of my ancestors. 'This is ridiculous,' I said to myself and tried to stop, but I couldn't.

There are some who get busy at a death; some who mourn and others who chat as if nothing had happened. And those who stand and watch. And I watched my relatives closely, wondering, 'What is a family?' There they were, the Zetters and Kopses, all at this family gathering. Change their expressions and their clothes and they might be at a wedding. And there was my mother in the box in the black car, outside the window, an empty shell. It was ridiculous. Is this all there was to life? I felt cheated. I remembered asking, for no special reason, two weeks before she died, 'Do you believe in God?' She thought for a moment: 'Yes, I think I do,' she answered simply.

The mirrors were covered and the low chairs were brought in. And I couldn't get out of going to the cemetery. So I went in the first car, following the coffin.

When we got out of the built-up area of the East End we sped more quickly towards Marlowe Road, her final resting place, a stone's throw from where she was born.

I was afraid that the coffin might slide out of the car. There she was, Jenny Kops, fifty-nine years old, going to the earth. Eight children out of her. Suffered all her life yet happy all her life, living from hand-to-mouth and now it was all over. She was dead forever.

'You always have time for your own funeral.' 'Shrouds have no pockets.' 'May you live long and die happy.' 'Please God by you.' 'I wish you long life.' 'By my mother in the grave.' 'When I'm dead then I'll get some rest.' All her sayings got mixed up together and ran through my mind.

In the same car were two of her brothers, my uncles, the rich one and the bookmaker. My mother's death had brought death closer. They feared their own death, like I feared mine. They started talking about horse-racing. I suddenly got angry and tried to throw them out of the car just as we reached the entrance to the cemetery.

Someone said talking about horse-racing was just to cover up grief. But then both of them started yelling at me, told me that I had caused her death, that I had worried her into the grave. I told the rich one that he could have helped her, that a little money would have alleviated her suffering, would have lengthened her life.

So I had to participate and help to push her towards the earth and then when the coffin was lowered I, with my brothers, were the first to shovel the earth onto the box. That dreadful sound of earth upon wood.

I suppose we had to do this to acknowledge the death and accept and embrace the inevitability of human fate.

Beside her grave my father had reserved some space. All his life he had been saving a few coppers for this.

I watched the birds in flight.

But I had other ideas about that burial. I pushed her towards the earth and I covered her with earth. I consigned her to dust. One generation pushes the other into the earth and to make sure the ones we love are out of the way, we put them in a box. We feel guilty, so we screw the box down. Then, we cover this box with earth, then a year later we press a marble stone on top. That's it. Over and done with. No tears would come. I tried forcing them out of me but it was useless. As I stood there I thought, 'How beautiful life is, why do we waste so much time?'

The nearest relatives washed their hands, and I washed mine. Then all the people at the cemetery came forward, leaned over and shook the hands of the chief mourners. This to me was the worst part of the ceremony. Some of my cousins had hands like wet fish. I was finished with the family, once and for all.

I had never believed in my religion but the words of the burial service had cut deep into me. 'As for man his days are as grass.'

We sped away from the cemetery and somewhere near Bow I saw two gasometers amongst the belching smoke. Being high I imagined that they were my mother's ankles poking up through the earth.

When we returned to the house our seven days of mourning began. The Shiva. In this prescribed time we were supposed to mourn and then, after a week, to get up from our low chairs and carry on living. Friends and relatives came to take our mind off things. They brought gifts of food because one is not supposed to do any cooking. They even joked about, to distract us. This was all part of the age-old ritual. But sometimes they got quite hysterical and every so often a great wave of weeping would overtake the room.

I agreed not to shave and to behave myself for my sisters' sake. And people kept on coming and going, saying what a wonderful woman she was. The best woman in the world, etc. I wanted to shout, 'shut up', she was my mother, she was all right. She wasn't the best woman in the world. Mind you, she wasn't the worst.

When people go to a shiva they are not supposed to say good evening or ask you how you are, and when they leave they are supposed to wish you a long life. Anyway, my rich uncle went along the line wishing us long life. I refused his hand. From that day to this I've never spoken to him. Mind you, he's very popular in the family. After all, he does live in Hampstead Garden Suburb and is a millionaire. But as my very late mother said: 'Look, you can be a very poor person with money, and a very rich one without.'

As he left the room he was the poorest man I'd ever seen. A little man puffing a cigar, with a diamond tie pin, all smart and grey and polished. A poor little man sitting on his heap of money.

When the shiva was all over we got up from our low chairs and my brothers and sisters returned to their own homes, and carried on living.

My father and I were the only ones to take care of. I moved in with Phyllis and Alf, and my father went to another sister. The days of Stepney and Bethnal Green were over, once and for all.

I drove my sister mad as I paced the house most of the day like a caged animal. Sometimes my contortionist came round and we'd make it in the sitting room where I slept. They let me alone. The loss of our mother had been such a shock that they didn't care if I worked or not at the moment. So I didn't.

I carved a huge wooden cross for myself, and wore it round my neck. And I wore a ring with a purple stone. 'To keep me safe from suicide,' I told them. Then I got on the Christ kick rather badly and grew a beard. After a few days I drifted back to the West End.

I sat in the café accepting cigarettes and tea from the arty hangers-on, but I hardly spoke to a soul and all the time I was spending myself writing. And I spent the evenings searching for a lonely girl to take back to Stoke Newington, without much success. I usually returned empty-handed.

I knew I was very ill and it was just a question of time before my mind would spill over. All my thoughts came tangled together. I no longer wrote to understand the situation around me; I wrote because I couldn't help myself. I had prayed for the artist to take over, I had called for him in the night, like Faust, and now he had taken over with a vengeance. But still I wasn't free of the family. Was I always to be torn? I wanted to trample across their tradi-tions and conventions, to provoke them to throw me out. But they put up with me.

Sometimes I reached a place of bliss where nothing mattered

any more, but most often I skirted the coastlines of death. For me the world was empty and destroyed already. The bomb had exploded in my brain. I felt I had burned an essential commodity away in my head and that my brain had burst and was spattered across the walls.

I had looked out of the windows into the streets of Stoke Newington until my head seemed to swell larger and larger and when it filled the whole room it burst. Over and over again Phyllis left my meals outside my locked door.

I became obsessed with the necessity to wear the colours mauve and green. I could stay alive with those colours on. And I started living a ritualistic life. Sometimes I ventured out but I couldn't go to the West End any more. I tried to make it one day on a bus, went five stops until I felt a metal band contracting around my head. So I rushed back and I sat in the middle of the room.

My distances became smaller and smaller. The main road and the immediate streets around; where I saw a dead pigeon. It became a new Hiroshima to me.

The street was full of the living dead. They spoke but no-one said anything; they walked but there was no movement; they breathed but they were not alive. Only children and animals were alive.

I became afraid of my hands for they no longer seemed connected to my body. I stopped going into the streets altogether, until at last I sat petrified, cornered, in the centre of my room. I could hear my family whispering outside.

When I ran out of drugs I chanced it Up West to get a bit more and rushed back again, thinking each heartbeat was my last. In the dubious safety of the room I lit up my cigarette.

Then I felt surrounded by inanimate objects, thought they were all out to destroy me. The chair with its arms would strangle me; the table might fly and crash my skull. The vase may shatter and pierce my eyes.

I was no longer in the world; I was in the universe. I ventured a bath one day, looked the length of my naked body, thought of my mother lying in a coffin, already decaying, I screamed, and rushed naked into my room.

The spores of death were all around me. There was simply no

escaping it. I burnt my cross in the fireplace but death poured through the electric light socket, death called me to the window-sill, death laughed in the radio, death screeched in the teaspoon and buzzed in the mirror. Everything meant death. Everything spelled its name.

I was trapped there, unable to move, unable to stay still. Unable to stand up, unable to sit down, or lie down. I couldn't go out and I couldn't stay in. The world outside was a blistered desert of streets. The world inside was closing in on me. I tied myself to the bed at night in case I sleep-walked. Still I wrote, but for no earthly reason.

Most of the time I visualized my mother under the wet ground, and the guilt of her death lingered with me all the while. 'What does she want of me? She still won't let me go. She's calling me from beyond.' I thought I would have to go to her.

Phyllis told me not to be so silly, my mother wanted only to help me. Yet I wrote, 'He who desires death by drowning will take great care crossing the road, in his journey towards the river.'

The room tilted over at a forty-five degree angle. I was certain that I was walking diagonally and I had to keep walking from one corner to another to try and balance the room. Or stand in the middle so that I wouldn't fall off the world. Two aunts came to visit my sister one day. Phyllis was out. I looked out of the window, saw them on the doorstep and they saw me, 'Well Bernie, aren't you going to open the door?'

I simply looked at them without saying a word, and went on looking as if I were hollow. At first they thought it a joke and laughed. Then they hurried away.

Then I was sure that I didn't exist any more. Everytime I spoke I uttered a cry at the end of the words. I started patting my fingers, my arms, my legs and my head to make sure that I existed. All the endless days my two hands patted my cheeks. Every time I sat on a chair I screamed for I thought I was going to disappear into the wood.

They implored me to see a doctor and finally I agreed.

The doctor had sporting prints on the wall. He told me to pull myself together. There was nothing wrong with me that a good brisk walk round the park wouldn't cure. I left his surgery feeling more desperate.

Back in the house I babbled on all the time. I knew what I was trying to say but it all came out different. With astonishment I heard myself utter words unrelated to my thoughts.

I think I understood then what the mad felt. They were really crying out for help but the words got jumbled on the way. 'This is where I get dragged off to the nut-house,' I thought to myself. I burned all the drugs in one last attempt at turning over a new leaf, but as the beautiful aroma of the stuff reached my nostrils I wanted some so I made flight to Soho where I met David Levine, and entered the bliss of the forbidden leaf.

Now we both made animal noises and he cried and laughed at the same time. In the early morning I was suddenly all alone in the street, kissing the window of a baker's shop. I would have gone completely to pieces there and then, but a taxi went slowly by. I hailed it and it took me home. My sister paid. I told her that I was going to look for a job the following day. I had taken her into my confidence. Only she and her husband knew about the drugs. The rest of the family couldn't understand why recently she had been defending me so vehemently.

The following morning I felt marvellous and utterly determined to settle down. I read an advert in the local newspaper. There was a job going at a tobacco factory near Bunhill Fields, off City Road. Phyl and Alf were pleased when I said I was going after it. We all had breakfast around the table; everything was going to be all right now. It was such a beautiful day.

I caught a bus and carried all my manuscripts with me in a carrier bag under my arm. I saw myself suddenly in the bus window. I looked wild but yet so terribly young. 'How are you not an old man yet, after all this? How can you still have a young face?' The bus stopped at the traffic lights; the engine reverberated, it got on my nerves and made me feel deeply uncomfortable. So I got out of the bus and crossed the road, and as I did I collapsed. Just fell to the ground. My legs wouldn't move; my whole body had become like rubber. The busy junction became like an undulating Disney landscape, pushing towards me like a nightmarish cartoon; I think people came to help but I crawled on all fours towards a side street. People in buses watched me.

I distinctly remember their faces seeming embarrassed; I tried throwing up my arms but they fell as if they had no bones within them. I saw a queue outside a doctor's surgery. They watched me as I approached and I stood up, went to the head of the queue and knocked at the door. The knocker, too, was like soft coagulating rubber and a coagulating face came to the door.

'I'm very ill,' I heard my voice say.

'If you're not on the doctor's panel you'd better go to the hospital.' She pointed and I heard myself shouting; then my legs carried me away behind a block of houses. Looking out of the window of a building I saw my mother.

'Mum! I didn't mean to do it,' I screamed. The face changed to an ordinary woman with white hair. The face seemed astonished. I crawled along the street then I realized the cause of all my trouble. It was my note books under my arm. I could feel the written words inside burning into my flesh, words had brought me to this. I hurled them away from me and all the while children played and the woman with white hair watched me.

The sky sang a terrible moaning song and the earth heaved. I started to gnaw the road, chewed the muck and spat it out again. Then I remembered the drugs on me. I crawled to a drain and slid the brown packets into it, turned and saw the woman again. She just stared at me as if she saw sights like that every day.

Some workmen were building on a bomb site. They saw me and three of them lifted me up. But it didn't seem to be my body they were carrying. I had no body.

They put me against a wall, told me they had called an ambulance and I was going to be taken to St Leonard's Hospital. I struggled up when they said that, for it was the hospital where my mother had died. It was only five minutes walk away. I collapsed down on the concrete again and spewed out my inside, thinking, 'This is not my own vomit.' It didn't seem to come from me. I could feel death dancing around me and I was shivering, yet I had no body. I could feel my soul being sucked out, sucked into the concrete wall; I was part of the concrete, squeezed dry, empty, finished. 'I just died,' I told one of the workman who was left with me. He was planing some wood and spoke very gently. I wanted to tell him he was the most beautiful man in the whole world. But the ambulance bells disturbed, crashed through the air. The other workmen had all been working on through all this and no-one had been looking out for the ambulance, consequently it whizzed right by. They shouted after it but the bell disappeared in the distance.

They returned, told me they would phone again. I begged them not to, pleaded for a taxi instead.

They carried me inside the cab and I was driven to my sister's. The taxi driver carried me into the house, where I was put to bed. 'I'm dead!' 'I've died.' I screamed. No amount of words, or logic could reassure me that I was still alive.

An old Jewish doctor came. He shook. I could see that he too was a drug addict. He injected me and I fell asleep, for two days. Two beautiful, dreamless days.

I was a little more reasonable when I woke up, though I still patted myself to prove that I existed. My sister pleaded with me to go somewhere for treatment. There was a hospital for neurotics. I hung on to those words. I wasn't mad or going mad. I wasn't dead. I was merely unbalanced, unable to cope with the world.

'Yes please, yes please. Please send me away.'

I would have gone anywhere, even to hell to get out of my own hell.

It was difficult to fix. England was full of neurotics, people waiting their turn to go to psychiatric hospitals. I wasn't so original after all. But this doctor knew someone who knew someone.

And I saw that someone in Harley Street. I sat cross-legged on the floor in front of him. 'I'm going to tell you all about my life and death.'

He sat there just nodding occasionally and fed me a few questions.

Two weeks later I was taken by my sister away from the worlds that I knew, away from the hell they had become.

13

Breakdown

It was almost springtime 1951 and I could see the buds on the wet trees as we walked along the long drive. Phyllis was crying. Ahead of us stood Belmont Hospital, a ghastly grey brick building. It looked like a Victorian workhouse.

Now I was really alone, alone for the first time in my life. The shaking heads of my family had stopped; now they were sure they knew what was wrong with me. My rebellion had been explained away. I was a drug addict. No-one questioned why I took to drugs in the first place.

So I walked lifeless along that path towards my destination.

Phyllis smiled but burst into tears when we said goodbye.

It was quite lively inside. Many people walked around—could they have been patients or were they staff?

I was a voluntary patient and knew I could leave at any time. But I felt very secure there. Suddenly safe.

The first day I was put to bed. The homosexual male nurse, with a kind face, asked me my name.

'Narcissus,' I replied.

'Here, drink this down Narcissus.' He offered me a glass of liquid. I can't even remember my head hitting the pillow.

I woke up the next morning and all seemed lively and very normal. Patients were sweeping the ward. A blustering, red-faced county man came to the bed, asked me how I felt. I told him that I was not so bad.

'Oh, you'll be up and about in no time.'

I thanked him, thought he was my doctor. Half an hour later I found out he was a patient.

And I was up and about that same day, and went for lunch to the rather bright cafeteria which was full of ordinary looking people. At least, at first sight it all seemed perfectly normal.

The man sitting next to me wasn't eating although food was in front of him. I prattled on telling him how I thought that neurotics were the first prophets of true sanity, 'After all, if you reject the world of today you must be sane. Draw a circle anywhere in London and you'll have a cross section as neurotic as us.'

I wondered why, in all that crowded cafeteria this table was empty, apart from the two of us.

The man stared glassily ahead, then he sharpened all his fingernails quickly with his teeth, and kept on looking to the left and to the right, over and over again as if he were an animal. Then, with one swoop, he fell on to his food, devouring it in a few seconds, guarding the plates with his hunched body. Rice pudding flew everywhere. He didn't use his utensils.

It was unnerving.

Wanting to find out the strength of him I asked another patient. The man had been blown up in France, found himself trapped with the dead bodies of his comrades. Rats came. To survive the horrible sight of his friends being devoured he had somehow submerged his personality and come to think of himself as a rat.

Belmont Hospital had been set up to help the mentally unbalanced soldiers during the war. There were two parts to the hospital. The Psychological Unit for psychopaths, where occupational therapy was the main treatment; there misfits were reclaimed for society. I, being psychotic, was in the other part where people needed more serious treatment. Here a Dr Louis Minsky was in charge. He had a wonderful reputation and the hospital's discoveries were changing the face of medicine, so I heard, and so I later knew to be true.

The men in my ward were very friendly. They acted as though nothing was wrong with them and joked about most of the time. On my second day I was already accepted. They called me Omar Khayyam.

The food was very good. Part of the treatment was to build you up physically. The outside world faded into unreality. This became the world. I once thought that people who suffered would be more understanding about suffering. This, I suppose was wishful thinking. One withdrawn old man made a point of praying at the foot of his bed, 'God bless all the family, and tell Mummy I've tried to be a good boy.' The men jeered and hooted at him. It reminded me of the treatment Oscar Wilde received.

A few days after I arrived I witnessed a most distressing sight. In the washroom a man next to me washed himself vigorously, then, about to dry himself, he thought he had made the tap dirty with his hands, so he washed the tap and then the sink again, then his hands again, then the whole towel, then the tap again; and then he started to wash the water. Then his hands and then the soap. It was a never-ending process. Every time he got to the door and touched the knob he'd imagine he had contaminated it again. I asked another patient how the man could ever get out of the bathroom. 'Sometimes he never manages it unless we haul him out,' was the reply.

But obsessions were not without comedy. One ex-sergeant-major liked to see all the beds in a straight row. He'd look down the line of beds with all the precision of his profession to make sure they were all level. Then he would see, perhaps, that one bed was a quarter of an inch out of line, so all the beds would be moved into line with it. Then he'd turn his back and feign indifference and suddenly whip around as if to catch a culprit bed in the act of moving. He was just like Grock.

I smuggled in some marijuana, so I smoked it in the grounds. It was great at first. Then I met my psychiatrist for the first time. I told him that I had some drugs hidden in the place. He didn't seem to mind, told me I would be pleased to give it up when I was ready.

My doctor explained that cure was the easiest thing. The most difficult part was finding out why I took to drugs in the first place and even if cured I was still not safe, for if I went back to the same social condition I was likely to start all over again. I acted up to him and over-dramatized my situation. For Belmont was security for me; it was a world within a world. People were free and easy there, the nurses kind, the doctors understanding.

I was to have no treatment for the moment, just food, rest and sedatives.

'You see,' Dr Wheeler said, 'you made a classic mistake. You should have been taking sedatives instead of stimulants.' I liked him and felt I could tell him everything. I was allowed, instead of occupational therapy, to continue with my writing.

'But I'll never want to leave,' I told the doctor. 'When you start feeling better, you won't be able to stand it here,' he replied.

Now I entered more fully into the life of the hospital.

We were not discouraged from mixing with the women. Often this killed two birds with one stone. There were many opportunities for near sex, for the grounds were rather large, with an abundance of trees and longish grass.

One lady asked me how I was, then suddenly she jumped into the air, and then she continued jumping all the time. But who was I to think this funny? I, who constantly tapped my forehead, I met her at Covent Garden Opera a few years later. She still jumped but not so noticeably.

At Belmont I met many people whom I liked enormously; librarians, actors, bus-conductors and physicists.

The grounds were idyllic. I watched the dragonflies as they emerged from their fibre shells.

There was a play-reading group and I started poetry-readings. I settled in. I started to contemplate the girls. The first was thirty-five. She walked around like a sleep-walker. I wanted to wake her up.

We lay on the grass and I touched her on the breast. I was the first man ever to do that to her. She told me she had seen her own father make love to her mother at the age of one. I asked her how she had such a good memory. She explained that they were using a new drug on her. It took her back and back. Right now she had reached the point before she was born, when she was eight months in her mother's womb.

In that place of dragonflies I attempted to take her but at the last moment I ran away over the grass. My legs seemed to make no movement, as if I were running in a dream, and was caught up in cotton wool.

We never spoke after that.

The next girl, Jane, had rosy cheeks. She seemed a picture of health. We got on well at first, but one night at a hospital concert she started to dance, fluttering scarves all over the place. Like a latter-day, watered-down version of a pale copy of an imitation of Isadora Duncan. I couldn't face her from then on.

Sometimes there were dances to gramophone records in the gymnasium. Men and women, obviously distressed, glided round the floor silently, stiffly.

Then my third girl. Tall and Lancashire, her golden hair cut like a boy's. A few days after she arrived I noticed her looking at me all through tea, then she came over, saying, 'I must talk to you urgently.'

We walked towards the grass and she said, 'I want your advice. I've fallen in love with someone. Shall I tell him?' I told her, 'Yes, yes, yes,' and she told me I was that person.

We rolled around under the sky and played about, but just as we got to the point of it she asked me to excuse her. She had to go up to her ward but would return in ten minutes when we would continue where we left off. I waited.

It got cold. She never turned up. She didn't turn up in the dining-room for weeks and when she did I waved to her expectantly, but she stared right through me. When I tried to speak to her she totally ignored me.

'Wish me luck! I'm so happy I can't be cured,' a queer boy said. He was being discharged that day. I kissed him on the cheek.

After a few weeks a great depression settled upon me. I was dead broke, had three shillings a week to buy my cigarettes with. Consequently I searched the hospital grounds for dog-ends.

The family had washed their hands of me. There seems to be some stigma about things of the mind. If I'd had tonsilitis or a broken leg they would have come with chocolate and cigarettes, but because I was able to walk about they didn't bother. They came once, but Phyllis was the only one who wrote and sent me a few shillings occasionally.

I lived in the eternal present, but life was becoming bearable again. Around me people were undergoing all sorts of different treatment. At that time leuchotomy was fashionable. Say 'knife' to a surgeon and he was already severing your pre-frontal lobes.

The man who thought he was a rat had this brain operation. I asked him how he felt. He didn't reply. So a couple of minutes later I wandered to the window, said it was a nice day. A few minutes later I said that I must be going. Then his reply to my first question came. 'Not so bad thank you,' and a few minutes after that, 'Yes, it is a nice day.'

He seemed empty sitting there with a high turban of white bandage covering his skull. He no longer fell on his food but ate it with extraordinary slowness.

I reckoned it was a terrible operation, that they were very much in the dark and experimenting. I told myself that I would refuse, no matter what, even if they threw me out. I preferred to die with an untampered brain.

I made a friend, a nice young man, serious and open-minded. He went up for treatment one day; an ether mask to evoke an abreaction. They were trying to find out what had caused his illness, wanted him to relive his past. When he came down he was out like a light. I sat by his bed and then suddenly he started to scream out, 'Sieg heil! Sieg heil! Sieg heil!' Apparently he had been in the Hitler Youth. He was an English boy but lived in Germany with his German mother before the war. I tried avoiding him after that, but we became almost friendly again. My doctor told me that I had to start thinking about getting back into society.

But for what? For me the lousy world had gone mad.

I wrote constantly and wandered the grounds. The prolonged contact with earth helped me. But beyond the gates was London. The great filthy disease called a city, and here we were, extreme examples of our kind, thrust up from the horror. Each face was a tragedy; and we clung together and played ping-pong. 'How beautiful that we couldn't cope,' became my theme song. 'Neurotics of the world unite, take over the world. You couldn't make a worse job of it.'

A padre came round one day selling religion. 'Let Christ come into your life.'

'Fuck off,' I replied. He smiled so I continued, 'Don't you see, if only I could? If only it were that simple.'

He told me to put my hands together and pray. I rolled a cigarette, told him Christ was a Yiddisher feller and the priests had perverted religion. 'Read Ouspensky and Blavatsky and Moisher Greenberg,' I said. He went post-haste to the next patient.

But I was feeling deep bitterness, for just one of my thousands of friends came to visit me. I realized then that friendship was a very over-worked word. Like the word 'family' it revealed itself to be a very rare bird indeed.

So I sat in the hospital, looking at the broken pieces of my life, trying to assemble them. None of the parts fitted. And even if they did I hadn't the glue. Drugs had made me see life in a different way. The sub-conscious was spilling into my mind. It was like Pandora's box. I couldn't tuck my thoughts back inside. All my fantasies were dancing around me and threatening my destruction.

I was truly obsessed. 'If I stand under that tree I shall be safe; under that, I shall be struck by lightning.' 'If I write magic words the sun will shine and the moon will not destroy me.' 'Now I must see the colour green every time I enter a room or look at anything.'

Belmont succoured me, became my mother and father and God. Dr Minsky was an archangel. I never met him but I prayed to him at night.

Now I considered myself a writer, fully fledged. I was making the sacrifice. I was in the arena, attacked by the lions from without and from within. I was writing to stay alive, I was writing for myself.

No-one had invited me to enter the arena. But now that I was there I had to fight for my life.

My doctor told me I could start going home at weekends. I told him I had no home but the hospital. But he persisted, said it helped us to acclimatize ourselves to the world. After all the world was there and had to be faced sooner or later. With much misgiving I left the gate one Saturday morning. On the other side of the wall the ground seemed to slope and again I was walking a gradient.

Being broke I had accepted the help of a fellow-patient. He paid my fare on the Green Line Coach and left me at Oxford Circus.

I stood there not knowing what to do. I wanted to run but was embarrassed, so I stood buffeted by the lifeless mass of people screaming my head off inside, with my hand over my eyes unable to move. Hell! There was a band tightening around my head. Oxford Street was a narrow ledge in endlessness. On either side was a deep abyss. I walked as if on a tightrope, thinking that the traffic would chase me up the walls or that the people would come

at me with knives, tear me to ribbons. To survive in the city one
needed to live by the laws of the jungle.

I've never been able to face Oxford Street even until this day.
I have to walk it sometimes, but mostly I run like hell.

I didn't go to my family. I reckoned I had no family. I went to
Soho where I sat with the old cronies smoking hash, waiting for the
inevitable party to begin; for a place to stay the night.

At that party I sat listless, watching the dead kids around me.
Boys and girls making love, sucking and pushing emptiness out
of each other.

I had lost my contortionist. She had gone off with a poet who
never wrote. But I again found my Jewish girl from Manchester.
We made love. She tried to bring me down to earth; instead I drew
her deep into my world.

I slept at the house of my friends, Pearl and Bop, and went back
to the hospital on the Sunday.

Later, I went to the dining-room for tea, where a nurse told me
I was wanted in the doctor's office.

Two shifty faces greeted me there. They were without doubt the
law. They had obviously followed me back from town.

I felt strangely calm, wanted to observe their technique. They
used that corny old line of one being very nice and the other being
a bastard.

'Now listen Bernard, we want to help you. Tell us all about the
drugs. Where you get it from, and you'll be in the clear,' the kind
one.

'Oh no he won't. We've got enough on him. We know all about
him. He's going to get it in the neck.' The contorted one.

'No George, he's a nice boy. Don't let's be hard on him.'

'Hard on him? Wait till he leaves this place.' They ding-donged
on like this.

It may have been a fifth-rate repertory performance but I found
my heart going out to the nice one. Then it occurred to me that
they had no right to be there in the first place. I opened the door.
'Good-day, gentlemen, don't call again.'

'We know all about your movements. We know everything,' the
kind one suddenly changed.

'If you bloody well know—why ask me? Now get out.'

And they did.

I screamed at the nurse for allowing them to come in, also at the man on the gate. What worried me was that they knew so much about me, had obviously been watching my movements for ages.

I still needed drugs and was no closer to a solution. I began to feel desperate again.

There were two suicides. One man went down to the local railway line, lay his head down on the rail and a train went over it. And a girl was found dead on the grass outside the hospital, a book was open beside her. It was called *Other Men's Flowers*. She died from an overdose of sedatives; had pretended to swallow her sleeping pill each night but instead hid it beneath her tongue.

After that we had to open our mouths to show the night nurse that we had really swallowed our knockout drops.

That weekend when I went to London was the most sickeningly memorable one of my life.

When I arrived all the ravers of Soho were going on about the hashish that was knocking around. 'It's the best shit in years,' David Levine exclaimed, his eyes all glassy. The bums commiserated with me about my stay in Belmont and bought me cups of tea, slices of bread and free sticks of that beautiful charge. Some of the characters, however, wanted to know how to get into Belmont. 'It sounds just the place,' they said.

The hashish was really terrific. All the Saturday I raved and floated; I hoped that it would let me down gently.

'I can't come down,' screamed David, tears rolling down his cheeks, yet he was full of ecstasy. The night exploded like a slow and beautiful bomb; nothing mattered any more. This was the life.

We sat in the café tapping the tables. Later Shirley and I went to Camden Town. As Pearl and Bop were away, we had the house to ourselves.

I couldn't make it in bed and lay on the floor feeling happier than any other time in my life. She was depressed. In the morning we went to Soho. It was Sunday and deserted except for the struck-off doctor, who sat alone in Tony's café. We joined him and sat drinking Turkish coffee.

This guy was always going around telling everybody he was Icarus. I asked him to reconsider, that possibly he was Daedalus. He left the café thoughtfully, turning the matter over in his mind. He drove off on his bicycle that was full of weird plastic contraptions, 'To catch the rays of the sun,' he said.

Shirley held my hand, appealed to me silently, but then I heard myself screaming. The drug had worn off. I was getting the most terrible reaction.

Some people call it blowing your top or flipping your lid; only those who have been through it can really know how terrible it is. I left my body. I was a lump of dead flesh spreadeagled over the table, unable to control a single muscle. 'Help.' My long drawn out yell took on a life of its own. I became an empty shell. This, I thought, was the moment of my death. This was the way people went out.

I poured the coffee over my hand to feel some sensation. I wasn't sure if it was hot or cold.

'Get me back to the hospital,' I heard myself screaming at her. But she couldn't move me and I stood outside my body for a long time unable to get back into myself, while she stroked my lifeless hands. The Greek owner of the café brought me another coffee.

Belmont Hospital can be reached at the other end of the Northern Line. You get a bus from Morden. I remembered the instructions.

She led me along the street, walking backwards coaxing me forward, holding my hands in a weird dance along the deserted Sunday streets. I remember a few people stared, but they must have put it down to the excesses of the young.

So we got down Goodge Street Underground Station.

Not a soul was down there. I sat in the empty station with the girl. Memories of the Blitz came back and I closed my eyes.

Memories of my dead mother. Now I was even lower than my mother and I prayed that the train would come. I looked along the tunnel, stood at the edge and looked at the live rail. It started calling me. I could feel the line pulling me, the way I felt the day my mother died. 'She's calling me,' I told Shirley.

But I didn't want to die; I just couldn't help myself. I was being sucked on to the line, magnetized. There seemed to be no way out.

But I didn't want to die. Christ, I wanted so much to live! I rushed back to the seat where the girl was, 'I don't want to die.' She held my hand, grabbed my wrists and neck, but it was no use, I was being pulled on to the line. The more I hugged at her and the seat the more useless it became. Now I stood on the edge and Shirley tugged at me, her arms around my waist pulling me away.

I could hear my cry echoing along the empty tunnel, 'I don't want to die. I don't want to die.' I was being sucked like a lump of useless metal on to the singing line.

A train came roaring through the station. That saved me. Its doors opened, like encompassing arms, and I fell inside and on to the floor. It was full of Sunday morning travellers reading *The People* and *The News of the World*. They pretended not to notice. All the way to Morden, I lay with my head in Shirley's lap crying and singing, she stroking my forehead.

'I don't want to die. I don't want to die.'

'You won't, you won't.'

'You saved my life.' I must have been shouting out for all the stodge of faces were peeping over the tops of newspapers.

Back at the hospital they gave me a drug to knock me out and as I sank into beautiful oblivion I promised every god there was, or wasn't, that I would never touch drugs again. I promised to Zeus and Jehovah, Jesus and Marx, Eros and Wodin, Mars and Venus. The last thing I remember was Shirley waving and leaving the ward.

The trouble was that the condition kept on returning, even though I didn't smoke. I wasn't able to control my movements. In the middle of an embrace, a word, an explanation, I'd lose complete control of my actions. 'Oooh.' A long-drawn out yell that frightened the pigeons but few of the patients. I rushed to the doctor. 'Look,' I said, 'I smash things.' I hurled a cup across the surgery. Smithereens. 'Please cure me.'

When he told me that my troubles were not so original I could have kissed him. Up till then I had thought that no-one had been in the dark places that I had been. But now that he assured me other people had been through the very same experiences, I knew there was some hope.

He asked me to undergo treatment but I refused electric convulsive therapy and deep narcosis, and deep insulin. I even refused my sleeping draught at night, becoming quite obsessive against drugs. So I fought with myself to get to sleep. Thoughts piled up like a crazy skyscraper, then they would crumble and start again. At four in the morning I was still fighting to empty my mind.

I discovered something about suicide, as I went backwards and forwards over my experiences. I did not want to die and yet I almost did. Something deep within me drove me to it.

There was an enemy deep within me trying to bring about my destruction.

How could I fight and conquer an invisible enemy? I knew that many people who committed suicide didn't really want to. Something deep within drove them. Bad enough to die when you decide to and want to, but more terrible when at the brink of death you're screaming to be allowed to live.

Like the world, a man was pitched in mortal combat with himself, the two halves of his nature struggling for supremacy. I was all alone with myself in the world, in the universe, and I understood a little more about myself. What price maturity? The closer I got to myself, the further I had to travel. I was overcome with the terrible knowledge that there was no way back. I choked back the universe and cried myself to sleep.

I started group therapy. Five of us sat around, from all walks of life we had come, and now we revealed to each other the true reasons for being at Belmont. It gave us a new sort of bond in the ward. One boy compulsively stole despite the fact that his father was a millionaire; another wanted to have his mother; and the bus conductor wanted to have anything. When the heat was on him he desired man, woman or child.

The whole ward was upset one day. A rather gentle man, who made the loveliest pottery, went upstairs for an abreaction. He asked the doctors to strap him down. They did. There were a few male nurses in the surgery plus a female nurse.

We heard the most terrible crash and we rushed out to find the patient collapsed on the stairs. The surgery was destroyed; he had snapped the straps, the two male nurses were knocked out; the doctor was unconscious and the girl nurse lay crumpled in the corner. Apparently she spoke with a German accent during the treatment. The patient had been tortured by the Germans during the war.

Deep within every man lies sleeping the strength of twelve. The doctor was a patient in a hospital for three months.

I was dreading being discharged from the hospital for I was warned that if I didn't accept any treatment there was little they could do for me.

Meanwhile, I got friendly with an ex-seaman who made the most magnificent iron sculptures. He was so strong, he bent metal with his hands.

One dusk we walked through the hospital grounds together. He told me how much he liked me; more than anyone else in the place. 'I'll never hit you,' he said. I started to sweat when I saw his clenched fist and jaw. 'I'd sooner hit the brick wall than hit you.' And with that he struck the brick wall with all his might. He held his lacerated bleeding fist towards me, 'I told you I'd never hit you.'

He was taken to the deep insulin ward, a place that looked like a medieval torture chamber. Here, with insulin, they took all the sugar out of your body. You lay in the deepest coma. Only your heart functioned. Then they gave you glucose to bring you back. If it didn't work through the mouth they injected it into the veins. As you came back into the world the doctors recorded your re-entry. You came first, up through the primeval slime of the soul. Slowly through the animal stages of moaning and grunting, until you took on a human personality and became yourself again. One patient told me that on coming round he saw his arm in front of him but didn't know what it was. He thought it might be a tree.

I was called to that ward one morning. The doctor warned me that an accident had happened to my friend of the lacerated fist. 'Things go wrong sometimes,' the doctor said.

The man I knew was no more; he was caught at the age of three years old and would never grow beyond it. He spoke to me like a little boy 'B-e-r-n-a-r-d, B-e-r-n-a-r-d'. That's all he would say; he was smiling but truly gone. He had become a human being, had crawled out of the beast within him but was forever locked at three. Things go wrong sometimes.

He was certified and taken to another hospital.

Little wonder that when this treatment was suggested to me again I refused.

In Belmont, every six months or so they reviewed an interesting case. My doctor told me that I had been chosen. I was delighted. I stood before more than a hundred people; doctors, psychiatrists and psychiatric welfare workers; I told them about my life and about my death. Went through my catechism 'Long Live Wilhelm Reich, Anarchy, Buddhism, and the poetry of Lorca and William Blake.'

A few days later my doctor broke the bad news. There was no point any longer in staying at Belmont.

'But what am I going to do?' I pleaded.

'Now your problems will really begin,' was the only answer he could give. I valued his honesty. I longed for a lead, a word of comfort, but I only got the truth. And a fat lot of good that was.

They gave me some clothes and suddenly I was walking to the gate.

They were some of the nicest people I had met in my life. For that I was thankful. But where did I go from here? As I stepped through the gate I knew that only Soho and despair waited ahead for me. Behind me, Belmont was a world that I could not return to, must not return to. I was utterly alone on a suburban train crawling towards London.

The hospital could not effect a cure for someone like me. My place was in the world. There was my battlefield and there was my answer.

There was no turning my back on that world, no matter how terrible it was. I wanted to live and give and get and grow out of my fear. I had to come to terms with life, with London, with what I was. I was determined, but when the train reached Victoria I stood in the station utterly confused, not knowing which way to turn.

14

Clutching at Straws

I drifted back to Soho, for it was the one place I could be accepted without question. You could have been away for five years and hardly anyone would bother to ask where you'd been. More likely they'd ask you to buy them a cup of tea, or ask if you wanted one.

It was the late spring of 1952 so sometimes I slept out in Trafalgar Square. You could sit with your eyes closed, as long as you didn't take your feet off the ground. Every so often the law came round and prodded you.

There was no longer any escape for me in drugs. All forms of locomotion became almost impossible. I couldn't cross water, not even the River Thames; neither could I stand on the Embankment. I couldn't travel by underground or go by bus; neither could I sit in a room higher than the ground floor.

People spoke to me but the words didn't mean anything. My one thought was that I must not return to the hospital. To go back was death. Yet here was the larger madhouse.

I wandered round the streets as best I could. At night I could cope best. It all seemed unreal, the city like a huge stage set; a cardboard cut out, where all the people were sleeping. There was no end to loneliness. Become aware of a thing and it exists everywhere around you. The one thing that kept me going was writing. I no longer deliberated whether I was a writer or not. I just wrote. All I had been through was my apprenticeship. I had prayed once for ability; prayed to that small spark within me to ignite. Now that spark was all there was of me. I learned then that the artist was in everyone; he needed to be awakened, but there was also the sacrifice. The spark could burn you to ashes.

There was no joy in my knowledge for I had been struck by real, utter loneliness. Its icy grip clutched my heart. It dragged

218

in the pit of my stomach. I had been battered against myself until everything inside me had been shattered.

How lonely the earth was; how lonely London. It appeared that all my life now would be an anti-climax, a passing of time; writing it all down for no purpose, for no one. There was no sense in living, no sense in dying.

I considered that the achievements of mankind would be swamped by the horror we had perpetrated. We would not be able to outweigh our crimes against ourselves. Hitler was not the end of something; he was the beginning. Man was alone without faith or God; terribly alone. I was outraged by my visions of the weeping children of Warsaw; by my mother's tears and by my indifference.

In the night-town of Soho I was accepted.

'Look Bern, anybody give you a spot of bother just tell me.' A boy with a blue serge draped suit and a kind cockney face offered me eternal protection. A week later he murdered someone and went to prison for life.

I got a job in a club washing dishes but lasted only a few hours. No sooner did I get there when the boss showed me the pile of dirty dishes reaching almost to the ceiling. I placed my hand under the steaming hot water tap and even though I scalded myself I didn't feel a thing.

The poets were still talking. The artists were still talking. The two rival splinter groups of four Trotskyists were still talking. The whores and the pansies, the tearaways and the Lizzies, the religious bums, were all still talking, talking, talking.

David Levine popped cocaine all the time now. One boy with a double-barrelled name told me that as I didn't smoke any more I might as well kill myself. A few weeks later he left the world himself, by way of the gas oven.

The pox was rampant, so it was a good thing I was leaving women alone for the time being.

I stood at Camden Town one evening and Bill suddenly stood before me asking me how I was. Before I could reply he emptied his pockets giving me all the money he possessed, about ten shillings. He was still living off the Camden Road, told me I was welcome to move in with him. I did not take his offer up immediately, for I was not the person that he knew before my breakdown. Then I used to talk all the time, fizzing like a rocket. Now I was silent, almost morose. And despite drugs being part of the past the nauseating effects would creep up on me and suddenly throw me into a cold, conscious coma for hours on end.

Dawdling one day, near Covent Garden I met a half familiar face belonging to a dancer named Peter. He lived near there with a rather impressive girl called Janice. Long red hair and Anarchist.

I felt secure in their flat even though it was five storeys high. At the top of the stairs there was a great statue of an Aztec corn god and inside the room the unreality somehow gave me real security. There was a skull with a wig on under a glass dome and so much furniture and so many books that we carried on a conversation without being able to see each other. There were great chunks of rose quartz lying around, shells and witchballs, several cats, guinea pigs and white rabbits. We dressed up, sat around the table eating with masks, wigs and helmets on our heads.

Peter read Gertrude Stein aloud till four in the morning.

'Listen to this dear.' He'd still be eating his soup as the first rays of dawn fingered the roof of the Masonic Headquarters. He also read from *Finnegans Wake*.

He made the most wonderful soufflés.

I stayed there a few days then I went to Bill at Camden Town, and took up his offer.

It was impossible for me to work, so he kept me. It was a great act of love for he worked at Wall's Ice Cream factory, nightwork in the cold room, which was one of the hardest casual jobs around. Bill never questioned, he just shared everything with me. He came home in the morning half-dead. I would roll out of the bed and he would roll in. We'd talk for hours over coffee. He spoke about conquering the world, all I wanted was to conquer myself.

Ordinary nice girls often drifted into the café. One day I noticed one of the religious boys trying to pass two suburban girls some hashish. I screamed at him. But I soon lost interest. I didn't want to get involved.

I applied for a job at Selfridges, right in the heart of my Oxford Street hell where there were vacancies for liftmen.

I arrived with my convenient loss of memory and decided I

wasn't going to be such a bloody fool this time. Now I was going to pretend to be an imbecile.

The personnel officer spoke to me slowly and loudly, 'There are no prospects in this job.'

'I—do not want—pros—pects.'

He was most kind and understanding, told me to follow him and when this didn't seem to sink in he repeated it as if he were talking to a deaf and dumb person.

I had always been so bloody clever, always made my life hell by becoming involved, but now I wanted to be completely shut off.

The foreman liftman spent nearly the whole morning teaching me how to make the lift go up and down. I could have learned it in ten minutes. At noon he told me he was most pleased with my progress. So they gave me a little side-lift that few people used.

But all good things come to an end and within a week, despite my imbecility, I was on one of the main lifts, flying up and down, endlessly.

'Are those lifts safe?' an American woman asked me one day at the very top floor.

'It's strange you should ask, only the other day an American lady asked me exactly the same question and I replied "yes madam" and at that moment we crashed to the ground and we were all killed.'

'Oh,' she exclaimed. We were alone in the lift and she backed against the doors. When she left I left also and went straight to the Personnel Department where I tendered my resignation, most eloquently.

I was always very elated whenever I left a job, happy to know my life was not going to take that direction.

Now I could travel on buses a little and I managed to get a job at Kingston demonstrating electric shavers. I only lasted two weeks, then I saw a job advertised to demonstrate waterless cookers in Birmingham.

I travelled by train to the Midlands, sitting on the edge of my seat with fear in case I suddenly opened the door and threw myself out. I engaged in frantic, stupid conversation with people who only wanted to read their magazines.

In Birmingham I stood before a group of middle-aged women. I barely knew how the contraption worked so I just spieled out any old patter. 'It all works by the principals of eternal combustion—' But their soggy faces put me off so I caught the next train back to London.

I got a job in Charlotte Street, a process block-making company. I was a general dogsbody to the etchers and I had a go at etching myself, but I was utterly useless. My hands were too shaky. The boss, a Jewish typical from British West Hampstead, turned out to be a freemason. I'd always hated Masons and here he was, a good and kind man trying to root out my prejudices. He sent me to his brother's shop to get a complete outfit. He told me it wasn't because I was Jewish but because Masons were supposed to help other people. Well, I still don't like Masons, like I never liked the Boy Scouts. And in a strange sort of way I hated him for what he did, for making me feel obligated.

Two boys from Belmont, with the help of my descriptions, drifted to Soho and soon settled in. It was home from home. One day they announced that they had managed to find a marvellous gaff. A caravan near Camden Town. There was another one vacant for only ten shillings a week.

Under the railway arches, along Kentish Town Road, stood Randall's Yard and the gaffer Mr Randall, a cockney with a mouth full of black teeth, a pocketful of black pound notes and an ominous perpetual smile.

There was a caravan, six feet long, three-and-a-half-feet across, just enough room for one bed, and six inches of floor space. That would stop me pacing the floor. I moved in. So there I was, standing with all my belongings; myself.

On that site lived a circus family with a string of monkeys; a scientologist with his line of new jargon, and the two boys from Belmont. Plus an army of rats.

Conditions were filthy, the nearest water was fifty yards away and there was no lavatory except the public one at Camden Town Junction.

I felt very safe there. The circus family was governed by an acrobat who was tough enough to keep any of the Camden Town boys at bay. But every night I had recurring dreams of destruction.

I had no sheets on the bed and I always slept in my clothes and shoes. One had to be ready for the holocaust.

I bought a second-hand guitar and learned to strum it.

Peter, the younger man from Belmont, loved animals. One day he stole a snake from a pet shop, cut it up into small pieces and chucked the bits around the site. Another day he returned from a visit to a small zoo in the country. He had stolen a huge white cockatoo and had blinded it in the process of getting it out of the cage. I loathed that white cockatoo. It jumped on my shoulders and pecked at my ears.

In Soho I met two girls. I invited them to my caravan for tea. One seemed intelligent, intense, the other was talkative and warm. They were both Irish way back. One wanted to be a writer, the other didn't. My attention went to her. Her name was Joyce.

I read them some of my poetry. Later I isolated Joyce from her friend and told her quietly that I wanted to see her again, alone. She came often but still I could not come down to earth.

Whenever I walked along the street I was afraid that I would float away. I always wondered how it was possible that my feet could remain on the surface of the earth.

Each moment was a dreadful experience, each word painful to write. Each letter not joined to the other and written with lopsided speed. I thought that each word was my last. 'This word! This word! This cannot be the last. This word—and this word. . . .' Each word held terror within it. The closer I got to myself the closer I got to destruction. Again thoughts of suicide obsessed me.

I remembered the words of my doctor: 'You need an anchor.' Even if I found no sense in the universe I needed to anchor myself in time and space. So I clutched at Joyce and I knew within that I was clutching at straws. I wanted to share my loneliness.

She was flesh and blood and I wanted to belong to someone before I evaporated in the black universe. We never made love fully. Strange that with my loose background I never pressed her to the conclusion. She was an anti-Catholic Catholic.

But enclosed in the caravan we shut off the universe for a while.

I was incapable of making decisions, needed someone to lead me and to help me out of myself.

I made a conscious decision. Up until now I had considered suicide. Now I considered the lesser of two evils—marriage.

She didn't know anything of this. I wept and laughed and read poetry and danced in that small space and called it love, and got caught up in it. And as I became enmeshed in her life I could see the horizon fading. The earth under my feet was not so shaky.

I thought my family were right after all. What else was there in life? I had been chasing something that didn't exist.

After all, there was a lot to be said for ordinary living. There was no use in fighting any more. You had to go with the tide.

I decided that would save me. A conventional ordinary life on earth was worth more than all the twisted nightmares of a displaced person. Perhaps yet I could live in the graveyard, if I could furnish a little tomb for myself. Who was I to want to change things? I couldn't even change myself.

I needed to deaden myself, to become a suburban blob, and have my offspring. So I finally decided to 'pull myself together' or, in the jargon of my family, 'at last I was becoming a mensch.'

'She isn't a Yiddisher girl, but believe me she looks like one.' That's what my family said. They were delighted, for at last I named the day of days. At last I had come to my senses. And the poor girl didn't realize what she was taking on. She had drifted into Soho accidentally and she was lonely like me. Two vacuums of loneliness lay together behind windows, reassuring each other this was inevitable and for ever.

Joyce was down to earth, practical, and good-hearted. She worked as an adding machine operator. I got a job trying to sell radios from door to door.

I bought a new suit and wore it, turned over my new leaf.

We found a flat in Stamford Hill, and I moved into it, stayed there alone, waiting for the day to arrive. In those few weeks I changed my job, became a statistical clerk and I fought the desire every night to run away from London, from England, from everywhere and everyone.

On the morning of the wedding I couldn't get the bath to work. I called the girl in from the next room. She was in her dressing-gown and as she leaned over I could see her bare breasts and I wanted her. Remembering the words of the prophet Freud, 'We're all a little more moral than we think we are,' I prepared for the ceremony without too much self recrimination.

And so in a Registry Office we were joined, simply and inhumanly. 'I know of no lawful impediment why I should not take—' It all seemed like a series of negatives as I repeated the words.

When the wedding guests went we made love immediately. But that little room in Stamford Hill clean and crisp smelled of polish and doom.

Nothing had changed, no magic curtain lifted. We quarrelled. There was a gap between us, a space. We hugged each other but we weren't close. We made love but it was nowhere in the room once we made it. It flew out of the window. I felt a world apart, a race apart. And I felt that she was bossing me, was pushing me down. I wondered if I could still fight against a path too hastily prepared for myself. Then I knew somehow I'd made a terrible mistake, but wasn't prepared to live with that knowledge, and so I pleaded with Joyce that we leave London. I was afraid of the planes throbbing in the night sky. Afraid of being confronted with the inevitable break-up. I told her stories I had heard about Jersey, about the money we could earn and save there. And so a few weeks after our marriage I was already on the move. We kissed goodbye and she cried and off I went. I was to get a job and she was to follow.

So I crossed the night ocean, trembling with fear at the thought of all that water beneath me. But I took sedatives to calm myself. And they worked.

The boat tossed and everyone was sick except me. I ventured to the rail, all around was the dark tossing sea, stretched out, heaving and retching, like my life.

I got a job in a potato stores and I sent for her. When she arrived it seemed everything was going to be all right. She got a job as a waitress.

Now real physical work began for me. Lifting and humping hundredweight sacks of potatoes all day. Grazing my knees and pulling my sinews. I soon started hating Jersey and the people in it. Maybe it was just me, for I realized that Jersey was just another straw I was clutching at.

We earned quite good money and when the potato season finished I got a job at the docks. I loaded wood into holds of ships and although the work almost broke my back, I found a certain release, my mind started to sing, I wanted to write again.

Jersey was physically beautiful and I wandered the shore-lines gazing into the rock-pools, looking for shells and catching shrimps.

The great sea seemed to put things into perspective.

I realized how far we had got away from natural things. We had tried to shut out nature and we couldn't, it sprang through us. This was our tragedy, this was the chaos in the world. We had not grown up but merely covered up and we turned a blind eye to our world of nature, but we couldn't get away with it for there was the sea waiting to pour down upon us. And there was the sea waiting within us. We would be drowned by one or the other.

My communing with chaos brought the usual and expected conflict into my private life.

We hadn't got away from anything, for we hadn't got away from ourselves. We had merely come face to face with our problems. Our argument broke through every situation. Two human beings trying to assert themselves, arguing incessantly over trivial things, soon lose all respect, all dignity.

I got a job as a labourer and worked with hundreds of Irishmen. We worked on the new drainage system which was being installed on the southern part of the island. We lived in digs with one of those Irishmen. He could quote from Socrates and Aeschylus and Shakespeare and Swift, but he swore like Camden Town.

As I passed his room he would drag me in, holding a bottle in one hand and a clenched fist in the other. It was drink or else. Then he would kiss me, great slobbering smacks on the forehead and then he would cry his soppy eyes out and smash up the furniture.

I smashed my thumb one day under a two-ton whaling board. The anti-tetanus injection caused me more trouble than the injury. It knocked me groggy for a week. I left the job and immediately got a position as a waiter. The hotel was crammed with holiday-makers from Lancashire; they would come and immediately lie in the sun, get all blistered up and smile through their terrible agony.

Several of the girls, married and unmarried, gave the come-on sign to the waiters. They wanted a little adventure, so a lot of the Italian boys were doing a lot of overtime.

I made tons of money, drank a lot and started to smoke ordinary cigarettes again. They were half-price in Jersey, so I smoked twice as many.

One day several of the waiters from the hotel were hired to wait on an official banquet in honour of the Duke of Gloucester. So there I was, with white gloves on. One waiter was assigned to five guests—five hundred guests in all. In they toddled, the royalty, and I sang 'God Save the Queen' for camp. So did the Italian waiters.

The food was marvellous. No sooner did we lay it in front of the guests when we whisked it away, in order to eat it ourselves in the passages. All the waiters became blind drunk. We swayed and rocked as we served the endless courses. The speeches started and I looked at the assembled guests, the sour cream, and I wanted to shout out 'Fuck you all'. Instead I scarpered into the passage where I danced a waltz with a boy from Milan.

Joyce and I drew further apart. It was pretty obvious that we wanted different things in life but we were unable to be honest with ourselves. We didn't want to admit our mistake to ourselves and others. We didn't want to let them down. Instead we took it out of each other.

One day, while serving lunch in the hotel, I thought that I would blow my top. I was rushing through the restaurant with four plates of soup in my hand. Suddenly my mind started to boggle, couldn't cope with the confusion of faces. I thought, 'In a few seconds I shall call out and everybody will look at me.' I saw myself then, in slow motion, as I threw the plates into the air and screamed. Five hundred startled guests watched me silently and the head-waiter came rushing over as I crumpled up.

They carried me out and I was out of a job.

I got another waiting job down on the sea front, serving coffee and drinks in a café. I made three pounds a day in tips but all the time I was aware of the sea which seemed to be spilling over the horizon and pouring into my eyes. Everything became more and more unreal. I started handing tips back to the customers. In the waiting fraternity those who don't tip are called 'Stiffs'. I called them all 'Stiffs'. I collapsed again in the middle of a busy evening, sat down at a table and just stared at the sea. The owner, a fat Lancashire woman, tried to be helpful. 'What's the matter luv? What's up?' How could you explain my sort of sickness to such a down-to-earth woman.

'It's nerves,' I replied.

She recommended a tonic. She was most kind but I had to leave the job. It was too close to the sea for comfort.

So I became a street photographer, a smudge merchant, as it is known in the trade, 'Two together smiling'. This became my theme song and I clicked away through July and August. I didn't earn a fortune but I made a few bob. The crowds started thinning and the leaves started falling and we decided to return to England.

When we got back I applied for a job as an assistant production manager in a lithographic factory. Because of my nomadic past I had to invent a history. I told them I had been living out in Australia for ten years. I got the job and the last traces of joy and hope left me. I developed terrible pains so I became a vegetarian and starved nearly all the time, becoming run down in every way.

One day, passing a fish-stall, I succumbed to a herring. I rushed home, tore its head off and fried it. Being a vegetarian had been so dreary. One had to think about food all the while. I love vege-tables. I just hate people who love vegetables.

Joyce and I argued all the time and I wanted to devote all my time to writing. I didn't want a hobby. I wanted to leave my job.

I started to hate the people at work. I wanted an argument as an excuse to leave. One day the boss called me in. The firm, it appeared, was moving to a new satellite town. They were pleased with my work. There was a good chance of advancement. Would I like to go with them and have a nice house in Sussex?

I thought it over for half an hour. At last I had an excuse to leave the job. I did. I was inevitably drawn, it appeared, towards chaos. Joyce and I never stopped arguing. Our friends stopped coming and started to avoid us. There was enough misery in the world, without us. So I started drifting out of our furnished room, wandered the streets and cried in cafés, shouting at the host of the assembled dead. 'Take a fucking Rimbaud at the moon.'

We decided to leave London.

In desperation we hoped to avoid our fate by going to Rickmansworth, which is near the soulless town of Watford. We lived in her father's house but I hated Rickmansworth where the living dead buried themselves completely at seven every evening and a stinking television sickness swept over the countryside in nauseous waves. Everybody was polite and nobody loved anyone.

Joyce's father was a nice man and her brother was a nice boy. We tried to patch the holes in our marriage but the ocean poured in too fast.

We bought some contemporary furniture and papered a room with contemporary wallpaper. But my hatred for those who travelled to Baker Street every morning was too strong and the swan song of Soho was the siren I was addicted to.

Joyce and I decided to return to London to have one final bash. When we got there we realized it was no good so we decided to return to Jersey and there, away from everyone, we would part. We would save some money to give us both a new start in life and then leave each other. There was a dreadful sense of failure, of time lost, of waste. More and more I was thinking of that frightful waste of time. This was the one commodity we could not afford to squander. And oh that feeling of failure.

Our marriage wasn't based on anything substantial. Loneliness is not good enough for a foundation. You start sinking into it.

So many people in the world meet and rub their bodies together, experiencing a little thrill and call it love. Mostly it was a desire for someone in the darkness. We weren't going all the way together. We were shooting off in different directions. We never touched.

We were both still quite young. If she could overcome her sense of failure, she might be able to start again. As for me, I was convinced I had reached my end. Before we went to Jersey we divided all our things. 'This is yours, this is mine. Do you want this?' 'No, no, no, you have it.' 'No, no, no, it's yours.'

What is mine? What was mine? This was the most hateful part of all, sharing out the accumulated objects of the past. Each item carried memories and wishes of so many people. How could I tell my family? When the things were finally shared out I decided not to take a thing except a vase I once made in Belmont.

Here was just another marriage on the rocks. Another shattered couple gone to the dogs, on the sliding sands of time with the great sea of chaos around us. I wanted my chaos, I wanted my waste-land, my own identity, my own way.

I screamed for separateness. I wanted to be alone, to go my own way towards my destruction. And so she cried and I tried not to, and we went together back to the Channel Islands where for the season we went our own ways. We shared the same room, the same bed, but slept head to toe. I never touched her ever again. And I counted up the loss as I lay awake at night. Eighteen months lost, another year and a half of my life down the drain.

When we returned to England a few months later we parted for always.

15

The Street Game

In 1954, when I returned to London, I visited my family. My
father was strangely delighted with the news of my separation
from Joyce. 'I told you so,' he said. Then he turned to the others.
'It just shows, you can't beat a Yiddisher girl.' I took it quietly,
with a pinch of salt.

My father had married again, an old Russian woman with milk-
white eyes. She was as blind as him, and could speak only Yiddish
and Russian.

They lived in a house in Hackney. It was full of old Jewish
people with hardly twenty words of English between them, yet
they had all been in England for more than fifty years. They
listened to Radio Moscow nearly all the time, ate matzos and
drank lemon tea continuously. Old Mr Adler was a very firm man
of eighty, looking more like fifty, with his grey-blue eyes. He would
completely ignore the criss-cross conversations about fried fish and
family and pigeon-hole me in a conversation from across the other
side of the room.

'I knew Gorki you know.' He sat silently for a while before con-
tinuing. 'He was no fool.' Then he just smiled at me, nodded his
head and shrugged.

'What do you think of the terrible news?' my father would say.
'What do you think of the terrible weather,' an old crony would
remark.

'What do you think of the wonderful progress in Russia?' 'St
Petersburg! There was a city!'

None of them listened to the other. They all spoke all day, all
lived in their own different worlds.

I was glad that my father had married again. For since my
mother had died he had been disappearing as a person, swallowing
himself alive, but now he managed to walk five miles every day.

231

He had started to collect silver paper for Guide Dogs for the Blind. It was about the only thing he could see in the street. I saw him once down Cambridge Heath Road stooping in the gutter. He spent several hours a week flattening it all out and rolling it into balls. He never took care crossing roads and was knocked over twice, but both times he stood up and walked on again.

He told me there was no other woman like my mother and one day he would lie beside her. 'Mind you, I'm not saying that Aunt Debbie isn't a good woman.' He was so preoccupied with that space in the cemetery, he spoke of hardly anything else and seemed to plan for nothing else. This seemed his only purpose in life—to die. His other hobby was reliving the family feuds; incessantly going on about past injustices.

He didn't fully trust his new wife. When they met at the Jewish Blind Society both boasted about the money they had saved. The money he had, turned out to be as much as the money she had, about a hundred pounds. They both thought the other had a small fortune.

'Don't think I'm poor,' he said to me. 'I'm taking care of all of you. I'm not short of cash.' He told my sister to share out the hundred pounds equally between the seven of us. He really did think it a great fortune, so who was I to disillusion him?

A great change suddenly came over London at that time. The American civilization had caught up with us. Everything was speeded up and slicked up, and there was a great deal of violence in the streets. A wave of bitterness and cynicism broke out. The whole surface seemed to be cracking. Prostitutes were thronging the pavements of Old Compton Street and policemen were walking around with hands open behind their backs for their dropsy and the Pornbrokers were raking it in. Cafés that we knew started closing, the leisurely ones where artists and anarchists argued all day. Coffee bars were opening in their place. The object was to get you in, make you feel uncomfortable under the harsh lighting, and then get you out as quickly as possible.

Skiffle swept through the streets. Groups of kids started twanging guitars under the arches near Charing Cross. Tommy Steele arrived.

Iris Orton was convinced that the millennium had also burst upon us, was sure that the great revolution of youth would break out at any moment.

In her wild cloak she went from cellar to cellar reading apocalyptical verse to the new crop of restless kids who had been spawned in war. And we, the old crop of the gone poets, sauntered the West End streets still thinking we would set the place alight and march on the citadels of the philistines.

We never went anywhere except the Coffee-House at Trafalgar Square where there were bad paintings on the walls and good girls trying to look bad around the walls.

The age of the week-end Bohemian had arrived!

But the desperation hadn't departed. Most of the boys I knew, the would-be writers and the painters, had gone the way of all flesh, into the ground. The toll was endless. I thought of their once smiling faces now rotting. Victims of the inner war. They were the unable, the unadjustable, the nothings, the unmighty fallen, the unsung, and I was waiting for my turn. I didn't see David Levine around, heard he was in a bad way, so I went to his room. He was completely gone, sat smothered in blankets saying over and over again, 'I'm so cold, I'm so cold.' He could no longer get high from drugs, but just needed them to stay alive. There was, however, still a tiny flickering of sensation when he stuck the needle in his veins. But he had no more conversation. Gone was his cry for compassion. He wasn't expecting anything except death. The once happy, mad, intelligent pianist sat with his teeth chattering, his glassy eyes fixed on nowhere. The little marijuana plant he had tried to grow in a little box of earth suspended from the electric light bulb, was all dead and dried up.

He died quietly. When they opened him up they found the biggest tumour they'd ever seen in a brain.

For the old-timers of Soho things got desperate. Some tried to fit into the new coffee-bar society, became characters, dispensing old anti-social tales to the newly lost. They held court, were lionized but remained pathetic. Most of them died alone somewhere, at night in a lousy room, and they were forgotten within days.

I stayed at that time near Camden Town. I always heard a man moaning as I walked up the stairs to my room. He would just give one long drawn out sigh of boredom. He stopped moaning one day, put ten shillings in the gas meter and took the gas-ring under the bedclothes with him.

But the kids in the streets. They represented something. Some people said they were living for kicks. I could see they were kicking for life.

So I wandered through that scene, feeling that I belonged to another time and soon I started recalling the old blissful really gone bohemian days. I was already part of the past and still hadn't begun. So I continued killing time, having the sad girls, wanting to reach across the black wasteland, yearning for a kiss to ignite the world for just a moment. But girls gave themselves without much joy. Just lumps of dough with open legs yawning through the act.

London was floodlit and in the Coffee-House the hot air reached up and mixed with the hot air of Whitehall, creating a great nauseous wave of apathy.

I saw a picture of the H-bomb on television. It looked like a great monster crawling towards the world. I was obsessed with an ugly vision of the impending holocaust. An American from *Life* or *Time* went to Moscow, came back with photographs and said, 'Do you know, those Russians are human. Ordinary boys and girls walk down the street and what do you know, they even fall in love, in Moscow.' I wanted to be sick. To have to be told that people in another country shared human emotions, showed to what extent we had descended.

I was thrown out of my room for the classical reason. Not having the wherewithal. So I wandered, slept around, and jawed the night away, until another day came inevitably around.

Girls are attracted to homeless poets. I sat in the Coffee-House, listening to all the shit about art and literature and the more withdrawn I became the more success I had. And I began exacting a sort of vengeance on them.

I began a novel. It started in the usual way. A boy and girl in bed.

One concave young friend had a tremendous facility for getting things done. 'Must get some money,' he suddenly said. Half an hour later he returned with fifty pounds. God knows what he did.

He started a magazine there and then and paid me for poems. It was exciting for a few months, but my concave friend stopped being a publisher and decided to be **a painter.**

He paced in front of his easel, saying, 'I must find next year's trend now!' Suddenly his eyes lit up. He got a nail and a hammer and started knocking holes in to the canvas. 'That's it.' The age of the gimmick had arrived.

My concave friend got tired of painting. He said he wanted to marry an heiress. Later I saw him driving around with one. It cost him an awful lot of money in taxi fares; for she never had any money on her. But they married and are now living happily ever after. I liked him tremendously.

Meanwhile, St Martin's School of Arts and tarts were setting the fashion trends in faces. One year it was Little Girl Lost and the next year it was the East of Eden look. Then the Zombie stare. Lovely girls whose perfume was blown by the wind. Provocative, evocative, yet suburban, playing at art. Arty. Ultimately they would marry artists or designers and become ordinary housewives.

Peter Fisk said I could move in with him and Janice. So I did. When he wasn't in his Orgone box he was cooking or reading from Gertrude Stein or James Joyce.

We wrote poetry together, each an alternate line. Nothing made sense; it was wonderful. Then we wrote a play called *The Madhouse.* All about a house that went mad.

A friend of theirs came visiting. A pathologist. She looked sad one day. I asked her why. 'I'm homesick for the dead.' She explained she was on holiday.

I told her she needn't be homesick for the dead—they were all around us. There was such a deterioration in almost everyone, everything.

I visited my family again, but they'd say, 'Shush' as I entered, pointing to their television screen. Conversation, even shouted conversation, had left the world of the Kopses. Something definitely was drastically wrong with the world. Now they were well off. Well, at least they had cash.

I'd gone through so much, felt so bitter, yet I wanted to continue. How could I live through this? How could I earn a living and leave my mind and body free and not too tired to find a way out? How?

I continued writing my book and poems, and lived for each moment. At nights we stayed up till four in the morning, usually wearing our masks and wigs and hats and listening to Peter making *Finnegans Wake* spring to life.

Winter pissed down. It seeped into the soul. I walked through Covent Garden picking up a few vegetables from the gutter, onions, carrots and cabbage leaves make a marvellous stew. One can live in a city for practically nothing, if you know how.

But I wanted to work, wanted to do something. I couldn't just wait for the end, even if the sky threatened destruction. Times of crisis hit the headline, the recurring boil of pus on the surface of the dying patient. Crisis frightened me, yet excited me. Like the river, I was afraid yet drawn to it. Down on the Embankment I watched the methy drinkers and down-and-outs gathering for the hand-outs from the religious. That seemed the logical conclusion for me. To become one of these. But I was still too proud. If ever I saw a crowd I walked in the opposite direction. I wandered alone, through the streets.

I tried crossing the river one day, thinking that the lines, 'Sweet Thames run softly till I end my song' would keep me safe. On Waterloo Bridge I panicked. I was half way across when I started to run for my life back towards the Strand.

But I thought to myself that there was no need ever to go to the south side of London. Nothing ever happens over there, except perhaps the Festival Hall or the National Film Theatre. But even that was getting so bloody pretentious. The last time I'd been there I laughed at something when someone leaned over from behind, saying, 'Shut up! This is significant.'

'Balls,' I hurled back.

People from the north side rarely crossed over, but I didn't realize how important crossing that river would be to me a few weeks later.

I met another sad Jewish girl. Her father was in smoked salmon. She was all mixed up with family and art and sex. And then I met a sad Irish girl. Her father wasn't in smoked salmon, but she too was all buggered up with family and art and sex. Autumn came and went and so did they. The leaves fell, but they didn't. Winter unnerved me. It's easy to live when you're broke in summer, but it's bloody tricky in winter. The hangers-on were most exacting in the Coffee-House. They expected conversation in return for a fag. I was all frozen up, had no more to say.

At Cambridge Circus one frosty day I saw some frosty flowers on a frosty flower stall, attended by a most unfrosty girl, something clicked and I got an idea. I spoke to her. She was alive and suspicious, rosy cheeked, plump and cockney. She laughed and was full of the language of the streets; not the swearing kind.

I asked her how I got a licence to sell in the streets. She told me to go to the Town Hall. On my way I wondered what could be my commodity, passed a bookshop, went back and looked in the window. The only things I loved were books. I would buy and sell the things I loved. I would earn, read and learn, and leave my mind free to dream and yearn. It seemed ideal. Excitedly I strode through the cold morning, trying to remember all the business advice passed on through the family, from one to the other, especially remembering how the secret of selling was buying. I entered the Town Hall and I got my licence. My pitch was smack next to the flower stall at Cambridge Circus. I rushed to tell my father that at last I was in business.

'Kops—Import, Export. Book specialist.' I could see it now. I was going to be the greatest bookseller in the world. But where was I to get the goods? Or the stall? Or the money to kick off with? I slept on it, with three cats and a shrunken head hanging from Peter Fisk's ceiling, staring down at me.

The next day I hired a stall from the Keeley family of Covent Garden for half-a-crown a day. The Keeley family were very down-to-earth London Irish and looked at me with suspicion. They were a very close-knit family and reminded me so much of my own Jewish family.

I kept my stall at Keeley's barrow yard near Seven Dials but so far it was practically empty. I scrounged a few books here and there, went to a jumble sale, borrowed two quid from my sister, browsed around junk shops and market places and gradually I built up a little stock. Every morning I pushed my barrow up to Cambridge Circus, and there I stood, next to the jellied eel and the flower stall. Maureen, the flower girl, at first treated me with suspicion. She was of the Keeley family, and such a marvellous character, always happy and bursting out singing for no reason. Soon I was calling her 'Moon' like her family.

But no-one came. Not a sausage. Not a customer. It was the very dead of winter. London was gripped by a freezing December. But I felt free at last, free to let my mind wander and watch the world pass by. And though I was hungry most of the time I felt that at last, I was doing something. Then a rather withdrawn woman came to the stall. She had some books to sell. So I went to her house in Kensington to see them.

Row upon row of books. My eyes lit up. I became excited and tried to hide it. I had the first symptoms of the disease known as book-fever. I held my chin and shook my head as I inspected them. 'I can't pay more than three pounds, I'm afraid.' I hadn't the vaguest idea what they were worth.

'Couldn't you make it a little more' she pleaded.

I knew I had her. I took out a book from a shelf, blew the dust from it, ' 'Fraid not. As it happens I'll have to scrap most of them.'

So I pushed my book stall all the way to Kensington, filled it up with the beautiful cargo and slowly pushed it back to Covent Garden.

Had I offered her thirty quid for those books I still would have been diddling her.

There was no one in the street when I got back, yet within seconds a swarm of book runners descended. They smelt books. They lived, slept, ate and dreamed books. And soon so did I.

'Come on, turn them over, all fresh, two bob each,' I cried out the way I remembered the dealers did down the East End and I was proud of myself, mustering all my acumen. One book was full of the most beautiful engravings and I could see the dealer trying to hide his excitement as he gave me the coin. I later found out the book was auctioned in Paris for three hundred pounds. I always meant to go back to that lady and give her some more money, but you know how it is.

My first success went to my head by way of food and wine and for several days I had a private feast. A week later came the awakening. My book stall was almost empty again.

A few bums ventured over from the French café to scrounge some money. There I was trying to graft, standing in the perishing cold, and they would come to tap me. Now I was a member of the working class so I told them what to do. My feet became so numb that I lost all track of them and night swept down about four-thirty and the wind howled along the street. I had no warm clothing to protect me.

I was reassured by one of the dear old ladies of 'The Dials'. It apparently was a very healthy spot, 'You see, the sea breeze rushes right along from the Thames, right up Savoy Street and down to Cambridge Circus.'

The man from the Town Hall came for his rent money. It was useless—I owed money left, right and centre and my remaining books were soggy. So much for me as a business man.

Twenty-eight years old with Christmas around the corner, and here I was again, face to face with my own failure, still not able to travel over water. As close to chaos as ever I was. This was the story of my life. And nobody ventured along the streets, not even the bums. Just the wind and the driving rain.

I did try to keep the books dry with a few old mackintoshes but they started to merge together in a pulpy mash. Though I still had a bed at Peter Fisk's. I was hungry all the time. A bag of chips became my only daily meal. Thoughts of suicide started growing in my mind again, there seemed no point in hanging it out. I reckoned I had seen it all, done more than most and I was singularly unimpressed with the world. Perhaps I would try the universe for a change. But the holiday was almost upon us and I thought, 'May as well have a holiday before retiring.'

So Christmas Eve arrived. People going home with parcels. 'Moon' at the flower stall doing a roaring trade in mistletoe and holly, people leaving offices early, drunk and laughing, and me penniless and without any hope. The sudden merriment of people emphasized my loneliness. 'So a Yiddisher boy comes into the world, what's that to me? I'm going out of the world.' A sort of exchange. I hated this holiday. People being sick in the streets on their way home, cars swerving with their drunken drivers in Charing Cross Road. 'What a way to remember their Saviour,' I said to myself, as I saw a business man vomit in the gutter.

I went down a coffee-bar cellar to see if a familiar face would buy me a cup of tea. Don Flowerdew was there. He bought me tea but we both sat in silence.

A girl came down the stairs. 'Oh no,' I said as I saw her, for she was such a beautiful vision. Her face hit me between the eyes. It was so familiar, though I hadn't seen her before. It was the face I had been doodling on table tops, between stanzas of poetry, anywhere where there had been an empty space since I wandered from my home after the war. She had on a short duffle coat, had beautiful shining dark hair and her eyes sparkled sadly. She was absurdly young. 'Oh no,' I repeated. 'I've had enough of women.' I hadn't reckoned on loveliness.

'Let's face it ducky. You and I are the older generation,' Don Flowerdew said to me.

It was true, I must have been nearly ten years older than her. I couldn't take my eyes off her.

I reckoned I had nothing to lose so I followed her through to the far end of the cellar, away from the others where I spoke, inviting her to a party that I suddenly invented. She told me she had been going to a party but it had fallen through. She sounded just as miserable as I was. I couldn't understand why a girl so beautiful, so young, could be so miserable.

I told her I was broke, I was a poet, I was Jewish. I could see she was Jewish and I wanted her to know that I wanted her. I was diving up to the surface again.

I couldn't take my eyes off her. I stared into her eyes which were the colour of amber, and I was trapped within like a prehistoric fly. At first I thought I didn't stand a chance. But it was Christmas Eve. After all, a Yiddisher boy was born that evening. Why couldn't I also be born?

'That's the wonderful thing about life,' I explained, exclaimed. 'The moment before something happens, you don't know you're in the dark and then suddenly it's light.'

I told her that I had been lost all the time, merely to come across this moment. Had I found myself earlier I never would have found her. I don't know what possessed me suddenly to speak like this. After all, I had never believed in love at first sight until this first sight. I felt as if I was about to be cheated again.

'Why did you say, "Oh no" when I came down the stairs?' she asked.

'I meant here's a beautiful girl. Someone I would love to love and I'm too bloody old. I'm beyond, and it's just my bloody luck. "Oh no" that I should miss it. "Oh no" that I should see you and never have you.'

We wandered through Soho looking in at the French Café, where I borrowed five shillings. I took her to the Swiss Pub and bought her a green chartreuse. I told her I was utterly broke and that there was no party.

Too many people were being sick in the street. I suddenly needed ceremony. Two Jewish people meeting on Christmas Eve, where should we go? 'Let's go to a midnight mass.' The idea came out of the blue, so I guided her towards Clerkenwell. The Italian church seemed an obvious choice. Don't ask me why.

I couldn't take my eyes off her and I reckoned my mother would have been pleased to know that she was a Jewish girl. As we walked I told her the lot. About the drugs, my marriage, my hopelessness, my writing. I told her I loved her. She didn't reply.

We got to the Italian church half an hour before midnight and sat right at the front of the congregation. By midnight the church was absolutely crammed with all the Italians of London. They were even more excitable than my family. So there we were, kneeling, two Jewish agnostics. The bells tinkled and the heady incense filled the air. I got quite high on that. And then, just as the priest began the ceremony, Erica slumped against me. She had fainted, her eyes going upwards inside her head.

I lifted her up bodily and carried her through the congregation as if it were part of the ceremony, as if she were an offering. So many people looked at me as I struggled through the mass towards the door. The priest was furious and seemed to ring the bell several times to regain the attention of his congregation, who were looking at the spreadeagled girl '*madonna mia*'.

I thought she looked like the madonna. And I wanted to call out, 'Make way for the virgin—here is the virgin.' It all seemed so natural, so linked. Christmas and us like this. For this reason I wasn't worried and I felt very vigorous but very protective towards her as I slowly edged out of the crush. A lot of those Italians who looked at her with such pity soon changed their expressions when they saw she was wearing slacks.

Outside we sat on the steps. It was already Christmas morning. A starlit frosty night, our breath covering the sky as we talked.

I took her back to the house in Neal Street. Peter and Janice were away for Christmas. She was a virgin, and as we lay on the bed together I did nothing to spoil it. The moon outside seemed to be racing through the icy clouds. I knew then that we would be together for always. I told her so. 'We'll be together always,' she replied. It was from that night the world was born. I had died several times to reach his new birth.

Erica told me all about herself. She came from quite a well-off Jewish family and lived just over Blackfriars Bridge. Her father was a doctor. She herself was at a teaching hospital and was hoping eventually to become a doctor. She loved her parents but wasn't very happy at home. I told her to leave home but it was obviously difficult. She had been going to a psychoanalyst since the age of eleven. I said, 'To leave home all you have to do is leave home.' I spoke as if it were so simple, as if it had been so simple for me.

She knew little about the world I lived in, the hard world of the streets. If I had told her that potatoes were five shillings a pound, she would have believed me.

On Christmas morning we wandered about the empty city. Usually, like all other people outside normal society, I curled up and died during holidays. But not that Christmas. I took her to a chum at Notting Hill Gate and we shared one boiled egg between the three of us.

It was the most wonderful day of my life.

When you meet someone three things can happen. You meet, collide and crash downwards. Or you crash head-on and get tangled where you are. Or you rush towards each other and in the embrace you soar upwards. We soared.

She told her parents about me a few days later. I went to visit them. I borrowed a suit from a friend, it was padded and draped and I guess I looked horrible. But they were quite friendly. The flat was very posh. Her parents had good taste. Her father, a general practitioner was a great huge teddy bear of a man who came from Riga, Latvia. Her mother was a small woman with a faint Scots accent and a charming manner. We talked of literature, of which she had an amazing knowledge. I was thrilled to be sitting in such a beautiful room surrounded by all the books that I had ever wanted to possess. Though now all I wanted to possess was the daughter.

I thought to myself, 'How strange that I, from Stepney, from my background, should be sitting here with a girl who had gone to a public school, who had been born into certain luxury, who had never known material poverty.' Yet we so absolutely, so simply, loved each other.

I took to her parents. They seemed good so I wished my father had been as gentle as hers, and though her mother intimidated me I admired her vitality and intelligence. But I could see that tiny as she was, she was a most formidable character.

Erica came from a household that had provided clothing for the Jewish Board of Guardians, clothing that my family had received. Erica, as a child, had a nanny and a maid. But she had never been happy.

That evening, again I asked her to leave home, telling her that we had to live together. She desperately wanted to, but felt she couldn't hurt her parents that much.

We met every day. She came straight from the hospital to help me at the bookstall.

The few shillings I made on the book stall I spent on gifts for her. I combed the East End markets and bought a pair of earrings, a small turquoise pendant and a Tibetan ring. She sported them in front of her parents, but was very hurt when her mother said, 'He's either paying for something he's had or for something he wants.'

But in that first week whenever I went, her mother was still nice to me.

'Erica gets very tired. Do please try and see that she's in by eleven.' The woman had such a winning way with her, I naturally agreed. But I felt then that I entered into battle for the girl I loved. Now I could see they were really worried. We were seeing each other at every possible moment. They could see that we were floating, happy and serious.

I didn't want to hurt them, and I thought about it a lot. Was I entitled to take what I wanted? The answer was always 'Yes'. First I had to break her from her analyst who kept on asking her about me. Erica refused to talk about me, afraid that words would destroy the magic. The analyst persisted, 'If you don't want to talk about him, it shows you're not very secure with him.' That was the end of that. Nine years of analysis had got patient and doctor practically nowhere. It was a great victory for me.

I was so pleased she was Jewish. We were on the same emotional wavelength. Here we were, from different worlds, yet we met so exactly in time and space.

So I crossed water for her. Blackfriars Bridge was a terrible ordeal, but we did several diagonals, she leading me by the hand until we got to the other side.

I became a man with her, wanted her to lean on me. Her fainting against me in the church on Christmas Eve had been most significant. I felt so protective towards her. If anyone in Soho as much as touched her on the shoulder I would growl like a wild beast and threaten to punch them on the nose. My friends as well.

February came and the falling snow settled. Erica developed a cold one day. We had arranged to meet, as usual, in the afternoon, but suddenly her parents forbade her to leave the house, under the pretext that it would be bad for her cold. Erica said in that case I would go there to visit her. Then they said that I wouldn't be allowed to go there again. She told them in that case she would leave home. There and then she left with just a basket stuffed with clothes and books.

I was sitting in the French café that morning, watching the thick flakes falling when I saw her at the door. 'I've left home,' she said. I lifted her up and swung her around, and all the snow seemed to melt, and the sun shone. No one in the café knew why we were so happy. In her basket I noticed her medical books. She said she had no intention now of being a doctor, so we took the books to Foyles and sold them.

Then we wandered through Soho and went to a little house behind Wardour Street where a composer friend was living. The Greek landlady let us a room, 'As long as this girl and no other girl you bring in.' I don't know what she was so particular about. Every other room in the house was occupied by hard-working whores.

So we lay together in that tiny room where you couldn't swing a cat. And working girls endlessly going up and down the creaking stairs with provincial men. 'Relax, relax,' I whispered to her. But she cried nearly all that night, as we clung to each other.

The next day Erica decided to go home to get all her things. I crossed Blackfriars Bridge with her, and waited in a café opposite. Then she came over and said, 'My mother wants to see you.'

So I faced the formidable lady in the drawing room while the doctor was hovering in the background. 'Sit down,' the woman demanded, pointing to a chair. I refused. I didn't want her walking around me laying down the law. On that low chair I would have been at a disadvantage.

Erica was packing in the other room, and I continued moving around the room, trying not to be fixed in a corner. 'These! These,' I said, pointing at the many books. 'You've read them all, cover to cover, yet what do you know or care about real life?'

There's a time in your life when you must be courageous, utterly. This was Erica's time. She grabbed the opportunity and embraced it fully. And it was my time too, but it wasn't very easy. I could see their point of view, and from their way of thinking they were right. For all they knew I was the most terrible bastard on earth; I might have been seducing their daughter away, only to leave her high and dry.

But I wanted Erica, wanted her for always. I knew that time would prove what I couldn't. So I disdained all argument, cut across all convention. I refused to argue any more, sat in the drawing room, silently, while the mother cried. I was sorry, yet I knew that I just had to do what I had to do. For some reason I had with me a framed Michelangelo print. I gave it to them before I left with her. They accepted it and all words ceased. And I took their daughter out of their house and down the stairs.

We struggled across the road with her suitcases, slowly we hurried through the deep snow. We caught a bus that crossed the river and took us to Charing Cross. And we wandered the streets hugging each other in that crazy way of lovers.

And we went back to our room in Peter Street where we made

love and soared over the world. But Erica, loving her parents, at the same time cried and cried all that day and some of the night.

16

The World is a Wedding

Suddenly I discovered there were trees in Charing Cross Road.
Walking along with Erica through the snow of that February the
whole world started meaning something.

The sky was the sky and the snow was the snow and life was a
bloody wonderful miracle. Erica was warm and gave herself to
me. And winter was not a death but a preparation for new life.

It had taken me twenty-eight years to reach myself, yet so many
people had destroyed themselves on the way. The world was only
just being created. Away went my bitterness. Sure, we were crawling about in the mud but mankind hadn't even started yet. We
were very young and at least we desired to get out of the mud.

The cold universe receded as we embraced each other. And we
discovered a new universe within, knew that living was now and at
no other time. Each day was for living and there was no other time.

I took Erica away from the café of Bohemians, wanting first
of all to cement our relationship before we could move amongst
the cynics. We wandered, broke and cuddling and sang, 'We're
having a heatwave', while all around people were shivering in the
snow and sliding in the slush.

I was on fire and I wrote my head off again; this time a new
kind of poem—love poems to the world. I had a vision that the
sparks of our love would light up the universe. Our marriage wasn't
made in the world; it was made in the universe. But we were not
so much out of the world that I didn't know what was going on
around me. As I kissed her in the street and whispered, 'Long live
love'. I was also whispering things like, 'Let's hurl our bombs of
love at those bastards who rule the world'; Let's rejoice with all
those who will not die with the age'; 'Let's sing over the wasteland
and wake the dead.' But once I got drunk and shouted along Old

Compton Street, 'You killed Lorca you bastards.' And I cried, 'Lorca's dead you lousy swine.'

Erica coaxed me back to our room by walking on ahead. I followed on, stopping every so often to call out at a corner, but every time she moved I followed.

And in the room she undressed me; that swinging little room in the universe, room for one bed and a sigh.

There's an old Jewish proverb, 'When the bedroom is happy, every room is happy.' But we had our own answer, 'When other rooms are happy the bedroom is happy.' It worked both ways. Every room and every street was happy.

On Erica's twenty-first birthday she was ill in bed and we were completely penniless. I searched through Soho, trying to borrow a few bob but everyone was in the same boat. Eventually I found a rotting pineapple in the gutter near Covent Garden. I took it back to her in triumph. Only three quarters of it was bad. The rest was delicious.

When she was better she sometimes visited her parents and smuggled me out a little food. We'd sit in the early hours, reading poetry and eating strands of chicken. Emissaries of her family came. Her sister, with a chicken, and her uncle, a respectable pharmacist, who nevertheless approved of what we were doing.

Her parents couldn't understand why we didn't get married. They didn't know we could not; didn't know that the terrible ordeal of the divorce courts was ahead of us.

The weather was far too horrible to do much business. A tattered tarpaulin covered the books. In between the rain, sometimes we earned a shilling or two which we spent on fish and chips. It was the time before the duffle coat had become respectable and we in Soho were the pioneers of this style. People stared at us and looked disapproving. We discovered that all the world does not love lovers.

Death had stopped calling on me. The river was once more a river; a bus was just a bus ride, but I still avoided the underground.

Erica had left the hospital, chucked in her lot completely with mine and we both felt completely free for the first time in our lives. We were our own masters.

And every day when night descended, we ascended and descended. We cuddled amidst the confusion of Soho and the crises of the world. In that little room in Peter Street I slept with my socks on, always expecting the sirens to blow at any moment, though God knows there was nowhere to run.

I had terrible visions of the authorities barricading the cities and all of us trapped like ants in a burning jar.

Having the barrow was great. The freezing cold wind did cut through us, but after an hour or two, after the nose disappeared from the face and the ears seemed to drop off, a great tingling started. Then we were suddenly as warm as toast. People passed by shivering and our bodies were tingling with inner heat. And the physical work was a joy, the sheer delight of pushing the barrow to and from the yard made me feel marvellous. For the first time in my life I felt healthy and vigorous. Often I pushed Erica along the road, around Soho on the barrow. Sometimes I would hold a one-man anarchists' meeting, happily addressing the grey, passing people, pointing at all the unsold books, 'Get cultured before the cataclysm.' People who worked in the open were much more open, happier. I struck up friendships with postmen, milkmen and barrow boys. And the whores. On Saturday nights they worked overtime and would pass the stall sometimes as much as twenty times in the one evening. One, who had a taste for Henry Miller and Dostoyevsky, would always wink as she went by, followed by her crumpled up customers; often she dropped me half-a-crown without saying a word.

Just as in the old days of Stepney, when the whore in the Buildings came to our rescue, these few shillings would give us our supper of fish and chips. It was hard to replenish the stocks because it was so difficult to part with the books, which I had mainly chosen because I liked them so much. I read more books than I sold.

My first novel was half finished. A regular customer of mine read it and suggested I ought to submit it to a publisher. I sent it to Leonard Woolf and he sent for me. He quite liked the book, but I never finished it. Instead I continued writing poetry. Every morning, when I woke I wrote down my dreams. I always slept with pencil and paper under the pillow, and sometimes I would leap out of bed in the middle of the night, and recall and record my dreams of flight. But I was never sure of what I was writing. I fell in love with words, got drunk on them. And a few of us got together to read our poetry in a public house. We were an esoteric group, reading to ourselves, apocalyptical poems in Old Compton Street.

Another of my customers was a printer. On his small press he produced my first volume of seven poems. It was reviewed in the *Jewish Chronicle*. 'Too bad that someone who works in the streets, like this, hasn't drawn from his background for his material.'

I cursed the reviewer at the time. Only later did I realize how much that review helped me.

Erica made me send my poems to an Italian magazine run by a millionairess. To our astonishment, instead of a rejection slip, they sent me a cheque for fifteen guineas. We went mad. It was a fortune to us. We had our first grand feast. Yet I didn't think in terms of writing as a career. Writing was something on its own. Being a writer and being published weren't connected. I was perfectly content to scratch a living in the streets, where I became aware of a new world.

The book-runners, Drippy Nose and Dirty Mac might have stepped straight out of Mayhew. They would perhaps start off the day with sixpence, buy a book in Berwick Street, take it to Foyles, flog it for a shilling, buy a book from me for a shilling, take it to Pooles, sell it there for two shillings and so on. Sometimes they might end the day with ten bob, sometimes they speculated in vain, being left with a worthless book on their hands after a long day's graft.

Sometimes they didn't even have sixpence to start the next day, so they'd take one of my books on spec. 'I think I know where I can place this,' Drippy Nose would say in his most refined accent. His name never belied him, his nose dripped forever along the rows of books as he inspected them. And there were marvellous characters along the street: Joe Bloom and his boxing boys; Charlie the wide boy, with his cronies, always flogging different gear along the streets to the provincial mugs, giant balloons and clockwork fur animals. Then there was 'Moon' the flower girl; Joe Pegg, the jellied eel man and all those weird characters, the book collectors, absolutely obsessed with their own particular subject to the exclusion of everything else. 'I'm only interested in books on bee-keeping,' said one woman, daily. 'I must have maps! Maps!' another man said. 'Pieces of parchment, only fourteenth century will do,' 'eighteenth century plays,' 'books on heraldry, I'm not interested in anything else.' I gradually got to know them, these people who were locked up in their private worlds. And I catered for them. 'Books for cranks at cut price' was my motto. But I never really made a living, we just scraped along. 'Times are bad' everyone was complaining, and people started saying, 'When the next war comes', instead of 'if it comes'.

There was much more violence in the streets and everyone seemed on the make. Strip clubs and pornographic bookshops mushroomed in Soho. Nearly all the bohemian cafés were now closed and most of the bums were drifting loose. Many of them couldn't avoid work any longer and became pornmerchants and book-thieves. It seemed as if all the rottenness of our civilization had come rushing to the surface, yet for the first time in twenty years I was happy, really happy. My family were delighted that Erica was a Yiddisher girl. 'Believe me you're better off with your own kind,' they said.

The American Fleet started steaming off Formosa and I started to panic, for now I wanted to live. 'Just my luck, just when I find you. Why do they pick on me,' I said to Erica, fondly mimicking my late mother, yet meaning it. All around the world violence was breaking through and marriages were exploding like bombs. When I was especially anguished like this Erica took me home. In bed the whole thing would fall into place.

We were still completely broke and every day was a hand to mouth struggle and every night a time of peace and achievement, for having got through the day and arriving at the night with such happiness. Even when we got a little money we treated it with little respect. I bought a vase for a shilling and sold it for fifteen shillings. That money, with care, should have lasted us four days. But it was cold and raining that evening so we went to a cinema in Leicester Square. It was beautifully warm in there. We spent the lot that evening. That was our attitude to money. I must have truly imbibed my mother's philosophy that 'something always turns up'. Erica got another cold and stayed in bed. Her sister came with a chicken and strict instructions from her mother. The chicken was meant only for her. She immediately offered it to me and we both devoured it.

In the springtime the American tourists started to come over. I stocked up with antique books, so I did a little business. But they would wave pound notes at me and try beating me down. As it was I was offering obvious bargains. Their whole way of life seemed larded with money; sometimes I would tire of a possible transaction and refuse to sell. For every book I sold gave me a sense of loss. It was just terrific to stand still and watch the world pass by, and to think and read, feel the upward surge of my love stirring new ideas within me; I wanted to talk to people, to feel contact. I wanted to start growing.

The bookstall gave me time to think, time to sort things out. It made me more aware of my place in the world, more aware of my true responsibilities. I could see that we in this world had grown up too fast, we couldn't keep up with our discoveries.

I recognized the beast within me once it had come to the surface, and though I had pushed it back it was still there. I began to accept myself. I was neither proud nor un-proud of my past, but I needed to accept the past in order to outgrow it.

I was a Jew, therefore I was a man. It is only by accepting I am Jewish that I am able to forget it. I, who spent my years running away, was taking a journey into myself, through myself, all the time. I who wanted to get away from the family wanted only to create a new family. I who lived in chaos, in this madhouse called the world, wanted to discover a new sanity. My responsibility was to achieve sanity, for this was the new purpose of the artist, or perhaps the old and the eternal purpose. The politician and the scientist had taken us all out on a limb, out of the laws of evolution and we were terribly alone. I prayed for the clarity, the strength, to remain vulnerable yet unflinching, to help to show people where we were situated. To show the danger and the hope. The possible and the probable. To help to show people that people were the same as people. So though I retained an extroverted and gay madness I started talking what is known as common sense.

It may have been all very well for the artists of 1900 to go berserk. Then society seemed stable. Today the very opposite was true. The artist needed a sanity, a cool stability. So I started to

stretch the limbs of my mind. Erica was my earth. I with my head
poking through the clouds needed earth desperately.

So the more Soho became depraved, the more we clung together.
The more bombs that were tested the more we clutched each other.

I couldn't see the world in terms of masses. I wanted my
humanity to begin in my own living-room. I wanted the man inside
myself to be as truthful as the artist. I wanted both of them growing out of the other.

It seemed that the divorce was going through. Erica's parents
had now heard all about it and they knew there was no stopping
our marriage, even though her mother appealed to her several
times. We decided to get married in a synagogue because we
wanted the ceremony. We needed the ceremony.

When the divorce absolute came through I could have kissed
every dirty stone of Somerset House. Phyllis was very pleased at
the news of our coming wedding, but my eldest sister told me I
was marrying above my station. Being broke, I asked my father
how much the ceremony would cost. 'They might ask ten pounds,
but take no notice. Bargain with them. They'll do it for three.'

So I went to the synagogue in Soho. Just along the street from
where we lived. I went up to the office. 'It'll cost you twelve,' the
official said. I told him I couldn't afford twelve. He asked me how
much I could afford.

'Three,' I replied.

'Out of the question.' He angrily turned his back on me. I
started to walk down the stairs. He called me back. 'Tell you what
I'll do. I'll do it for ten.'

'Three,' I replied.

He got furious. 'For that money go to the East End.'

I continued walking down until I heard him calling me back.
'Eight,' he said, 'and that's my final word.'

'Three,' I replied.

'You're mad! Who does it for three these days?'

'Three,' I replied and again started walking.

And again he called me back—'Seven, and that's my final word.'

'Three,' I replied.

'You're out of your mind,' were his final words.

This time when I started walking down the stairs he didn't call me back.

So I went straight to the East End to Stepney Green Synagogue. Of course this had to be the place. I must have been out of my mind. This was the obvious place for our wedding. The synagogue where I had sipped the wine, queued up for sweets and pretended to pray. Where as a child I had plucked the mulberry leaves from its garden for my pet silk worm.

They told me they'd be pleased to do it for five. I said three. They said four. I said three. They said three ten, so who's arguing over a lousy ten shillings? They agreed to three.

As I left the synagogue I walked past the buildings in Stepney Green. The bomb-sites were all cleared now and high blocks of flats reached into the sky. It all seemed so cold. Gone were the narrow streets and the old women arguing on the doorstep; gone the faces leaning out of windows and the old excitable men on the corners. Gone the children playing hopscotch and swinging around lampposts. Television antennae were stretching up to receive the new message. The community was dead. And my mother was dead, and her world was dead. It had gone into always. My only regret now was that she never lived to see this day when I was ordering my marriage.

So on February the ninth 1956, a year after Erica came to live with me, I left my book-stall in charge of a friend, Marcus. I had five quid in the pocket of my second-hand ginger tweed suit that made me look like an Irish labourer on St Patrick's night.

'Moon,' the flower-girl, gave Erica a small bouquet of flowers at cost price. Being a Catholic she was naturally pleased that we were finally making it kosher.

Erica's mother still had not relented and they were not coming to the synagogue, where they too had been married.

February ninth was one of the coldest days for years. It had real style. It started snowing as we set off for Stepney Green. Kenneth, an artist friend, was my best man.

There he stood, a dada artist from Kensington, in a black skull-cap. Phyllis was there, and Essie and Ivor, my brother Dave, and Rose, and Erica's sister, Gillian.

Nobody else was in the synagogue except the Rabbi and the

cantor. The ceremony, and that morning, symbolized a moment of light in the darkness around the world, a sprinkle of time in space.

We stood under the Canopy and I smashed the glass with a very positive and much too hard thump of my foot. The small congregation shouted, 'Mazeltov'.

'The world is a wedding,' The Talmud says. Life is the time of affirmation, of celebration in the middle of chaos. In the Talmud it also says that all brides are beautiful.

That may be so but mine was the most beautiful of all.

'But isn't she beautiful? Isn't she the most beautiful girl in the world?' I buttonholed my brother, I asked everyone. They had to agree with me.

Erica phoned her parents after the ceremony. To our great joy, they invited us for dinner the following day.

Outside the synagogue they all suddenly had to leave. It was a weekday and they all had to go back to work. So off they went in their cars. Erica and I, my friend and her sister stood alone in Stepney Green. The snow was so heavy that for a moment we just stood looking at the blanket of white. I had never seen the flakes so large. Our clothes became pure white in seconds but the huge flakes melted on our faces.

'It's our confetti,' I said.

Some workmen in a hole in a road waved at us. Then we got a taxi. 'Take us to the Café Royal,' I said grandly. There we blew the lot—the whole fiver. Erica's sister bought champagne and when we left the restaurant we started Chagall-floating, zooming over Regent Street, looping the loop over Eros. Then we danced along the street through Soho, through the snow, gathering people as we went along.

Erica took her flowers and asked me not to look back as she threw them over her shoulder into the snow.

When we got to my barrow I could see Marcus lying across it with a bottle in his hand. He had sold a few books and with the proceeds was downing a couple of bottles of cider in our honour.

So we went to a house in Seven Dials where we danced and danced and danced to the music of one scratched Yiddish record. It was the loveliest dancing night of my life.

Faces and bottles endlessly until the dawn. It was always like that in Soho. The party started with six people and now all Soho was there. Faster than sound was the Soho grapevine.

'Isn't she the most beautiful girl in the world?' was the only thing I said as we danced into the day.

The disenchanted lonely of Soho loved nothing more than a wedding. We started a whole string of them.

When we walked out in the morning I saw the bookstall still there. 'Moon' told me that Marcus had been too drunk to push it back. The law had come but she handled it all right. 'Don't nick them officer, it's their wedding night,' she said. The policeman had smiled and walked away. For the first time in my life I even loved the police force.

We then went to her parents' home where all was forgiven over a chicken dinner and sparkling wine. Now I decided to accept them without argument. I realized you can't change the older generation.

As I sat eating I wondered about my own family, for now I was starting a family. I always believed that parents owed their children everything and children owed their parents nothing. Like the birds of the air the parents' joy was to see the fledgling fly away, vigorous and happy. 'If I have a child all he will owe me is in living his own life fully,' I thought. And so we began to live with each other in the eyes of the law and nothing had changed. The struggle was still there, the poverty and the respect we had for one another. And I pushed the barrow, bought and sold, and feared the headlines and loved the nights and lived every inch of the day.

Erica became pregnant.

So the rains of an English spring passed. And sometimes the sun shone and all the while her belly stretched and her face became more beautiful.

The clouds of war got thicker and blacker as did the newspaper headlines. Yet we were very happy. Never once did I question the value of bringing a child into the world, for again I was rediscovering old truths, 'The world survives by the breath of young children,' the Talmud says.

I, who had spent all my life looking for something, had found what I was looking for. I, who broke away from the family, had merely wanted a place in the sun for my own family. I could

no longer see things in universal terms but only in specifics.
I wanted to follow my own star—I wanted to think for myself, to live simply, to work in peace with my wife. To live peacefully and die peacefully in my bed, of old age. There was so much to do. And I had merely started. Surely there would be time?

Suddenly madness again, as in the beginning of my life. Now at this new beginning a new madness—Hungary and Suez.

Erica nearly eight months pregnant insisted on going to the demonstration, to Trafalgar Square where a mass protest was being held. It was a very black Sunday. On the bus going there the conductor said, 'Good luck to them Israelite boys.' I told him not to give me any of that crap, for if the politicians wanted he'd be loving the Egyptians, the Germans, the Peruvians, the Aztecs and so on. I thought of our child inside, hearing all this noise. What a world it was coming into. There was no escape, no turning back. We had to go through with it. We were committed, involved, naturally. Everyone on earth was involved.

The demonstration reminded me so much of my childhood. Placards outside St Martin's in the Fields called for 'Prayers for world peace'. World peace? What could we do about it? Was it just a dream? But the time for talking had passed. And so we marched with the crowd because emotion was the one true flame that burnt like a miracle within us. 'Eden must go! Eden must go!' As a socialist, anarchistic, mystical atheist I agreed with this. I shouted it. But as a Jew I wasn't so sure.

I wanted Israel to succeed. I was completely split. My ideals and my emotions clashed on the battlefield of me. I was the victim. What could one do in the modern world, when one was moved by an ancient faith that had nothing to do with religion but everything to do with a beautiful life on earth? For I was a Jew. I had embraced what I was and what I had to be. I had taken a journey into myself back to the beginning. To ignore my roots was to get tangled in them. This was my entrance visa into the world. When you acknowledge your roots you become at one with the earth and with all people. When I dashed back from that protest meeting I sat listening with my ear glued to the radio to the Voice of Israel. I rejoiced to hear about the advance of the Israelis into Sinai. I was at one with them but when I heard about the bombing of Cairo I was outraged. This was my schism. In my father's house they talked over their lemon tea.

'He's a clever boy, that Khrushchev.'

'He's an anti-Semite.'

'So Bernie, you making a few bob?'

And in my father-in-law's house I felt extremely restless. From the window I could see the Thames, the beautiful floodlit buildings and London stretched peacefully in sleep. All this could get blown away in one flash. And inside, Erica, reading on the settee, almost bursting with child. I smiled at her, trying to appear calm. But she could see inside me and tried reassuring me, 'It will all blow over, you'll see, It's all a game of bluff.'

If only I had her faith.

She seemed so calm, so sure of herself. All I could do was to write little poems, yet there she was really creating, creating life! I thought, 'She goes through the crisis, soothing my brow, reassuring me, and look at me, what am I doing? She creates and I do nothing.'

That night in our own crowded room, I couldn't sleep for thinking, 'What have I done with my life? What have I created? I hadn't died, I hadn't committed suicide. Sing you silly sod! Sing over the abyss. Sing that life is worth while because it is. Sing that a flower is a flower and the world is a wedding. Sing because we are for no apparent reason suddenly illuminated in the darkness, reaching up for the sun. Even if we are going to be annihilated that was no reason to die before you died. Sing to wake the living and the dead. Just sing. Say yes to life. Yes! yes! yes! and yes again. Spit on the darkness.'

I rushed out of the bed. I saw a dramatic situation, a comedy about tragedy. The essential humour of my life, the people I knew, the life I loved, my world. And I was surprised and I laughed with it as it emerged, as one character in it said to another, 'You remember Mr Miller?'

'Not off-hand.'

'He was killed the other day by a van; he was worried about the world situation and was reading a newspaper as he crossed the road.'

So many times I had almost been in that position.

I knew that if I had but a few days left on earth I wanted to embrace those days, not curse them. To make something of them, of myself. To achieve dignity through affirmation. And for three days, at a white heat, I wrote the first draft of my first play. It seemed to be all there inside me, waiting to emerge. It seemed to write itself.

And when I had finished for the first time I was absolutely sure that I had written something worthwhile.

I knew a man named David Archer. He had a bookshop in Soho. I told him about the play and he told me about an American who was in London looking for new plays. So I phoned Mark Marvin that evening, told him I had just written something that I just had to read to him without delay. He said his wife was out and he was baby-sitting, and although it was a little irregular he would be delighted for me to go over.

He told me I looked like a gaunt, starving, possessed apparition when I appeared at the door of his luxurious apartment. He offered me whisky, but I refused, and I started to read the play. He puffed a long cigar as I acted through all the parts.

At the end of it he said, 'Son, you've written a beautiful play, but what's the premise?' I didn't know what the hell he was talking about.

Nevertheless, there and then, he gave me a cheque for fifty pounds. I could hardly believe my eyes and I walked home staring at the cheque and thinking perhaps the whole thing had been a practical joke. But we danced round and round the room for joy when I got back home.

For four days I kept on going back to his place to give him what I thought was the premise.

'No son that's the plot.' 'No no, that's the dénoument.'

I just couldn't find that premise, but I later found out that Americans love a premise. He gave me a book on playwriting to learn all about premise. It almost ruined me. My second play was terrible because of it.

Threats of war and headlines and Erica got bigger. So now I had three things to worry about. She was taken to the London Hospital just along the road from Stepney Green. My son, in no

hurry to enter the world, had been induced, had been helped in
with forceps. Erica had a bad time.

I saw her lying there as if she had been through a life and death
struggle, and she looked as if she had given all a human being
could ever give another.

I went in to see him ten minutes after he was born. When I saw
his cone-shaped head I winced, but was relieved to hear that all
babies were born like that. He yawned when I looked at him. At
last I had achieved immortality! Yet part of me was so afraid.
I had passed on the spark, the torch, the essence of myself. All
life was contained in him. I could see the membrane throbbing on
his head. The body was a dam, holding in life, keeping out death.
Skin and bones and a dream, separating space from space. I was
afraid to hold him, afraid that I might drop him or throw him out
of the window. His utter dependence! Suddenly I felt the sheer
responsibility. How fragile, how tenuous, how miraculous life is.

We decided to call him Adam; a substantial name for the
troubled time.

When Erica came out of the hospital the leaders of the world
were still behaving like imbecile children. 'Ya! Mine is bigger
than yours.' The city put the wind up me, but like life you just
had to put up with it. I tried joking, 'If you'll get through life
safely without dying you'll be lucky.' But I was dead scared inside,
but here was my security. Here, where we were, was my home.

Now came the waiting for news about the production. Meanwhile I carried on at the bookstall. On the first day when Erica
brought Adam there we didn't sell one book. She fed him in the
cellar where I stored the books. That evening we were cold and
hungry and utterly miserable. But the whore of the street stopped
between customers, 'What a lovely baby,' she said, and pressed
two half-a-crown coins into Adam's palm. He clutched them tight.
I quickly packed up, pushed the barrow back, singing, and we had
the most wonderful supper of fish and chips and pickled onions.

A few weeks later I was awarded five hundred pounds by the
Arts Council; 'Enough for you to live on for a year, so just write
whatever you want,' they said. There I was at the end of another
phase, poised on the brink of space like a vulnerable explorer,
afraid, excited, desperately and naturally involved, obsessed with

work, for work and love and the world were the same thing; I was trying to grow, to keep in touch, trying not to be destroyed by anything, not by the things within nor the things without, wanting a good life on this earth for my own family and therefore for all other people.

So I pushed the barrow away for the last time and when we went home Adam fell asleep early.

After we made love I sat up late into the night, thinking and writing, being too excited to sleep, possessed with the feeling that I had just started out in life.